Against the Odds

During the writing of this book, Klaus Serr was Associate Professor of Sociology at Addis Ababa University in Ethiopia, having previously taught in Australia at the Australian Catholic University, La Trobe University and RMIT University. Klaus has actively been engaged in the areas of homelessness and poverty since the 1990s. He is a founding director of Social Work Services P/L and has worked in the human services sector for more than twenty years in Australia, England and Hong Kong. His books include *Zerstörte Träume: Anfänge eines Armutsberichts von Unten* (2013); *A Study into the feasibility of a social enterprise project: the coffee shop development* (with D. Rose, 2008); *Shattered dreams* (2006) and *Thinking about poverty* (2001).

With studies in Australia, Germany and now Ethiopia, the author constructs a mosaic picture of poverty in the world as part of the impressive project called 'Shattered Dreams'. This unique combination of three detailed but different faces of poverty calls us to action, not just in each locality, but globally. Through social research, Against the Odds *creates once more the extraordinary, bringing the reader a touching tale that lets people speak about their lives and deprivation.*

Professor Dr. Ulrich Bartosch,
Katholische Universität, Eichstätt-Ingolstadt, Germany

Against the Odds

Poverty in Addis Ababa

Klaus Serr

AUSTRALIAN SCHOLARLY

Royalties received from the sale of this book will be sent to the Missionaries of
Charity in Ethiopia to support their poverty work.

First published 2014, Australian Scholarly Publishing Pty Ltd
7 Lt Lothian St Nth, North Melbourne, Vic 3051   TEL: 03 9329 6963   FAX: 03 9329 5452
EMAIL: aspic@ozemail.com.au   WEB: scholarly.info

ISBN 978-1-925003-54-3

Design and typesetting Sarah Anderson
Cover photo by A. M. Friala

The main chapters of this book are typeset in Minion Pro 10.5pt

For Marie,
with gratitude and friendship

CONTENTS

FOREWORD

Then, the conviction that the economy must be autonomous, that it must be shielded from 'influences' of a moral character, has led man to abuse the economic process in a thoroughly destructive way. In the long term, these convictions have led to economic, social and political systems that trample upon personal and social freedom, and are therefore unable to deliver the justice that they promise.

Pope Benedict XVI, *Caritas in Veritate*, 2009, n. 34.

In this 21st century, humans journey through space, build computers of amazing power and eradicate diseases that only recently were fatal. But humans have not eradicated poverty. In fact, 2.6 billion people around the world are greatly deprived, many struggling to survive on under $2 per day. This human crisis of vast proportion has an enormously damaging impact on individuals, families and communities. Paradoxically, the crisis persists in the shadow of immense accumulated wealth, where the turnover of some corporations is greater than the GDP of entire countries, where in 2011, 1,210 billionaires command a record $4.5 trillion profit, and where the world still spends an estimated $1,500 billion on weapons each year.

In this context, *Against the Odds: Poverty in Addis Ababa* shows in its early chapters how the current economic system of international finance and trade has promoted inequality and unfairness, and how it leads to ever increasing wealth and poverty disparities between nations and individuals. Inextricably linked to the global economic system, Ethiopia remains one of the world's poorest countries, with an absolute poverty rate of 40–50% and currently 40% inflation. This dire situation continues despite Ethiopia's strenuous efforts and real achievements in social and economic development, while other nations and individuals have benefitted to a much greater extent from global economic arrangements. This imbalance is unacceptable, and it is imperative that positive and effective measures be developed to address these inequities. In reporting the results of in-depth interviews with some of the poorest in Addis Ababa, as well as with a number of professionals working in poverty-related areas, this book contributes to finding these measures.

Against the Odds: Poverty in Addis Ababa contributes to the current public debate on social protection and to an increasing awareness of the need to provide public assistance and services to protect the vulnerable and needy in the greater African region and in Ethiopia. For example, recognising the importance of the issue of social protection, the recent 7th Annual National Conference of the Ethiopian Society of Sociologists, Social Workers and Anthropologists (ESSSWA), held in Addis Ababa, was devoted to the theme 'Social Protection and Safety Nets for Vulnerable Social Groups under Economic Growth'. The need to make greater efforts to assist the poor is also recognised by the Catholic Church, whose projects deal with both rural and urban poverty alleviation with the participation of the poor in view of their integral human development. For instance, as Pope John Paul II and Pope Benedict XVI have pointed out: 'The poor are not to be considered a "burden" but a resource, even from the purely economic point of view' (*Caritas in Veritate*, 2009, n. 35).

Against the Odds: Poverty in Addis Ababa breaks new ground by giving a voice to some of the victims of the system, comparing and contrasting their views with those of professionals. In doing so, the book's insights, findings and recommendations spring from a data set that is broader, deeper and more inclusive than most other studies. It not only identifies the kinds of services needed by the poor, but also the roles and functions many organisations can play in poverty alleviation, including the different levels of government, churches, NGOs, the many parts of society and the poor themselves. The book's conclusions and recommendations have, therefore, important policy implications. Its overall recommendation for all relevant stakeholders to work together in partnership, for instance, is of vital importance, as many Ethiopians continue to experience great hardships, a situation that has become ever more uncertain and perilous for so many.

Against the Odds: Poverty in Addis Ababa offers a vision of humanity in a world that is too often unfair; it deepens our understanding of the poverty crisis affecting many Ethiopians and can assist our efforts to overcome the scourge of poverty. This book is rich in the way it uses its information to reach towards a better future for the poor in Addis Ababa and elsewhere.

+Abune Berhaneyesus D. Souraphiel CM
Metropolitan Archbishop of Addis Ababa

PREFACE

Against the Odds: Poverty in Addis Ababa is the third and final part of the international poverty pilot study called *Shattered dreams*. Conducted between 2005–06 and 2008–09, this research took place in three communities: in Melbourne, Australia (in partnership with Catholic Social Services Victoria); in Munich, Germany (in partnership with Caritas Germany) and in Addis Ababa,[1] Ethiopia (with assistance from Hope Enterprises and the Ethiopian Catholic University of St Thomas Aquinas).

The impetus for this project stemmed from the fact that most studies on poverty are undertaken by 'experts in the field', while people living in poverty are rarely consulted about their experience and understanding of poverty. Research such as this is of critical importance, because unless anti-poverty policies developed by professionals include the expressed needs and experiences of the poor, solutions are unlikely to be effective.

While each study had a different local context, representing different kinds of poverty, all studies aimed to gain a greater understanding about poverty by enabling the poor themselves to speak about their experiences and then contrasting these views with those of small groups of professionals working in the poverty area. The purpose was, thus, not to test or build on established poverty concepts or theories but, by using an explorative and open-ended approach, to increase insight into the conditions of a very deprived group of people.

BRIEF COMPARISON OF POVERTY EXPERIENCED BY THE POOR

While interviews with the professionals in all three locations demonstrate their awareness of the suffering of the poor, the relevant social conditions applicable in each location and also the kind of supports needed for the poor, it was the interviews with the poor and disadvantaged that showed most of the differences.

All the groups of poor were clearly deprived in their own right in the community they were living in. However, while categories such as multidimensional aspects, lack of income and so on appear similar in the way poverty was seen in each location (see Table 1), there were clear differences in terms of severity between the relative poverty in affluent Munich and Melbourne, and the absolute poverty experienced in Addis Ababa.

TABLE 1 Poverty experiences identified by the Poor according to location

MELBOURNE	MUNICH	ADDIS ABABA
• Multidimensional aspects	• Multidimensional aspects	• Multidimensional aspects
• Lack of adequate income	• Lack of material and financial resources	• Lack of money
• Substandard accommodation	• Social and cultural exclusion	• Lack of food
• Family conflict/ breakdown	• Social disadvantage	• Substandard accommodation
• Lack of social/ community networks	• Lack of physical and psychological well-being	• Social isolation
• Personal problems		• Emotional and psychological aspects
• Negative outlook on life		

The complexity and difference of how poverty was experienced across the three sites is perhaps best illustrated by participants' comments. For example: Poverty for Jemma[2] in Melbourne is:

> ... a total castration of the soul, depressing, claustrophobic, with some good days, bad days, where the pressure is constantly on, and you always carry a

weight, juggling funds and resources. It is like robbing Peter to pay Paul, a downward spiral, slipping further and further away and ever getting harder to get out of the mess.

Poverty for Agatha in Munich is:

> ... often a situation one cannot grasp, where one feels intimidated and unprotected. This is why we can say that whoever cannot be heard [in society] will just go under. ... Poverty is therefore not only concerned with money and food but it also involves relationships with other people and the kind of life chances which result from these connections.

Almaz in Addis Ababa described poverty in the following manner:

> I feel always so inferior because I have nothing. It is difficult for me to talk in front of people. When people talk to me I prefer silence. I have no confidence to talk and feel ashamed of myself. ... People looking at me think I am able-bodied but I cannot use my arm and I am afraid of hospitals and needles. ... Wherever I have slept I saw rapes ... it is not safe in the streets for girls and women. There are younger men roaming the streets who are also poor, looking for women. ... Younger girls in particular are moving from place to place and that makes them unsafe.

Poverty in both Melbourne and Munich was less severe than in Addis Abba, where people struggle to survive on a daily basis, with relatively little support provided for them. In Addis Ababa, lack of money was therefore more crucial than in the other locations, representing major difficulties to many who still rely on begging for their daily survival. The poor interviewed in *Against the Odds: Poverty in Addis Ababa* also lived in much more precarious situations than the other two groups, often without being able to meet their daily needs. This kind of absolute poverty contrasted markedly with the emerging poverty problem in Munich, where all people interviewed had a higher standard of living than those in the other two locations. Most disadvantaged in Munich also had access to permanent subsidised housing, compared to those in Melbourne and Addis Ababa who did not. Participants in Melbourne, in particular, had to live in depressing, often run-down boarding houses and cheap rental accommodation, whereas most people interviewed in Addis Abba lived without adequate shelter. Research participants in Munich had also fewer personal problems and addictions than those in Melbourne and Addis Ababa, and felt much more socially excluded by comparing themselves with the better off in their affluent city.

Against the Odds: Poverty in Addis Ababa gives a voice to some of the most deprived people and victims of poverty, and it is hoped that the voices presented here are heard and understood by society and relevant policy makers alike, so that, ultimately, the lives of the poor can be improved. To this end, this publication intends to make a positive contribution to the public debate on poverty in Ethiopia and elsewhere, not only by showing the plight of the poor but also by demonstrating their strengths and their ability to be part of the solution to their problems.

However, due to the global financial crisis and related negative trends such as high inflation and strong rises in food prices, it needs to be noted that many of the figures presented in the text as well as those given by the informants regarding stated earnings, estimates of living costs etc, are likely to have changed significantly since this study was undertaken. In some instances, government policy/programmes may have also changed since the time of writing.

Klaus Serr
Addis Ababa, 2013

ACKNOWLEDGEMENTS

The author is a recipient of an Australian Teaching and Learning Council (ATLC) Citation for Outstanding Contributions to Student Learning, and is grateful to the Australian Catholic University (ACU) for allowing the award money attached to the award to be used in support of this publication.

I gratefully acknowledge the numerous contributions made by the many people supporting the research and the publication. I especially appreciate the work and time of all participants who really form the heart and soul of this book. Amongst these participants, special thanks are due to the poor who so generously allowed the researcher to see parts of their lives. I am also greatly indebted to the following people.

Staff and students at ACU, in particular, to Gabrielle McMullen, Yoni Ryan, Phoebe Palmieri and Anne Cummins, who strongly supported my nomination for the ATLC Citation. Many thanks to Margot Hillel, Michael McKay, Shurlee Swain, Sue Rechter, Peter Camilleri, Sabine Hammond, Jean Mukasa, Nancy Reid and many others for their support and interest in this work. Special thanks to Peter Rendell and John Ozolins for helping with a complex ethics application.

Staff and clients of Hope Enterprises, with special thanks to Zenebe Ayele, Dr Minus and others, who generously gave access to their clients and helped in many ways, including the organisation of appointments.

Staff from the Ethiopian Catholic University of St Thomas of Aquinas, who assisted in some of the organisation of the research, with special thanks to Jose Rogelio Alarcon O.P.

Staff and students of the School of Social Work, Addis Ababa University (AAU), including Abye Tasse, Melese Getu and Deborah Zinn, with special thanks to Meron Ayele and Rahel Shiferaw for interpreting the interviews with the poor, and to Ashenafi Hagos, Wassie Kebede and Berihun Mekonnen, who helped in many other ways.

Staff of the Department of Sociology, AAU, including Getnet Tadele, Abeje Berhanu and others, with special thanks to Yeraswork Admassie, whose comments on various parts of the manuscript were invaluable and very much appreciated.

All those who have generously supported and advocated for the publication, including Berhan Ahmed and Bekelech Habteselassie, African Think Tank; Fernanda Claudio, Australasian Association of African Studies; Jonathan Makuwira, RMIT; and Karen Crinall, Monash University. Also, Dirk Hoekstra, International Livestock Research Institute; and Richard Pankhurst, who read and commented on specific sections of the book.

Australian Scholarly Publishing (ASP), especially Nick Walker for his interest and strong commitment to publish this book and the ASP team for their continuing advice and support.

Special gratitude to Marie Lawson, who has read all chapters, made valuable editorial suggestions and has been enormously supportive throughout the entire process. Marie has been a wonderful friend over many years and this book is, therefore, dedicated to her with love and friendship.

Special thanks to Eric Porter, RMIT, who reviewed many parts of the manuscript and helped in numerous ways, which was greatly appreciated.

All those who provided generous personal support during the journey of the writing, especially Ling and Toby, David, Jan, Julie, and Susanne and Richard.

BOXES AND TABLES

LIST OF TABLES

ABBREVIATIONS

ALDI	Agricultural Development Led Industrialisation
BMAS	Bundesministerium für Arbeit und Soziales
CIA	Central Intelligence Agency
CSA	Central Statistical Authority
ECA	Economic Commission for Africa
ECEA	Ethiopia Commodity Exchange Authority
EU	European Union
FHEW	Female Health Extension Worker
GATT	General Agreement on Tariffs and Trade
GDP	Gross Domestic Product
GTP	Growth and Transformation Plan
GNP	Gross National Product
HDI	Human Development Index
HICES	Ethiopia Household Income and Consumption Expenditure Survey
HIPC	Heavily Indebted Poor Countries
HPI	Human Poverty Index
ILO	International Labour Organisation
IMF	International Monetary Fund
MDG	Millennium Development Goal
MEDaC	Ministry of Economic Development and Cooperation
MoFED	Ministry of Finance and Economic Development
MPI	Multidimensional Poverty Index
NGO	Non-Government Organisation
NIC	Newly Industrialised Country
OECD	Organisation for Economic Co-Operation and Development
PASDEP	Plan for Accelerated and Sustained Development to End Poverty
PSNP	Productive Safety Net Programme
SAP	Structural Adjustment Programme
SDPRP	Sustainable Development and Poverty Reduction Programme
SIPRI	Stockholm International Peace Research Institute
UN	United Nations
UNCTAD	United Nations Conference on Trade and Development
UNDP	United Nations Development Programme
UNICEF	United Nations International Children's Education Fund
UNMS	United Nations Millennium Summit
WCED	World Commission on Environment and Development
WCSDG	World Commission on the Social Dimension of Globalisation
WHO	World Health Organisation
WMS	Welfare Monitoring Survey
WTO	World Trade Organisation

INTRODUCTION

Right around the world, there is evidence of recent high unemployment, dramatic price rises of food, fuel and other basic commodities, and strikes (Seabrook 2007; International Labour Organisation (ILO) 2010). Together, these phenomena give reason for a growing sense of dissatisfaction with existing arrangements in the global economic system. It will be argued here that this system produces inequalities, such as unprecedented wealth and poverty, between and within countries, leading to an ever more divided world. This is a world in which many corporations have higher annual turnovers than entire countries, and where inequality between people is extreme. Indeed, the data in the latest Forbes rich list (Forbes 2011) show the degree to which global wealth has not been shared or distributed fairly. For example, the now 1,210 billionaires command a record $4.5 trillion[1], and just one man's wealth of $74 billion is almost fifteen times the combined resources of those 2.6 billion people who live at the margins of existence—and have under $2 per day.

Growing discontent among ordinary people around the world follows the 2007/08 global financial crisis, in which an estimated $14.5 trillion was wiped off the stock market with 'a world credit loss of $2.8 trillion in October 2009' (Shah 2010). Called by the World Bank (2009) the biggest crisis since the Great Depression, this crisis was the result of large-scale speculations by institutions such as banks and corporations. World trade declined about 6% in late 2008 (European Union 2010a), and further decreased another 0.6% in 2009. Although difficulties emanated mainly from the US and other developed nations, economic output also decreased in developing economies, down 6.1% in 2008 and 2.4% in 2009, with further losses expected (IMF 2010). As the crisis spread around the world it crippled economies, forced millions out of work and dramatically increased 'precarious employment situations ... and the ranks of the working poor' (ILO 2010, p. 6). It also increased the wealth of some corporations and made many of the richest people even richer.

Despite the prevailing economic doctrine, which preached against government regulation and intervention, Western governments were quick to assist corporations with huge tax-payer-funded bailout packages. The US alone is said to have spent $10 trillion, while Europe initially assisted with $1.5 trillion. The 'sovereign debt crisis' required government assistance for entire countries—including Greece, Iceland, Spain and Portugal (Shah 2010)—and public debt in developed nations rose dramatically. Whereas the US bank bailout of $700 billion increased its deficits to almost $13.5 trillion by late 2010, in Germany, the biggest European economy, generous bank rescue packages of €400 billion increased national debt to €1.7 trillion in 2009 (Frankfurter Rundschau, 19 Oktober 2009, p. 1). Thus, stimulus spending to support the market in Europe escalated overall public borrowing and debt accumulation, with total consolidated gross debt for the EU-27 area of 61.5% of GDP, with the largest proportions of debt accumulated 'in Italy (105.8%), Greece (99.2%) and Belgium (89.8%)' (European Union 2010a, p. 112).[2]

While private debt became public through state bailouts, huge profits in the US and Europe made afterwards have been 'privatised' and are unlikely to support workers and public services needed; nor are they likely to be used for productive purposes to create employment (Freeman 2010; Schultz 2010). For example, despite the crisis, annual corporate profits in the US are now the highest on record at $1,208 trillion, an increase of 26.5%. The Standard and Poor's 500 Stock Index also rose 38% from last year, the sixth highest on record. This was largely achieved through massive unemployment with a current rate of 9.8%, where 'companies laid off hundreds of thousands of workers, closed less profitable units, shifted work to cheaper regions and streamlined processes' (Rampell 2010). As Rampell (2010) further reports, corporate cash holdings are now estimated to be around $1.6 trillion, monies likely to be 'invested' in renewed speculative activities, company mergers and stock buy-backs, rather than the creation of jobs. Although corporate super profits have not yet been noted in the Eurozone, apart from the strong economic performance by German industry due to the low value of the euro, profits of billionaires in Europe have also again risen strongly (Forbes 2011).

While the repercussions of the crisis are still uncertain, people in both underdeveloped and developed countries are suffering immense deprivation and hardship. Through the implementation of the existing economic orthodoxy, often called the 'Washington Consensus',[3] unfair global trade arrangements have had major negative effects on poor nations, especially in Sub-Saharan Africa. Indeed, countries like Ethiopia—the focus of this study—find it difficult to trade and receive a fair deal in the global economy. Although supporters of current arrangements see the financial crisis as a temporary problem, believing that the 'global recovery will continue, despite more financial turbulence' ahead (IMF 2010, p. 4), others disagree. For critics of the system, the current crisis raises renewed concerns about the nature and viability of economic globalisation and its negative effects. They also point to the systemic contradictions of capitalist development and flaws in the neo-liberal policies underpinning it (Stiglitz 2006; George 2010; Social Watch 2010; United Nations Conference on Trade and Development (UNCTAD) 2010). Whilst economic globalisation generates unprecedented economic output, the cost associated with its development is often mass poverty and inequality, environmental degradation/climate change, arms race/global conflicts and human rights abuses. Although these concerns have been examined by a number of United Nations (UN) enquiries since the 1980s, little progress has been made to address these issues (UNDP 2009; Social Watch 2010).

As Chapter One thus argues, the latest financial crisis has simply intensified existing structural problems noticed for decades. For instance, several UN Commissions, such as the Brandt Commissions (1980 & 1983), the World Commission on Environment and Development (WCED 1987) and the more recent UN Millennium Summit (UNMS see UNDP 2001), all recognised the crisis faced by humanity. Indeed, some, including the Brandt Commissions, considered the situation so pervasive and critical that they thought the future of the entire human race was at risk.

In this context, poverty has been recognised as a global crisis since the 1990s. This crisis is not limited to developing countries but increasingly involves the most industrialised nations. Following the international forums, the Millennium Declaration committed 189 countries to collective action to alleviate the suffering of those 1.2 billion people then living in extreme poverty by 2015 (see UNDP 2001).[4] Despite these well-meaning efforts and enquiries, this work has not led to the kind of concerted efforts required by governments, corporations and international institutions needed to change existing structures. Some commissions, such as the WCED, clearly operated within prevailing economic thinking, pushing for a continuation of orthodox capitalism as a way out of the economic and other crises. Even the UNMS failed to acknowledge the structural causes of poverty and inequality, ignoring the need for redistribution of incomes and resources. In addition, these international organisations simply defined poverty in monetary terms, without due regard to poverty's complexities and without consultations with the poor themselves.

This book develops the theme of poverty in several ways. Chapter One sets out the history and conditions of poverty, establishing the global economic context into which individual nations must fit. It also argues that while economic globalisation affects poor countries the most, the implementation of the Washington Consensus impacts on all societies, even the wealthiest. Chapter Two then focuses on poverty in Addis Ababa, Ethiopia, showing how such a poor country, already disadvantaged through environmental degradation, famines and other problems, finds it difficult to progress under current international trade arrangements.

In the following chapters, the victims of this unfair economic system speak for themselves. They demonstrate that in many ways they are the real poverty experts, defining their own deprivation as well as developing possible solutions to the problems experienced. In-depth interviews with the poor, therefore, show a much more complex picture than that offered by mainstream poverty studies based on monetary measurements. We learn that the lives and experiences of the victims of poverty are multifaceted, and that poverty includes both lack of income and basic needs, as well as social and emotional/psychological distress. To compare the voices of the poor, relevant service providers and policy makers are also interviewed. Synthesising the findings from the three groups provides a small but significant insight into the experience of some of the most marginalised people. Taken together, the findings present both a powerful societal analysis and an instrument of public policy.

Chapter One

POVERTY IN THE GLOBAL CONTEXT

The persistence of poverty in Ethiopia arises from several causes, many of them operating on a global level. Developments in the global economy since the 1970s have added greatly to existing problems. The return of free market economics after the crises of the 1970s fuelled belief in neo-liberal 'economic adjustment' as the cure for poverty in the 1980s. This required not just economic restructuring but cultural change in developing countries to instil values conducive to economic growth, with growth itself treated as the cure for all ills. For ordinary individuals on the streets of Addis Ababa, the results have been disappointing at best, disastrous at worst. Tracing the impact of these broader developments on the daily lives of the poor gives vital insights into the nature of poverty.

Since the Industrial Revolution, the capitalist system has been characterised by instability, with '130 years of unstable employment with sharp alternations between high and low levels' and 40 years of war (Jones 1991, p. 27). The only exception was the 'golden age of capitalism' (1945–

1973–5), where rapid economic growth and the rebuilding efforts after World War II created near full employment (Bello 2010; UNCTAD 2010). Importantly, many economies then operated highly regulated Keynesian state interventionist policies,[1] rather than the laissez-faire approach advocated by many economists since the 1980s—an approach that minimises regulation and the role of the state.

In the face of the recessionary trends in mid-1970s, policy makers reverted back to the old ideas of classical economics developed in Europe around the 17th–18th centuries (Wallerstein 1980; Weber 1985). The modern version—often called neo-liberalism—relies heavily on assumptions about the behaviour of the market and people themselves. Based on notions of supply, demand and ideology rather than on concrete evidence, governments around the world committed themselves to economic growth at all cost, via privatisation, rationalisation and deregulation (UNCTAD 2010). By doing so they ignored the lessons of the Great Depression, which in many ways was caused by lack of government regulation, the speculative behaviour of capitalists and the fundamental contradictions inherent in the capitalist economy. For example, while the capitalist system produces vast economic output in terms of goods and services, it is prone to boom and bust cycles via expansion and stagnation (Wallerstein 1980). To survive, businesses must constantly strive to become larger, maximise profits and reduce costs. As predicted by Baran (1973) and others in the 1970s, this process invariably results in monopolistic corporations (reducing competition) and wealth accumulation for a minority. In the 1970s, it helped fuel stagflation—a combination of high inflation, low growth and high unemployment. As wealth accumulates in the hands of few people and corporations, oversupply of goods and services (overproduction) becomes more pronounced as wealth is not shared (inequality) and/or invested in more productive activities, so that unemployment increases.

Thus the golden age of capitalism did not last. As major post-war economies, such as Japan, Germany and other newly industrialised countries (NICs) such as Brazil and South Korea, added vast production capacity to the global economy, this period of high economic growth came to an end in the mid-1970s (Bello 2010). When stagflation and the first big recession since the Great Depression emerged, policy makers resorted to drastic changes to deal with the crisis of overproduction (Bello 2010; UNCTAD 2010). In the first instance, many who disagreed with Keynesian state interventions (see Hayek

1960; Rostow 1960; Friedman 1962, 1968) became drivers of a new direction, influencing economists and governments all over the world to implement the ideas of free market policies, similar to those which had proven to be so disastrous leading up the Great Depression (Ellwood 2006).

The free market approach, adopted to rescue the capitalist system in 1980s, basically included three features. The first feature was neo-liberal restructuring in developed countries. The second was increased globalisation through the integration of other areas on the periphery of the global market; these areas include major markets such as those in China and India, adding further to production. This globalisation meant more markets opened in developing countries, gaining access to cheap labour and resources. Achieving this aim meant pushing policies of economic adjustment (monetary policy, trade liberalisation, deregulation, removal of trade barriers) via the Western-dominated Bretton Woods organisations (International Monetary Fund (IMF), World Bank, the General Agreement on Tariffs and Trade (GATT)/Word Trade Organisation (WTO)). The third feature was financialisation. Increased interest in the latter occurred since, despite neo-liberal and global restructuring, corporate profits continued to dwindle in the real economy, as more and more production capacity was added to the global economy from the semi-periphery/periphery (e.g. China, India). In order to maximise profits not paid out in wages (via takeovers and cost cutting), vast sums of money were diverted from 'real markets' into financial markets where money is mainly used in unproductive and speculative activities (Ellwood 2006). The more money/left over profit flows into the financial sector, the greater the accumulative effect, as speculative behaviour builds bubbles which ultimately burst (financial crises). This strategy also drains further resources from productive activities in the real economy, as only real production can create additional value in the economy (Bello 2010). As the latest financial crisis demonstrates, financialisation hurts real markets, which depend on companies and banks to invest in production rather than on speculation, and which employ people who, in turn, can buy the goods produced.

In no other country have neo-liberal principles been more wholeheartedly embraced than in the US, the dominant economic power in the 20th century. Here, unregulated and speculative excesses of the market had already sparked the Great Depression in the 1920s. The more the US pushed for the adoption of this neo-liberal model around the world, the more markets were exposed to short-term speculation (also known as Casino Capitalism), leading to the crises of the 1990s and 2000s (Ellwood 2006). As governments failed to control and regulate corporations and markets, these crises were globalised, creating increased suffering for people who had nothing to do with these decisions and activities. The restructuring of the global economy thus resulted in vast accumulation of wealth by a few corporations and individuals while impoverishing billions of people around the world, destroying livelihoods and working conditions and reducing public services for ordinary people.

IMPACT ON RICH COUNTRIES

The global experiment with 'market fundamentalism', which began in the 1980s, was quickly embraced by Anglo-Saxon countries like the US and the UK, where the Reagan and Thatcher administrations eagerly deregulated economic frameworks. In this process, the role of government was minimised and states were stripped of their public assets (Stiglitz 2006). The free market doctrine also called for the reduction of trade and financial barriers and the deliberate redistribution of wealth upwards. While the associated 'trickle-down theory' predicted that when the wealthy do well they would invest, create jobs and so benefit everyone in the long run, little evidence supports this theory. Instead, income inequality has risen over the last two decades and wage earners in 60 out of 110 countries have lost about 60% of their share of income (UNDP 2010).

The failure of the model was most obvious in the US, where the excesses of wealth and extent of poverty remain the greatest among industrialised countries. As Krugman (2004) demonstrated, while the distribution of middle incomes ($41,000–45,100 per year) in the US only rose by 9% during 1979–1997, incomes of the top 1% ($420,200–1.016 million) rose 140% (about 23 times the income of an average family). The US has also one of the most concentrated distributions of wealth in the developed world. By 2007 the top 1% of households commanded about 34.6% of wealth, 'the next 19% had 50.5%, so that just 20% of the people owned a remarkable 85% of the nation's wealth, leaving only 15% for the bottom 80% of the population (wage and salary workers)' (Domhoff 2011).

This trend was mirrored in the corporate sector in most industrialised nations, where corporate tax fell from 37.6% to 30.8% between 1996 and 2003. In 2007, corporations in the US, for example, only paid 24% of national tax, and workers the rest. Looking at this issue, multibillionaire and the richest man in the world in 2008, Warren Buffet—then worth $62 billion—concluded that his own income tax was far less than that of his secretaries and office clerks, saying that: 'There's class war, all right … but it's my class, the rich class, that's making war, and we are winning' (Buffet 2006, cited in Patel 2010, p. 84).

The neo-liberal model thus worked well for rich individuals and corporations alike. For instance, the number of billionaires steadily increased during and beyond the 1990s. Despite the global financial crisis, their extraordinary riches have accelerated from the year 2000 when 306 billionaires commanded $1.27 trillion, to 1,210 with a total net worth of $4.5 trillion in 2011 (Forbes 2011). Global corporations did equally well out of the Washington Consensus model, so much so that Korten (1995) suggested in the 1990s that 'corporations rule the world'. Their economic power and annual turnover was larger than that of entire countries, and by the mid-2000s '51 of the 100 largest economies' were run by corporations. For example, Walmart was bigger than Sweden, Austria, Norway and Poland; General Motors bigger than Saudi Arabia; BP bigger than Denmark or Indonesia (Ellwood 2006, p. 61).

While the restructuring that began in the 1980s benefitted the wealthy and corporations, many working people lost their jobs. By the end of 1998, more than 150 million people were unemployed around the world (UNDP 2000). This number climbed to 188 million by 2003 (World Commission on the Social Dimension of Globalisation (WCSDG) 2004) and to 212 million by 2009. Despite the predicted economic growth of around 3.1% by the IMF (2010), unemployment rates are estimated to rise globally to 6.5%, and in developed economies to close to 9% by 2010–11. The latest financial crisis eliminated another 34 million jobs during 2007–09, with the largest increases in developed countries, where close to 14 million additional people found themselves unemployed, with almost 7 million in the US alone (ILO 2010).

As unemployment and inequality rose in rich countries, poverty was especially noted in the Anglo-Saxon nations. In the US, studies have found a range of poverty rates, depending on their measures and definitions of poverty. For example, Harrington (1962, 1984) found substantial poverty in the 1950s and 1980s, with rates between 20% and 25%. This rate did not change over the 30-year period despite massive economic growth and the US reaping the main benefits of the global economic system. While strongly pushing the free market model, the post-war period in the US has been marred by stark social inequalities and the highest incidence of poverty in the industrialised world, with poverty rates (50% of median income) on average around 15–17% since the 1970s (see Mishel *et al.* 2003; UNDP 2005; OECD 2010). Even measured with an austere poverty definition, which still 'relies on an "absolute" measure of poverty defined in the early 1960s … and held constant in real terms since that time' (Smeeding 2005, p. 4), the current poverty rate of 14.3% in the US (almost 44 million people) is the highest since 1994. Other Anglo-Saxon countries at the forefront of neo-liberal restructuring have had a similar high incidence of poverty in the mid-2000s: for example UK 12.5%, Canada 12.8% and Australia 14.3% (UNDP 2005).

While Anglo-Saxon countries had particularly high rates of poverty, other major industrialised nations also showed increasing poverty levels. As Japan and Germany abandoned their alternative socio-economic models for the Washington Consensus during the 1980s and 1990s to compete in the global market, poverty also increased in those rich countries. For Japan, this meant poverty levels rising from about 11% in the mid-1980s to a major increase of 15.3% by the mid-2000s (OECD 2010), where one in six Japanese (about 20 million people) lived in poverty in 2007 (Fackler 2010). In Germany too, poverty became more noticeable in the 1980s, and then increasingly in the 1990s (8.5%). Unemployment rose from 4.3 million in 1998 to 5.29 million in 2005, the highest since 1932 and the Great Depression. Rising poverty also led to the first German national poverty enquiry in 2001, and by 2008 about 13% (one in eight) of Germans fell below the national poverty line (60% median of income) (Bundesministerium für Arbeit und Soziales (BMAS) 2008).

In other countries of the European Community, poverty has also been noted since the 1970s, when concerned member states launched the European Poverty Programme via the Commission of the European Communities (see Dennett *et al.* 1982; Brown 1984). Working parties and researchers invariably painted pessimistic pictures of the extent of poverty in Europe then and the possibility of relieving it since: 'such a goal would imply substantial economic and social change, likely to be strongly resisted by many whose interests were served by present structures, including those to whom governments looked for support' (Brown 1984, p. 9). As structural changes hinted at by Brown were not undertaken, poverty estimates in Europe continued to rise from 30 million income-poor in the 1980s to 50 million in the 1990s (Eurostat 1990) and 60

million in early 2000 (European Communities 2002), when national poverty
varied from the lowest rates (Finland 5.4%, Norway 6.4%, Sweden 6.5%) to the
higher rates (Ireland 12.3% UK 12.5%, Italy 12.7%). By the late 2000s income
inequalities had also markedly increased in all EU-27 countries, so that the 20%
with the highest disposable income had five times more than the lowest 20%. By
2007, the European Union (2010a) reported that about 80 million (18% and one
in six people) were materially deprived and about 23% at risk of income poverty
(below the 60% median income threshold), while 8% of the population in work
were also considered as income-poor. Measured by the 60% threshold, the latest
poverty rates in Europe range from the highest in Romania (25%), Bulgaria
(22%), Latvia (21%), Greece, Spain, Italy (each 20%) and the UK (19%), to the
lowest in the Czech Republic and the Netherlands (both 10%) (European Union
2010b, p. 301).

IMPACT ON DEVELOPING COUNTRIES

While the 1980s restructuring of the global economy created unemployment,
inequality and poverty in industrialised countries, the results of the crisis
of overproduction in underdeveloped nations were much more dramatic.
Poor countries at the periphery of the capitalist system were seen as a
kind of 'safety valve' for capitalism—to be integrated and exploited for the
continuation of the system, a process Frank (1972) famously called the
development of underdevelopment. This process saw the creation of huge
debts and economic dependencies, and eventually produced stringent
economic conditions under what is known as 'adjustment' regimes in poor
countries (Ziegler 2005; Stiglitz 2006). Unfortunately, Ethiopia was one of
these countries.

In order to open markets and aid exploitation of resources in poor nations,
the concept of 'development' became useful and was initially applied in the
form of economic (and cultural) prescriptions known as 'modernisation'
(Hettne 1990).[2] Being a Western (mainly American) model, modernisation
related to the neo-liberal paradigm and free market principles, with its
central idea of economic growth, adopted in industrialised nations. However,
development had also a cultural and political agenda; non-Western cultural
values and communist systems were seen as obstacles to Western-oriented
development and 'progress' (Hettne 1990). 'Developed' thus meant being
'advanced' in the Western sense, whereas 'underdeveloped' meant 'being

backward'. The widening gulf between rich and poor countries was then, at least to some extent, explained by development theorists in terms of cultural differences such as 'punctuality, hard work, achievement and other "industrial values"' (Seligson 1984, p. 5).

Development

The model of development was strongly promoted by the international institutions set up at Bretton Woods in 1944 and proponents included the IMF, the World Bank and GATT, later to become the WTO. While most of the 44 countries present at the gathering were trying to draw the lessons from a speculative, unregulated capitalism and the chaos that led to the Great Depression in the 1920s, the resulting agreements favoured an American model, which made the US dollar the global currency by linking it to the value of gold. Since about three-quarters of the world's gold reserves 'was stashed away in Fort Knox' (Hill and Scannell 1983, p. 14), and all international transactions had to be exchanged in US dollars, this agreement gave the US enormous advantages. Equally, the Bretton Woods institutions, which were to play a major part in international development in the future, favoured the US and the other Western powers in many other ways. As voting rights, for instance, were allocated according to a nation's financial contributions, and changes to the rules of the institutions required 60% of all members' votes, it guaranteed the dominance of the US and other Western powers (Corbridge 1986).

In this way, the IMF arose as the most powerful Bretton Woods organisation. Its brief included the regulation of exchange rates between the US dollar and other currencies, and the lending of money during financial crises. The US, which dominated the Fund from the beginning, thus gained control over world monetary policy (Hill and Scannell 1983). In contrast, the World Bank's role was to assist the global economic capacity and the development effort, especially in underdeveloped nations. Under GATT the world economy acquired the framework on which global trade was to be conducted after the war. At least in theory, GATT was to raise the living standards of the global population through free trade—that is, by the reduction of tariffs and trade barriers. The new trade arrangements that followed under GATT (and later WTO) were based on complex and legally binding regulations, underpinned by free-market policies often benefitting a small and powerful number of stakeholders in the global system. Pushed by multinational corporations and the Bretton Woods organisations, these stakeholders have increasingly limited government interventions and regulation since the 1980s (Galbraith 1995; Thurow 1996; Ellwood 2006). Although the Bretton Woods institutions have consistently claimed to be interested in the reduction and alleviation of poverty, especially in the Third World, their projects have drawn heavy criticisms in this regard. Many thus argued that the very policies underpinning their operations represent the ideas of the free market, demonstrating little success in actual poverty alleviation (see George 1986; Hancock 1989; Trainer 1996; Social Watch 2010).

The debt crisis of the 1980s prompted a transformation in the role of these Bretton Woods institutions. The crisis stemmed initially from Western banks lending large sums at cheap variable rates to poor countries, which local elites often wasted on Western luxury items and weapons rather than on productive activities. Then the US raised interest rates to enable it to finance its huge deficit (already $2 trillion by the mid-1980s) and its military expansion, both of which had helped fuel inflation (George 1988). As a result, highly indebted countries were no longer able to pay their debt and the collapse of the entire financial system was threatened (Hettne 1990; Korten 1995). To deal with this crisis, as recurred with the bailouts in the 2007/08 crisis, the loans were refinanced, mainly through US government bailouts of US banks. In this context, the IMF, in its role as 'international receiver', firstly assumed responsibility for private debt, and secondly 'set the terms of financial settlements between virtually bankrupt countries and the international financial system' (Korten 1995, p. 164). In addition, the World Bank also started to own debt and, with its twin organisation, allowed additional lending under certain conditions. In the early 1980s Third World debt stood at $854 million, and between 1982 and 1990 poor countries repaid more than $1.3 trillion (George 1992) to their creditors. Despite these vast repayments, countries accumulated more and more debt, reaching $2.2 trillion by 1997 and more than 2.5 trillion by 2004 (Ellwood 2006), crippling many economies and destroying millions of livelihoods.

With debt came IMF/World Bank conditions and economic adjustment programmes such as Macroeconomic Adjustment (usually undertaken by the IMF) and the World Bank-led Structural Adjustment Programmes (SAPs). These are modelled on neo-liberal trade policies that asked countries to restructure their economies to meet the rules of the global market and, hence, suit Western interests (George 1992). Economic adjustment invariably meant opening the doors for the exploitation of local resources by foreign companies, exposing local markets to competition and importing significant quantities of foreign goods, though developing countries had little to sell on the international markets. IMF/World Bank requirements also called for devaluation of currencies, a reduction of trade barriers and of protective measures for local markets, deregulation (Seabrook 2007) and liberalisation of 'financial and labour markets and a smaller economic role for governments' (UNCTAD 2010, p. 115). Policies were also directed against public subsidies and services to local people, promoting privatisation of state-owned enterprises and utilities, which foreign companies then could buy cheaply. Under this economic regime, public financial institutions, which could lend money for local development, were shut down or privatised, and countries were often not permitted to borrow even to aid their own development (Green 2008). Further prescriptions included the reduction of the role of the state and reductions in social and other public services, such as health care and food subsidies (Ellwood 2006). Invariably, the enforced conditions stipulated 'flexible labour markets', leading to severely reduced working conditions and wages for the average working families.[3] In many regions, such as Africa, fiscal policies thus adopted in the 1980s and 1990s had enormous social costs, where the reduction of public services and agricultural subsidies, for example, increased the number of jobless substantially (Economic Commission for Africa (ECA) 2010).

As many poor countries traditionally relied on their large agricultural bases for export earnings, IMF/World Bank conditions were particularly disruptive in those sectors. In order to increase exports, those countries were often advised to rationalise agriculture by concentrating on specific high-yield crops for export. As a result, many nations grew similar crops and other agricultural commodities, with two unfortunate outcomes. First, such countries reduced their domestic food production, thus losing the capacity to feed their own people and having to import what they needed at great cost. Second, these developments subjected countries/farmers to the increased risks and volatility of world markets and prices over which they had no control. Due to increased competition for the same export markets, commodity prices fell, simultaneously reducing national incomes within poor countries and providing cheap goods to Western nations. As the WCSDG (2004) pointed out:

> ... from 1980 to 2000, world prices for 18 major export commodities fell by 25% in real terms. This fall was particularly significant in the case of cotton (47%), coffee (64%), rice (60.8%), tin (73%), cocoa (71.1%) and sugar (76.6%) (WCSDG 2004, p. 83).

By the early 2000s, falling commodity prices for coffee alone had destroyed the livelihoods of more than 20 million households (UNDP 2005). Following the neo-liberal blueprint, farmers in poor countries grew and exported ever more coffee and other agricultural products, as global export earnings for coffee alone fell from $12 billion in the 1980s to $5.5 billion by 2003. To make things worse, trade agreements enforced by GATT/WTO imposed significant trade barriers, as explained below. Such barriers stifled the economic progress of poor countries as they found it hard to reach markets in the US and Europe, a situation persisting today (Chauffour 2008; Social Watch 2010).

While developing economies were told to reduce both the protection they gave to their economies and their subsidies to their fledgling industries, major Western trading blocks continued to protect many of their own sectors. As the UNDP (2005) suggested, the highest barriers to trade are directed against the poorest nations, which face tariffs three to four times higher than those faced by rich countries when they trade with each other. For instance, in the early the 2000s rich nations spent about $1 billion per year assisting the agricultural sector in underdeveloped nations, but $1 billion per day on subsidising overproduction in their own countries (UNDP 2005). The World Bank's chief economist Nicholas Stern highlighted the problem further, stating that 'while the average European cow is subsidised about $2.50 per day, and the average Japanese cow is subsidised $7.00 a day, 75% of the population in Sub-Saharan Africa live on less than $2.00 a day' (cited in International Development Research Centre 2003). Poor farmers in poor nations are thus hit most severely because unfair competition in this global market prevents them from making a living. For example, as the UNDP reports: 'Cotton farmers in Burkina Faso are competing against US cotton producers who receive more than $4 billion a year subsidies—a sum that exceeds the total national income of Burkina Faso' (UNDP 2005, p. 10). According to the World Bank (2009), in 2007 developed countries subsidised their farmers to the tune of $258 billion (23% of their receipts), leading to an overproduction in those supported markets and an underproduction in poor nations.

Partly fuelled by Chinese demand but also by speculative behaviour of investors, commodity prices rose sharply towards the mid-2000s (Social Watch 2010). The volatility inherent in financial markets also caused drastic fluctuations and distortions in price levels, with various results. The impact of commodity price movements can have positive or negative trade effects on a nation's economy, largely depending on the overall export and import composition. Poor nations, often faced with unfair trade subsidies and restrictions that support developed nations, have little control in this market and effectively become 'price takers'. The effects of the dramatic increases in domestic food prices have therefore been very negative, especially for those countries relying heavily on food and fuel imports. As shown above, trading arrangements in agriculture are highly distorted, discriminatory and non-transparent (Chauffour 2008), and the consequences for many developing countries included the following scenario: 'Import bills increased and balance of payments deteriorated. In all countries, consumers, especially vulnerable consumers, were negatively affected by the rise in food prices' (World Bank 2009, p. 140).

World Poverty

As a result of unfair trade practices and agreements, the income ratio between rich and poor countries widened enormously from 1:3 in the 1820s to 1:72 by the early 1990s. As George puts it: 'by 1983 the trickle-down from rich to poor had become a "stream-up" from poor to rich: the transfer of resources from the developing to the developed world' (George 1986, p. 20). Not surprisingly, by the late 1990s the richest 20% of countries commanded 86% of global GDP and 82% of export markets, with the poorest 20% nations having to manage with 1% GDP and 1% of export markets (UNDP 1999). Since the 1970s, the national income of countries in the top 25% averaged about 23 times that of the bottom 25%. This percentage increased 29 times by 2010. For the same period, the richest nation is now three times richer than it was in 1970, but the poorest is 25% poorer in 2010 (UNDP 2010). At the same time, the global economy grew steadily from $30 trillion in the late 1990s to more than $60 trillion by 2008 (UNDP 2001, 2010).

While the Washington Consensus has increased the fortune of the rich nations, corporations and some individuals, its policies have negatively affected the lives of billions of people. Existing trade arrangements increased unemployment and working poverty, and made millions of workers vulnerable to losing their jobs. The ILO (2010) estimates, for instance, that there are about 633 million people working and living on less than $1.25 per day, with a real risk that this extreme working poverty could rise another 7% (an additional 215 million), especially in South Asia, South-East Asia and Sub-Saharan Africa. Using $2 per day as the criterion, the number of working poor climbs to 1,183 million with an expected rise of almost 6% (an additional 185 million). The ILO estimates also suggest that the number of people at risk of unemployment could be as high as 1.59 billion, making them all vulnerable to severe poverty, as many poor countries lack the social services required to assist them.

Despite global poverty declining between 1990 and 2000 (1,237 million down to 1,100 million), this fall is mainly accounted for by China and India. During the same period, the incidence of poverty increased in other regions, including Sub-Saharan Africa (by 82 million), Europe and Central Asia (14 million), and Latin America and the Caribbean (8 million) (WCSDG 2004, p. 44). However, recent poverty estimates vary. In 2008, for instance, the World Bank changed its long-held $1 per day extreme international poverty line from $1.08 international purchasing power parity (1993 prices) to $1.25 (2005 prices). This changed the poverty estimates from 935 million people (about of 17% of the global population) to 1,375 million extreme poor in 2005 (25% of the population) (see Shaohua and Ravallion 2008; World Bank 2009). The World Bank (2009) also estimates that there are 1 billion people without enough to eat and 2 billion facing undernourishment; it also finds that the situation is made even worse by the recent 'triple jeopardy of the food, fuel and financial crises [which] is pushing many poor countries into a danger zone, imposing rising human costs and imperilling development prospects' (World Bank 2009, p. 1).[4] Thus, the Bank anticipated a further 55 to 90 million people slipping into severe poverty during 2009, with about 40% of developing countries highly exposed to increased poverty effects. While the World Bank (2009, p. 4) thus laments that 'the world can, and should, do better', given the vast resources available, the UNDP (2010) poverty estimates are even higher. Using a new multidimensional poverty definition (with at least 30% of the indicators reflecting acute deprivation in health, education and standard of living) it estimates that 1.75 billion people live in severe poverty and about 2.6 billion under $2 per day. This kind of poverty exists in a world where there are 1.5 billion people who are overweight and 500 million obese (WHO 2011). However, poverty and deprivation affecting poor nations are also expressed in other ways. For example, the average life expectancy of people in Africa is only 53 years, compared with 75 in Europe. Life expectancy also divides globally by income groups: people with low income can expect to live about 57 years compared with 80 years for high-income groups (WHO 2010). In the poorest countries 'life expectancy is now below 51 years; in Lesotho it stands at 46—similar to that in England before the Industrial Revolution' (UNDP 2010, p. 32).

Other poverty-related conditions affecting poor people in developing countries include the many preventable illnesses and millions of deaths (UNDP 2009; WHO 2010). This heavy burden of disease and death in poor nations could partly be relieved through more medical facilities and filling the chronic health worker shortages. According to WHO (2010), inadequate medical facilities and the lack of medicines make life more difficult in more than 30 poor countries. Following the privatisation of medical systems and the introduction of fee for service in health (and education), promoted by the World Bank (see UNDP 2010), generic medicines cost about 630% more in private facilities than in the public sector, and 'common treatment regimens can cost a low-paid government worker in the developing world several days' wages' (WHO 2010, p. 20). While the world spent more than $1,500 trillion on weapons in 2009 (Stockholm International Peace Research Institute (SIPRI) 2010), UNDP estimates from the mid-2000s suggest that the:

> ... amount needed to lift 1 billion people above the $1 a day poverty line—is $300 billion. Expressed in absolute terms, this sounds like a large amount. But it is equivalent to less than 2% of the income of the richest 10% of the world's population (UNDP 2005, p. 38).

Poverty in Africa

Stiglitz (2006, p. 47) suggests that by the 1980s many African countries, like other regions, had 'fallen on hard times' and, often, undemocratically installed regimes ran up an enormous so-called 'odious debt'. As the debt burden became unsustainable, many countries turned to the World Bank and IMF for help and became subject to the stringent SAPs, creating many problems.

During a substantial part of the 1990–2009s, 46 Sub-Saharan economies were managed under IMF conditionality, and 'by the end of the 1990s the production structure of the sub-region had become reminiscent of the colonial period, consisting overwhelmingly of agriculture and mining' (UNCTAD 2010, p. 122). By the late 1990s debt had risen to 108% of regional gross national product (GNP) with an average of 30% repayment of export earnings (United Nations International Children's Education Fund (UNICEF) 1999). Lack of economic diversification and real economic development led to considerable economic stagnation, unemployment/vulnerable employment, increasing inequalities and poverty. Indeed, the UNDP (2002) found that while there had been impressive growth in some parts of Asia, the income of Africa as a whole had dropped significantly during 1975–2000. Comparing Africa's income with OECD nations, Africa's income dropped from 1/6th of OECD countries to 1/14th. Sub-Saharan Africa fell even further behind, its income reduced to 1/40th or less of the OECD region. A similar assessment of the impoverishment of Africa (and other poor regions) is made by UNCTAD (2010, p. 123), suggesting that neo-liberal policy reforms adopted in these regions have either reduced economic development or at least hindered 'crucial investment in physical and social infrastructure' (ibid., p. 123). Today, already high unemployment rates, vulnerable employment and working poverty are on the increase in this region, putting ever greater pressures on peoples' livelihoods (ECA 2010; ILO 2010).

Though international pressure mounted for debt relief for the most indebted countries, international institutions such as the World Bank and the IMF were reluctant to implement change. Nevertheless, the late 1990s saw a programme of debt reduction as part of the Heavily Indebted Poor Countries (HIPC) initiative for those countries whose debt was more than 250% of their export earnings. While a welcome initiative, in 2003, the 27 countries in the scheme still paid $2.8 billion to service their debt, an average 15% of revenues which in the worst cases, Senegal and Malawi, rose to more than 30%. Due to the financial crisis, African debt increased between 2008 and 2009, with the average ratio of debt and GDP rising from 22.4% to 25.4% during that period (ECA 2010). As the ECA points out:

The global financial crisis has reinforced Africa's weakness vis-à-vis the world financial architecture, where it is not a party to most decision-making regarding rules governing global financial flows (ECA 2010, pp. 11–12).

Where economies had made some improvements in the mid-2000s, it was not because of the IMF economic reforms but because of debt relief, price rises in some commodities and fewer armed conflicts. Better economic management also played a major part in countries such as Ethiopia, Tanzania and Uganda (Stiglitz 2006), which chose to place more emphasis on social development. While the incidence of poverty in Sub-Saharan Africa has been reduced between the 1990s and early 2005 from 58% to 51%, progress since has been slowest in this region, with the number of people in absolute poverty increasing from 296 to 388 million (World Bank 2009). Countries such as China, Thailand and Malaysia, which avoided IMF/World Bank policies, did better, in sharp contrast with those that followed their advice.

As will be discussed in Chapter Two, the struggle against poverty in Ethiopia is located within this broader context. The changing fortunes of the international economy, the huge imbalance between rich and poor, the ideologically driven policies of the World Bank and IMF and the endless and often destructive competition inherent in modern capitalism all combine to increase the difficulties of the poor living in one of the most disadvantaged regions of the world.

CHAPTER TWO

POVERTY IN ETHIOPIA

Ethiopia is one of the poorest nations in the world. Its economy largely depends on agriculture, which accounts for 45% of its GDP and 85% of its employment. The country has a population of about 88 million, of whom 17% live in urban areas (CIA Factbook 2010). Ethiopia has a history of famines (e.g. 1972–74; 1984–85; early 2000s), droughts, civil wars and crippling foreign debt, coupled with a low economic per capita base. These disasters have made Ethiopia a prime candidate for international assistance. While significant improvements in many areas have been noted, especially from the late 2000s onwards, these are more the result of debt reduction via the HIPC Programme, major Ethiopian Government initiatives and the work of NGOs, than of the efforts of multilateral institutions such as the IMF. Indeed, as argued by some commentators (see, for example, Dessalegn and Aklilu 1999; Stiglitz 2006), IMF restructuring has largely been counter-productive, even undermining some government policies. One factor, however, limits the impact of both domestic and international efforts: their shared understanding of what poverty means. Although economic and social policy strategies differ, sometimes markedly, all these agencies rely upon the same restrictive measures. This study is an attempt to provide the groundwork for an alternative and more effective understanding of poverty. As part of this attempt, this chapter first considers Ethiopia's place in the globalisation process over the last few decades, showing the effect of the developed world's neo-liberal policies and practices on this country. The concept and measurement of poverty is then discussed, with particular reference to its application in Ethiopia.

ETHIOPIA AND PRESSURES FROM THE DEVELOPED WORLD

As the Washington Consensus and the Bretton Woods institutions gained ascendancy over the international economic system, Ethiopia, like other developing countries in the 1990s, underwent a process of market liberalisation. This process shifted public policy away from a command-based to a market-based economy. Although the former had shortcomings, the free market policies pushed onto the country ignored the complexities of local conditions and, in many respects, made things worse. As we have seen earlier, neo-liberal restructuring had become a prerequisite for countries seeking international financial and economic assistance. With mounting public debt, the results in Ethiopia were no different, and the consecutive 'rescue packages' offered by the IMF entailed the usual adjustment directives. In this context, the IMF imposed restrictions on how foreign assistance could be used (Stiglitz 2006), forced large-scale redundancies on public sector workers, created few jobs, and so increased the incidence of poverty and inequality (Dessalegn and Aklilu 1999; Asmamaw 2004[1]).

As with other poor nations, the Ethiopian economy is predominantly based on agriculture, with a relatively small manufacturing sector. In step with IMF trade-led policy, rather than diversifying its economy—for instance, building up its manufacturing base—the country concentrated on exporting agricultural products. The focus in the 1990s was Ethiopia's Agricultural Development Led Industrialisation (ALDI) strategy. While this had some success, the growth of agricultural production was patchy (Asmamaw 2004). Indeed, some elements of liberalisation undermined others.

In the mid-2000s coffee was still Ethiopia's major cash crop. Despite yielding 60% of the nation's foreign exchange earnings, this sector only employed about 25% of the population directly or indirectly (UNDP 2005). Following the Washington Consensus model of competing in the global

Against the Odds

market, state subsidies on goods such as fertilisers were phased out. Despite increasing its coffee production by two-thirds, Ethiopia saw its income from the sale of coffee decrease from $494 million in 1985 to $178 million by 2003. According to UNDP (2005), the price for a kilo of Ethiopian coffee dropped from an average (over the last 15 years) of $1 per kilo in 1998 to 0.30 cents, with estimated losses to Ethiopia—one of the poorest nations the in the world—to the tune of $200 per household and about $400 million overall in 2003. Not only were the incomes of many coffee farmers reduced below subsistence levels,[2] but the drop in prices also decreased Ethiopia's ability to finance vital spending on social and health services. While the country was thus both dependent on and exploited by the international market, in the mid-2000s, a handful of multinational corporations controlling more than 50% of the sale of coffee increased their profits from $30 billion in 1990 to $80 billion by 1995 (UNDP 2005; Ellwood 2006).

As world coffee prices have steadily increased from the mid-2000s (UNCTAD 2010) Ethiopia's revenues have also benefitted.[3] However, as already discussed, agricultural commodity prices fluctuate and are affected by the volatility of global financial markets. Emphasis on growing commercial crops thus exposes farmers to risks in a market dominated by bigger actors and a process that cannot be controlled by Ethiopia. The production of coffee also varies due to climatic variations and is estimated to have only expanded about 3.9% between 1990 and 2008 in Ethiopia. Production has also slowed as some farmers decided to grow alternative crops due to the very low prices in the early 2000s (Ethiopia Commodity Exchange Authority (ECEA) 2008). According to the ECEA (2008, p. 34), local farmers still receive comparatively little for their produce as most of the local profit 'goes to marketing middlemen'. Likewise, on the international level, '... coffee roasters such as Starbucks are those who obtain the lion['s] share of the margin in marketing of coffee products without the recognition of the coffee producers' (*ibid.*, p. 34).

Muchie (2008) also observed negative trends in other agricultural activities, such as cut-flower businesses, springing up in Ethiopia and other cash-strapped East African countries. Here, big companies set up flower farms in many locations where increased competition between the sites led to higher supply and, ultimately, lower prices.

The problems in agriculture in Ethiopia are exacerbated by the fact that manufacturing is concentrated in only four sectors: food, beverages,

Poverty in Ethiopia

textile leather and shoes. Moreover, these sectors contributed only about 15% of foreign exchange earnings (Ministry of Economic Development and Cooperation (MEDaC) 1999, cited in Asmamaw 2004, p. 12). While unemployment rates in the rural sector were low, in urban areas they increased substantially between the mid-1980s and the mid-1990s, from 7.9% to 22% (ibid. 2004). Given a large informal sector, current official unemployment rates are unclear and only 47% of the population was considered to be in formal employment during the 2000–2008s. Of those formally employed, 51.8% were at risk of becoming unemployed, with 45.8% living on less than $1.25 per day (UNDP 2010).

The concentration of manufacturing in four sectors in the 1990s mentioned by Asmamaw (2004) above has thus changed little over time, with only some additional production in chemicals, metal processing and cement (CIA Factbook 2010). Trade liberalisation has thus largely failed. Although the nation is predominantly agricultural and has sufficient arable land to feed the population (Muchie 2008),[4] the country still relies on food and animal imports and aid to feed itself.

As part of trade liberalisation, policies on currency devaluation and the removal of impediments to local and foreign private investment also changed (Dessalegn and Aklilu 1999). During 1990–2000 the Ethiopian economy had a sluggish average per capita growth rate of only 2.4%, with a 13.9% debt service ratio to GDP (UNDP 2002). Following the path of other African countries, Ethiopia's external debt increased dramatically from $5,206 million in 1985 to $10,352 million (160.4% of GNP) by 1998 (UNDP 2002). In 2001, external debt was 46.2% of GDP, more than 280% of exports, and repayments exceeded 55% of export earnings, despite widespread food shortages experienced at the time (International Monetary Fund and International Development Assistance Staff 2001). Despite the HIPC Programme initiative reducing debt to about $3 billion, by the mid-2000s Ethiopia's debt service still amounted to about 7% of government revenue (UNDP 2005). By 2008 Ethiopia's external debt had climbed back to about $4.289 billion, and by 2009 the ratio of public debt to GDP was 39.3% (CIA Factbook 2010). Ethiopia's GDP was only $88.23 billion and the nation has one of the lowest GDP per capita incomes ($1,000) in the world (UNDP 2010). Estimates of 2010 also confirm the poor state of the economy: imports were $7.517 billion compared with $1.729 billion of

Against the Odds

exports, while the current account deficit amounted to about $2.232 billion (CIA Factbook 2010).

Precipitated by the Global Financial Crisis, interest rates in the US in 2008 fell to almost zero and the US dollar fell dramatically. As a result, food prices in Ethiopia increased dramatically and inflation soared to over 25% in 2009 (IMF 2010). While the government's efforts to restrain prices initially reduced inflation to about 18%, it has recently risen to 29.5% when price controls were lifted again (Muluken 2011, p. 1). The danger now is that the continuing impact of the financial crisis will make the country slip further behind. Given its limited ability to protect itself from the negative effects of economic globalisation and unfair trade arrangements, as well as imbalances of payment, the debt spiral may start again, prompting another round of IMF borrowings with the usual conditions, such as privatisation and selling off state assets, which exacerbated problems before.

WITHIN ETHIOPIA: PROBLEMS, POLICIES AND ADVANCES

In the existing situation, chronic underlying problems in the economic structure are exacerbated by the famines, droughts and civil wars mentioned above. In the mid-1980s alone, an estimated 1 million people lost their lives and between 1994 and 2003, and 5 to 14 million were in need of food provisions every year (Green 2008). In the 1990s and early 2000s, Ethiopia often experienced extreme poverty rates of above 50%. By the early 2000s, Ethiopia was still ranked 168 out of 173 countries according to the UNDP Human Development Index (HDI) (UNDP 2003). As the restructuring of the global economy was under way, the early 2000s saw 49% of the Ethiopian population undernourished (40% of children), 47% of children under the age of five underweight and 51% of children under height. Life expectancy was below 44 years, and the adult literacy rate was only about 39%. Poverty rates were equally stark, with 31% of the population living on less than $1 per day and over 76% under $2 per day; only 15% of the population used adequate sanitation facilities, 24% used improved water sources, about 6.4% suffered from HIV/AIDS, the malaria incidence was 635 per 100,000 and tuberculosis 118 per 100,000 (UNDP 2002).

While Ethiopia has seen many improvements since the early 2000s, one in eight children (about 321,000) still dies before the age of five, more than 18,000 women per annum die of pregnancy-related complications and a further 500,000 pregnancies lead to disabilities (Save the Children 2010). A contributing factor to these problems is Ethiopia's rapid population growth. Of 80 million, 83% live in rural areas. The median age is only 18, 44% of the population is aged under 15 and only 5% are over 60 (WHO 2010). This skew has lead to an inadequate infrastructure. For example, there is only one doctor per 42,700 people, a health worker shortage of almost 168,000 and 33.8% of family planning needs are not met (*ibid.*). In 2008, the number of reported cases of infectious diseases included 3,862 for cholera, 4,170 for leprosy, 2,532,645 for malaria and 3,511 for measles (WHO 2010). Although undernourishment and food deprivation of the total population have been reduced, these are still significant issues (Save the Children 2010). While life expectancy at birth (for both sexes) has increased from 48 in 1990 to 58 in 2008, it is still low by international standards, especially since the expectancy of a healthy life is just 50 years (WHO 2010). For adults, mortality rates from disease stand at 817 per 100,000, at 51 per 100,000 for malaria, at 61 per 100,000 for tuberculosis among HIV-negative people and at 51 per 100,000 for HIV/AIDS sufferers (*ibid.*).

Impressive Progress

Since the early 2000s, Ethiopia has made considerable efforts to reduce poverty and to improve living conditions for the population. From the time its debt burden was relieved, the county has seen higher economic growth, and improvements in living conditions have been noticeable. For example, undernourishment overall fell from 71% during 1990–92 to 44% by 2004–06, and food deprivation (average shortfall of dietary energy requirements) fell from 25% in 1990–92 to 18% by 2004–06 (UNDP 2010). The extent of children (under five) being underweight was reduced from 47% to 38% by the late 2000s. The population using improved drinking water has risen overall from 17% in 1990 to 38% by 2008 (77% to 98% in urban areas and 8% to 26% in rural areas). Access to sanitation has improved over the same period from 4% to 12% (21% to 29% in urban areas and 1% to 8% in rural areas) (WHO 2010). Expansion in the educational and health sectors has also shown impressive progress. Primary school enrolments, for example, have risen from 33% in 1991 to 95% by 2007 (UNDP 2010). Female health extension workers (FHEWs) in rural areas have improved the health and lives of women and children (Save the Children 2010).

Overall, Ethiopia has had significant achievements in delivering basic services. Thus, in the recent UNDP report, Ethiopia has improved its position on the UNDP HDI to 157 out of 169 countries. It shows the 14th highest improvement in health services and demonstrates the 11th fastest improvement overall in the HDI (UNDP 2010, p. 108). All of these achievements put the nation in a good position to achieve the UN's Millennium Development Goals (MDGs) (see Ministry of Finance and Economic Development (MoFED) 2010).

This impressive progress results from conscious government efforts to implement anti-poverty measures and strategies. For example, in 2000 Ethiopia initiated a poverty reduction plan which led to the Sustainable Development and Poverty Reduction Programme (SDPRP) for the period 2002–05. This was followed by the second phase of the poverty reduction scheme, the Plan for Accelerated and Sustained Development to End Poverty (PASDEP) for the 2005–10 period. The PASDEP's direction was to meet the MDGs, improve human development and infrastructure in rural and urban development, health, education and food security. It calculates an absolute national poverty line, and the strategy is also informed by some 'consultations with civil society, non-government actors and partners' (MoFED 2006, p. 1) in areas such as agriculture and rural development, health, water and sanitation, education and employment generation. In the PASDEP, there is also a greater focus on capacity-building, small-scale enterprise development and micro-finance, greater commercialisation of agriculture and private industry development (see MoFED 2006). In 2005, the Ethiopian government introduced a Productive Safety Net Programme (PSNP) to support over seven million of its poorest citizens through a combination of public employment schemes and grants to elderly people, and expecting and nursing mothers (Green 2008).

MEASURING AND DEFINING POVERTY

While the Ethiopian government policies were more effective than the IMF/ World Bank adjustment programmes in reducing poverty, their shared definition of poverty in absolute and monetary terms limited the successes of both. It can be argued that this understanding of poverty is too narrow and too abstract, consisting of a set of concepts developed at an arm's length from the realities of the lived experience of the poor. Such concepts are not without merit; they highlight key factors in how poverty develops and persists. But they also tend to lie within the assumptions of neo-liberal policies while curtailing efforts to find alternatives. Above all, they encourage policy-makers to concentrate on the material dimensions of poverty and, in this way, neglect structural inequality and disadvantage, and overlook the social and cultural complexities that shape the needs and priorities of the poor themselves. This narrow vision is nowhere more evident than in the way prevailing approaches develop a poverty line. As this study demonstrates, direct consultation with the poor themselves quickly pinpoints the inadequacies of current indices. Poverty data is collected in Ethiopia by the Central Statistical Authority (CSA), which conducts the Ethiopia Household Income and Consumption Expenditure Survey (HICES) every five years and the Welfare Monitoring Survey (WMS) every three years. Whereas the former mainly collects income and consumption-related information, the latter collects data on non-monetary items such as education, health and other related deprivation (Tassew 2004).

As shown in Table 2.1, the Ethiopian 2005 absolute poverty line is set at 1,075 birr[5] per year, a figure left at 1995/6 average constant national prices. This poverty line is constructed by 'choosing a bundle of food typically consumed by the poor' using 'the cost of 2,200 kilocalories per day and essential non-food items' and applying this against 'per adult household consumption expenditure' (MoFED 2006, pp. 21–22). However, the real per capita household consumption for 2004/5 (at 1995/96 constant prices) was 1,256 birr (577 birr for food and 678 for the non-food component), an increase of 19% since 1999/2000. The average kilocalories of 2,746 consumed in 2004/5 per adult was also higher than in previous periods (*ibid.*).

Using this measure, MoFED (2010) suggests that absolute poverty has steadily decreased from almost 50% (1994/95) to 45% (1995/6) to 44% (1999/2000) to 38.7% (with 39.3% in the countryside versus 35.1% in urban areas) during 2004/05. It anticipates further reductions for the 2009/10 period to the level of 29%, and even more optimistic progress in the order of 22% for the future, to meet the MDG targets (MoFED 2006, pp. 20–21). Although the Ethiopian national poverty strategy has improved the living conditions of the population and, apart the from income/consumption measures, has deliberately targeted such areas as education and health, the national poverty line would benefit from an annual revision given the current high inflationary pressures and the increase of food and other prices, particularly noticeable in urban centres such as Addis Ababa.

TABLE 2.1 Ethiopian poverty lines used in the 2005 PASDEP

POVERTY CLASSIFI-CATIONS	FOOD POVERTY LINE IN BIRR PER ADULT PER YEAR	KCAL PER ADULT	TOTAL POVERTY LINE IN BIRR PER ADULT PER YEAR	TOTAL POVERTY LINE IN BIRR PER ADULT PER MONTH	TOTAL POVERTY LINE IN BIRR PER ADULT PER DAY
Poverty line	647.81	2,200	1,075.03	89.58	2.94
Moderate poverty line	809.76	2,750	1,343.78	111.98	3.68
Extreme poverty line	485.86	1,650	806.27	67.18	2.20

Poverty rates 1995/96 and 2004/05, measured at 1995/96 national average prices (MoFED 2006, p. 22)

TABLE 2.2 International absolute poverty lines

INTERNATIONAL POVERTY LINE BY PURCHASING PARITY POWER STANDARD	POVERTY LINE AMOUNT IN BIRR PER YEAR	POVERTY LINE AMOUNT IN BIRR PER MONTH	POVERTY LINE AMOUNT IN BIRR PER DAY
$1.25 per day (severe poverty)	7,528.12	627.34	20.62
$2.00 per day	12,054	1003.75	33
$2.50 per day	15,056.25	1254.68	41.25

Exchange rate of American dollar to Ethiopian birr is 16.5 at time of writing

Source: National Bank of Ethiopia, 2 March 2011

An increase in the national poverty line would also be in line with the 2011 pay rise of 39% for civil servants (from the lowest scale of 1,499 birr to 4,343 birr per month) 'to regulate the living standards of civil servants given the inflation rate and rising cost of living' (Mahlet 2011, p. 22). Table 2.2 shows the monthly and yearly poverty line amounts of the World Bank's current international standardised poverty lines (using purchasing power parity) of $1.25 per day (severe poverty) and respective amounts of $2 and $2.50 per day. Using 2011 exchange rates, the severe poverty line for Ethiopia would be 7,528 birr per year, 627 birr per month and 20.62 birr per day. The extent of poverty (or the amount of people considered not to be in poverty) increases quite dramatically when lines of $2 and $2.50 per day are used.

Table 2.3 shows some grocery items which the government had decided to keep constant in early 2011 due to rapidly increasing food prices, but which now are no longer capped. Based on the Ethiopian national food poverty line of 1.77 birr per day, one would not be able to buy anything on the list. Even using the total amount of 2.94 birr per day (food plus expenses) one could only buy some tea leaves. Managing the food budget alone would still be difficult on the severe World Bank poverty line of $1.25 per day (20.62 birr), as other expensive items such as coffee were not controlled, while housing and other expenses such as utilities are not yet accounted for. As suggested by Eden (2011), even at fixed prices in Gotera, a one-bedroom condominium apartment[6] costs between 700–900 birr per month (1,400–1,600 for two bedrooms). Rising rents make it increasingly difficult even for people on reasonable incomes (*ibid.*, p. 31), especially since utility prices such as electricity and water are also expected to increase substantially, with water prices to rise up to 300% for some users (Groum 2011). A poor person is also unlikely to afford even cheap meals. The same applies to low-income workers (earning in the vicinity of 600–800 birr per month) such as daily labourers, cleaners, maids, *zebegna*s,[7] receptionists, waitresses, etc., many of whom are women.

As demonstrated above, using the absolute poverty line is highly problematic, and the PASDEP[8] (and future poverty reduction programmes) would benefit from further development and consultations with the poor to see how they identify their needs and if these needs are the same as those defined by the experts. For instance, are the items chosen for the food bundle 'typically consumed by the poor' really the ones the poor would actually choose themselves? Are the non-food items selected adequate and do they meet the needs of the poor? Have the required items changed over time?

The Ethiopian national poverty line is devised based on an old conceptual framework of absolute/subsistence poverty, a definition derived from the early British poverty studies of the late 1800s and early 1900s, conducted by Booth (1969) and Rowntree (1901). This framework reflects these early researchers' belief in laissez-faire economics, and directly influences the way poverty came to be narrowly defined, namely in relation to 'income, subsistence or the maintenance of physical efficiency, and consumption' (Taylor 1992, p. 101).

TABLE 2.3 Selected grocery items

SELECTED FOOD ITEMS WITH GOVERNMENT PRICE CEILING		
FOOD ITEM	UNIT	PRICES IN BIRR
Bananas	1 kg	5
Beer	330 ml	7.10
Bread	350 gm	3.4
Meat	1 kg	50
Oranges	1 kg	7.50
Pasta	1 kg	18.5
Rice	1 kg	12.5
Soft drinks	300 ml	4.2
Sugar	1 kg	14
Tea (leaves)	100 gm	2.50

Source: For food items with government ceiling see Binyam (2011, pp. 38–39)

The minimalist approach to human need (where life is reduced to basic survival) has also influenced other concepts such as basic needs and relative poverty (see Smeeding 2005), all of which relate to the ideas of the market economy (see Townsend 1993; Seabrook 2007) and the economist's view that economic principles are the best way to organise society (Korten 1995). These old conceptions and views of poverty continue to influence public policy not only in developing countries, but also in affluent societies such as the US, Britain and Australia (Pusey 2003). Underpinned by neo-liberal economic thinking, mainstream poverty definitions ignore structural issues such as inequality, and so help to maintain it (Townsend 1993). This in part explains the focus on economic growth in mainstream poverty discourse, where, to a large extent, the cause of the problem is prescribed as the cure. Absolute poverty (mainly used in poor countries), therefore, tries to measure income/consumption to cover basic necessities such as nutrition/food, shelter, clothing and some utilities. By contrast, relative poverty (mainly used in developed nations) looks at disposable income in relation to other people in a particular society (see Saunders 2005); those with disposable incomes below this level are deemed to be in poverty.

Although there is still no clear consensus among policy makers on how to measure and define poverty (Hauser 1997; Saunders 2005; Serr 2006a, 2006b), expert definitions use monetary (quantitative) poverty measures to classify someone as either below or above a poverty line. Despite claims of objectivity, these classifications really depend on the value judgements of experts in the form of their perceptions of basic necessities and how populations should live. Recent poverty calculations by Shaohua and Ravallion (2008) make this clear. If instead of $1.25 per day, $1.45 per day is used, the numbers deemed severely poor would rise from 1.4 billion people and 25% of the global population (2005 figures) to 1.72 billion (26.6% of the population). A figure of $2 would make it 2.6 billion people (40.2% of the population), using $2.50 would make it 3.14 billion (48.6% of the population), and $10 would put the majority of the world's people in poverty, with 5.15 billion (79.7% of the population). As policy makers use the minimalist approach to save money, the poor are condemned to the lowest denominator, having barely enough to survive. The rich, on the other hand, are never subjected to the same treatment in terms of 'what is enough'. While a substantial part of the global population is missing out on a decent life, poor people are hardly ever consulted about whether this global economy actually works for them. Instead, mainstream poverty definitions are usually constructed by experts without asking the poor about what their needs are.

Criticisms of purely economic indicators have led to the development of alternative poverty definitions. For instance, the HDI, devised by the UNDP in 1990, focused less on GDP and introduced some socio-economic aspects, such as school enrolment and literacy rates (see UNDP 1990). In 2005, partly influenced by Sen's conception of human capabilities (Sen 1992, 1999), the UNDP introduced its Human Poverty Indexes (HPIs) for poor and rich countries; these indexes include factors similar to the HDI, and add measures which reflect decent standards of living in selected nations (see UNDP 2005). In its latest report, the UNDP (2010) presents a Multidimensional Poverty Index (MPI) which measures the number of poor and the intensity of deprivation through ten indicators in three dimensions: living standards (electricity, sanitation, drinking water, floor, cooking fuel, assets), health (child mortality, nutrition) and education (schooling, enrolment). Poverty here is defined when someone is deprived 'in at least three of the ten weighted indicators' (UNDP 2010, p. 224). While still clearly influenced by conceptions of basic needs, this index is a welcome conceptual addition in the poverty discourse.

While poverty definitions based on monetary calculations have their uses, they cannot capture the more normative and qualitative aspects of deprivation and the daily struggle faced by poor people. This aspect was already noticed in the 1960s by Henderson *et al.* (1970) in their major quantitative survey in Australia; they commented on their results based on the income poverty line, findings which:

> ... have all been stated in terms of an artificial concept, the income unit. As a consequence, perhaps they may have lost meaning and impact and it may help to restate them in terms of people, for it is human beings, not concepts or theories, that are the ultimate concern in our study of poverty (Henderson *et al.* 1970, p. 34).

Alternative Approaches to Measuring Poverty

Awareness of the pitfalls of purely quantitative measures has grown steadily since the 1970s and 1980s (see Dennett *et al.* 1982; Gordon *et al.* 2000; Saunders 2005). While reliance on quantitative factors remains predominant in the mainstream, more recent approaches try to refine those measures by drawing on additional qualitative factors. A number of researchers have also begun seriously to explore alternative definitions. Much of the impetus for early alternative developments was the result of Peter Townsend's pioneering work on the relative deprivation index. Later revised by Mack and Lansley (1985), relative deprivation considers the poor as 'those who are excluded from social intercourse: the isolated, the invisible, the hidden and the overlooked' (Townsend 1984, p. 57). Despite its many limitations, the relative deprivation index was important, since it focused on the need for 'an explanation or understanding of poverty as the outcome of the irresponsible exercise of overly concentrated social, economic and political power' (Dennett *et al.* 1982, p. 159). Amartya Sen (1992, 1999), a proponent of the absolute poverty approach in the early 1980s, later developed a notion of human capability (which influenced the UNDP HDI), identifying those abilities required to function in society. This also conceptualised poverty more broadly than just income. While, in Europe, the search for better ways

29

to understand poverty continued and conceptions of social exclusion were developed (see, for example, Gordon *et al.* 2000), these models still miss important non-monetary categories such as emotional and psychological well-being. Other useful ideas, for example Maslow's hierarchy of needs and holist approaches to human needs such as that of Max-Neef (1991) and others (Doyal and Gough 1991), are not utilised.

However, ideas based on peoples' participation are gaining more credibility. Informed by notions of small-scale and alternative development (see Friedman 1962; Freire 1970; Schumacher 1973; Dag Hammarskjold Foundation 1977; Max Neef 1991; Serr 2001, 2004), there is growing recognition of the importance of taking the voices of the poor into consideration when defining and developing solutions to poverty (Neumann und Hertz 1998; Peel 2003; Serr 2006b). The great potential of this participatory approach has also been demonstrated by the pioneering and large-scale World Bank study called *Consultations with the poor* (see Narayan *et al.* 1999, 2000), conducted in 23 countries. This research revealed that poverty is increasing for many people, and that their needs are much broader than just money; these needs include 'happiness, family, children, livelihood, peace, security, safety, dignity, and respect' (Narayan *et al.* 2000, p. xv). Most importantly, the study suggests that by the late 1990s:

> There are 2.8 billion poverty experts, the poor themselves. Yet the development discourse about poverty has been dominated by the perspectives and expertise of those who are not poor—professionals, politicians and agency officials (Narayan *et al.* 2000, p. 2).

While the Ethiopian national poverty line relies on quantitative HICES and related data, there are also participatory studies using either qualitative or a mixture of qualitative and quantitative methods. Such studies include the above-named World Bank consultations with the poor, titled *A study to inform the World Development Report 2000/01, on poverty and development* (Dessalegn and Aklilu 1999); the child poverty study *Young lives* (Tekie *et al.* 2003; Tassew *et al.* 2008) and *Destitution in Ethiopia's Northeastern Highlands* (Sharp et al. 2003). Since some of these studies were conducted in some of the poorest areas, they found a higher incidence of poverty than did the income-based surveys (e.g. Dessalegn and Aklilu 1999; Sharp *et al.* 2003). Others, such as Tassew *et al.* (2008), also confirmed that Ethiopia is making progress in its fight against poverty.

Further, as briefly shown below, approaches that draw on the participation of the poor themselves enhance our understanding of poverty issues. In 1999 the World Bank study consulted directly with the poor at six rural and four urban sites, and documented four dimensions. The first dealt with how poor people perceived/defined well-being (or lack of it). The second showed how they prioritised their problems (and changes over time). The third showed which institutions were important in their lives (and their relationships to them). Finally, the fourth was concerned with their perceptions of gender-related tasks and responsibilities. As that research showed, all participants described their lives as a state of ill-being. As shown in Table 2.4, the poor defined their poverty in terms of 'no future', 'desperation and hopelessness', and 'hunger and food insecurity'. The terminologies used illustrate their experiences and depth of deprivation. 'No future', for example, refers to a life that 'is from hand to mouth', without any chance to make plans for the future. The 'desperation and hopelessness' becomes clear as people have no hope and are left to 'dream' of having a better life, being forever hungry.

TABLE 2.4 Participants' poverty definition, World Bank study 1999

POVERTY CATEGORY	TERMINOLOGY USED BY PARTICIPANTS
No future	Life is from hand to mouth We live only for today It is a life of no thought for tomorrow We envy the dead
Desperation and hopelessness	We are between life and death Waiting to die while seated We are full of debt We have neither a dream nor an imagination
Hunger and food insecurity	We eat when we have the means, and we go to bed hungry when we don't We live on coffee We live as dependents on others We are pitiful Life of hunger is as bad as the hyena

Source: Adapted from Dessalegn Rahmato and Aklilu Kidanu 1999, pp. 27–29

Conducted within Ethiopia, the 2003 destitution study of the Northern Highlands included three zones of the Amhara Region (North and South Wollo and Wag Himra).[9] The mixture of qualitative and qualitative findings described poor peoples' perception of destitution, which comprised three main elements: inability to meet basic needs, lack of assets and dependence on others. When the poor were asked to rank wealth in their community, they described the poorest in the community as 'those who have nothing' and those who 'have nothing to boil except water' (Sharp *et al.* 2003, p. xi). The study asked people to self-assess their situation via four categories: destitute, vulnerable, viable and sustainable (from the time of interview to ten, two and one years ago)—and found some disturbing trends. As Table 2.5 shows, levels of negative states rose: destitution rose from 5.5% to 14.6% over the ten years to 2003, and vulnerability climbed from 17.4% to 54.9%. Correspondingly, levels of positive states dropped: viability dropped from 45 to 27.5%, and sustainability from 32.1 to 3.1%.

TABLE 2.5 Self-assessed levels of destitution and vulnerability over time, expressed as number and percent of sample

CLASSIFICATION	10 YEARS AGO	2 YEARS AGO	1 YEAR AGO	TODAY (2003)
'Destitute'	85 (5.5%)	333 (16.4%)	307 (14.6%)	310 (14.6%)
'Vulnerable'	267 (17.4%)	932 (45.8%)	1,119 (53.3%)	1,167 (54.9%)
'Viable'	691 (45.0%)	672 (33.1%)	605 (28.8%)	585 (27.5%)
'Sustainable'	494 (32.1%)	96 (4.7%)	70 (3.3%)	65 (3.1%)
Total households	1,537 (100%)	2,023 (100%)	2,101 (100%)	2,127 (100%)

Source: Sharp et al. (2003, p. 71)

Despite the limitations and subjectivity of self-assessment, including several possible interpretations of the frequencies shown in Table 2.5, this study gives insights into many issues of deprivation not captured in solely income-based surveys. Findings from qualitative methods thus include lack of basic needs such as clothing and food shortages, housing quality, and health and nutrition, plus factors such as lack of land/farm resources, payment for work, availability/usage of food aid, availability of social, institutional and financial support, access to health and other services, rural–urban linkages (including issues of migration) and causes of destitution.

The aim of the current study is to gain a greater understanding of poverty. It follows recent trends in enabling the poor themselves to speak about their own experiences. It then contrasts these views with those of small groups of professionals working in the poverty area. This project is part of *Shattered dreams*, an international pilot study conducted between 2005–06 and 2008–09 in three communities: Melbourne, Australia; Munich, Germany; and Addis Ababa, Ethiopia (e.g. see Serr 2006a). The purpose of the study is not to test or build on established poverty concepts or theories. As we have seen, their reliance on quantitative, material aspects of poverty is too limiting. Instead, this study sets out to increase insight into the conditions of a very deprived group of people by using a direct, explorative and open-ended approach that focuses on the lived experience of poverty. The basic method was simple and direct. The same core questions were asked of all participants from each of the three groups—the Poor, the Providers (service providers) and the Advocates (academics and policy makers):

1. How do you define poverty?
2. What are the causes of poverty?
3. What are the barriers which prevent fuller participation of the poor in Ethiopian society?
4. How could poverty be relieved or solved?

The presentation of findings in the following chapters is arranged in the order of the four main research questions asked of the respondents. For each question, the responses of the Poor appear first, followed by those of the Providers and the Advocates. All poor participants are represented with a fictitious first name, while the two professional groups are referred to either as 'Provider' or 'Advocate', distinguished by a number.

Chapter Three

DEFINITIONS OF POVERTY

This chapter looks at responses by the Poor and the professionals, and discusses how these different groups define poverty. The issues that emerged cover a range of areas. Apart from the expected income poverty, respondents identified problems with unemployment/underemployment, substandard accommodation, lack of food, social isolation and emotional/psychological problems. These observations paint a diverse picture of poverty, demonstrating that for both groups interviewed, poverty is multidimensional and means much more than just lack of money. In the first part of the chapter the responses of the Poor are discussed, followed by a discussion of the responses of the professionals—first the Providers, then the Advocates.

3.1 THE POOR

> [The poor are those] who have no house, no food … have nothing to eat all day and can only eat here [at Hope Enterprises]. … [The poor] are not considered by the government as real citizens (Befekadu).

As Box 3.1 shows, from the data generated by this study, six categories of poverty were identified, providing the main themes for the discussion.

The Poor defined poverty as a multidimensional experience, not simply as lack of money and basic necessities. Therefore, as well as the five specific categories, a general and overarching category was identified and labelled 'Multidimensional Aspects', as only this latter category seemed to capture the complexity of poverty. This category provided the conceptual tool to demonstrate how the poverty experience consists of many combinations of needs, hardships and emotional/psychological states, which all interact.

Box 3.1 Poverty categories identified by the Poor

- multidimensional aspects
- lack of money
- lack of food
- substandard accommodation
- social isolation
- emotional and psychological issues

Each of these categories is discussed in turn below. However, when the data were analysed, another issue became apparent—the women tended to be more vulnerable and deprived than the men. Contributing to this gender difference was the fact that all women were single parents, raising children under difficult circumstances, while none of the men was responsible for children. In addition, homeless women are particularly unsafe and often at risk of being raped. Thus, despite many similarities in male and female experiences of poverty, the female participants seemed to live lives different from their male counterparts. To demonstrate these differences and similarities, the discussion below always starts with the definitions of poverty offered by the women, followed by those of the men.

MULTIDIMENSIONAL ASPECTS OF POVERTY

I feel always so inferior because I have nothing. It is difficult for me to talk in front of people. When people talk to me I prefer silence. I have no confidence to talk and feel ashamed of myself. ... People looking at me think I am able-bodied but I cannot use my arm and I am afraid of hospitals and needles (Almaz).

While at first glance, poverty for the participants can simply be described as the lack of necessities to survive, interviews conducted with the Poor brought out the complexity of their poverty experience. The interviewees demonstrated the multidimensional nature of poverty by suggesting that their experiences are a combination of interacting factors, which include lack of work and adequate income, lack of basic necessities such as food, housing, clothing and sanitation, and their more complex and subtle consequences, such as being insecure, afraid and lonely, losing hope, and feeling ashamed and humiliated. While this pattern of destitution and hardship holds for both males and females, women in particular are very vulnerable, especially when they are homeless.

The Women

The immense vulnerability and deprivation of the women is highlighted here by Almaz, Kedega, Aster and Belaynesh.

As Almaz lives on the streets, one of her main concerns is safety:

> Wherever I have slept I saw rapes … it is not safe in the streets for girls and women. There are younger men roaming the streets who are also poor, looking for women. … Younger girls in particular are moving from place to place and that makes them unsafe (Almaz).

As Box 3.2 demonstrates, Almaz begs for her living, like many other participants in the study. She stated that people at the local church give her bread and sometimes even *injera* for breakfast. She eats her lunch at Hope Enterprises[1] for 60 cents, and sometimes saves half of it to take back to her sleeping place at the police station for dinner. Being homeless, Almaz is not only insecure but also at the mercy of the weather, with little protection against the cold and heat of the seasons. Like the majority of people interviewed, Almaz has no access to sanitary facilities such as clean drinking water, toilet, shower, or washing amenities. The facilities she can access by paying for them are normally very unhygienic and inadequate.

When Almaz expands on her experiences, she illustrates well the multidimensional nature of poverty. Being poor for her means:

- going two or three times per week without any dinner
- being unable to afford any clothes and shoes
- having nowhere to live

- having no flat or house, bed and cooking utensils
- having nowhere to keep any of her belongings, even if she had some
- having no blanket to keep her warm
- having a broken arm but being too afraid to go to a doctor
- living in fear, feeling unsafe living on the streets
- having no friends or family in Addis Ababa
- being extremely lonely and isolated
- being unable to afford to visit her daughter and family in the countryside.

Box 3.2 Case example: Almaz

Almaz has been sleeping in front of the Federal Police Station for more than one year. She sleeps close to the station's gate so as to be safe at night. She chose this location as she was afraid of what might happen to her living on the streets. Almaz has no friends. She is so concerned about her safety that, most days, she stays at a local church (St Michael's), before going out for lunch, eating *injera* at Hope Enterprises. After lunch she begs for money in the streets and then goes back to the church, listening to religious education, or tries to sleep there as much as possible before night-time. This helps her to be half awake at night, just in case someone wants to hurt her. Before she settles for the night, she puts a cardboard box underneath and covers herself with her shawl. She points out that she used to have a blanket that had been given to her by a foreigner, but someone stole it. During the wet season, when it constantly rains, she covers herself with plastic sheets to escape being wet. During the religious festivities, she is allowed to sleep at the church. As she has no facilities she tries to use the toilet at the church (paying 25 cents), which is a 30-minute walk from the police station, or to use the public toilet nearby[1]. If she has enough money she will walk for 50 minutes to use the public shower once or twice per week, paying 1 birr[2]. Almaz states that there is a broken water pipe that leaks in Piazza[3], where she can wash her clothes.

---

1   According to the informant, this kind of toilet is often a small, corrugated, unsanitary hut with two wooden planks placed over a hole on the ground. People squat over this hole and there is unlikely to be any toilet paper or much water for cleaning up. The informant states that the stench emanating from this 'public toilet' is very strong and it is usually surrounded by flies and other insects.
2   All figures given in birr are unlikely to be current due to the major price increases since the study was undertaken.
3   Piazza is in the centre of Addis Ababa.

While being homeless is very difficult for a single woman, it is even harder for those with children. For instance, Kedega lives on the streets with her two girls (aged seven and 10) and is afraid of the roaming youths at night, not so much for herself, but for her girls. Like Almaz and other participants, Kedega suggested that even young girls get raped on the streets. These girls then invariably fall pregnant, so precipitating the cycle of poverty for women. Kedega's children also do not have the opportunity to go to school. They go begging during the day and sometimes try to sell chewing gum to generate a little income for the family. Kedega therefore explained that she worries about her children, as their future looks very bleak. Overall, *dihinet*[2] for Kedega means:

- inability to care for and educate her children
- lack of a house/shelter
- lack of food items such as *injera*, potatoes, *shiro wot*,[3] onions or pepper
- lack of water, toilet, shower
- lack of personal hygiene items.

As all women interviewed in this study were single parents, their poverty is much exacerbated by the difficulties of having to care for and raise children on their own. Many of these women have great difficulty supporting their children through school.

For example, Aster said that she constantly worries about her children and how to feed and house them. She stated that until recently, she lived on the streets with two of her five children, where they were sleeping under a tree near a church. She explained that life on the streets was very hard. At night they put cardboard boxes on the ground, and since they have no blankets they use their *gabis*[4] to keep warm. They have no toilet, showers or drinking water. During the day they all beg so as to have something to eat, and the children cannot go to school. Even now, sharing a house with another woman, they still have to use the toilet in their local church or a public one. Whenever they can afford it, they pay 1 birr each to use the public shower, and must buy drinking water outside the church in a bucket.

Another example of poverty's multidimensional character is described by Yelfu. Poverty for her is:

- not enough money
- no well-paying and regular job

- not owning a house to live in
- not enough food and basic necessities
- no land
- no stable married life.

Thus, apart from issues already discussed, poverty entails the lack of family, friends and social networks to give support through the difficult times, as well as feelings of dejection, unhappiness and hopelessness. Thus, Belaynesh, for example, thinks that 'there is no way out' of her situation, and feels so hopeless that the only thing she can do now is to trust in God: '... there is no way out and until God intervenes I will have to wait' (Belaynesh).

The Men

While problems with safety and childcare make the lives of the women more complex than those of the male participants, the men's poverty experience is also characterised by multidimensional deprivation. As most of the men live alone, their poverty experience includes feelings of loneliness and hopelessness. For some, these feelings are accentuated by lack of self-worth, health, money and resources.

For example, Bizuayew and Melaku have lost hope; they reported feeling lonely, ashamed and cut off from people. Melaku considers himself 'able-bodied', but has no work, no friends and no support from others. He feels ashamed about his appearance and the dirty clothes he has to wear. He really wants a family:

> I don't even have a girlfriend because I am poor and have no money. Girls don't like dirty people and they don't come near me. But if I have money I will marry and have a family. Having a family is very important (Melaku).

Melaku also explained that even if he has a little money saved he still lacks the confidence to go and drink tea in a shop: 'I would not dare. People would stare at me and the owner and waitress would not be happy to receive me because of the way I look.'

Bizuayew also was dissatisfied with his life circumstances, including his estrangement from his relatives in Addis and his family at home: 'I often get angry about my life and feel pain because of the situation I am in. All my relatives are in the countryside—apart from those in Addis, but I really don't like them.'

Other aspects of poverty in this multidimensional category were outlined by Tesfaye and Melaku. For Tesfaye, poverty means:

- ill health and the inability to do more work
- lack of money and inadequate income
- lack of family, friends and community involvement.

For Melaku, poverty means:

- being dejected and very unhappy
- being uneducated
- feeling hopeless
- lacking self-confidence
- being unable to accept oneself the way one is.

In contrast to the men described above, Getachew was quite philosophical about his life; he has not lost hope and stated that: 'I don't feel anything most of the time and just hope for a better life. We always must have hope that one day we will be okay. I even dream to be a millionaire one day.'

LACK OF MONEY

> Poverty is the opposite of wealth—when you are poor you cannot do anything. But if you are rich you can do everything. Poverty can also be described as 'Matate' [and in terms of] absence and shortage (Belaynesh).

Many of the participants saw the lack of money as a major issue. The shortage of money meant inability to meet adequately some of their basic needs, including food, housing, basic sanitation and hygiene; lack of money, in other words, involves a range of further deprivations.

First, lack of money often related to the lack of opportunity to earn an adequate income. Participants were either unemployed or underemployed, having only some casual work that was ill-paid and irregular. Second, insufficient funds meant that most of the Poor could not afford many of the things they identified as necessities. Third, lack of money often meant daily food shortages. Many of the participants struggled to have enough food; some even stated that they had no food at all on some days during a given week. As lack of work played a large part in the experiences of the Poor, the issue of unemployment/underemployment is discussed in more detail below. Since unemployment/underemployment necessarily entails inadequate income, that section is followed by a discussion of the implications of lack of money.

Unemployment/Underemployment

Unemployment and underemployment was seen by all participants as a major issue and reason for the shortage of income. As there are no universal welfare state provisions in Ethiopia, none of the participants received any income-related social security benefits.[5]

To demonstrate participants' predicament, Table 3.1 shows the stated income-generating activities of each of the Poor, and their earnings in relation to these activities. As the table makes clear, women's earnings are far lower than their male counterparts. This discrepancy arises because six of the women said that they relied entirely on begging, and four supported themselves by a combination of begging and casual work. In Kedega's case, her children helped the family income by selling tissues and sweets.[6] While all the women informants engaged in some form of begging, all men said that they supported themselves through various casual labour activities. These jobs were irregular and almost never paid enough to support them adequately. Based on the figures in Table 3.1, it is estimated that each day the women's average income is 2–3 birr, while the men's is 7–12 birr (figures have been rounded).

The women

Examples of how underemployment and unemployment lead to shortage of money are illustrated below by Almaz, Aster, Belaynesh, Genet, Samira, Yelfu and Zinash. Belaynesh reported that she lives mainly from begging and only earns 2–3 birr per day. While she considers herself lucky because her daughter is supported through school by a local NGO, this assistance is expected to stop in about one year's time. Belaynesh will then have to support her daughter herself, including buying the school uniform and other necessary materials, which are currently paid for by the agency. Thus, she stated that she often cannot meet her basic needs and those of her two children (a 15-year-old girl and 10-year-old boy). She explained that whenever she has not made enough money, she buys only bread[7] and tea for breakfast. She also goes to Hope Enterprises every day for lunch and takes food home for the children. But since Hope Enterprises is not open on Sundays, Belaynesh and her children have nothing to eat at least once per week.

TABLE 3.1 Income-generating activities and related earnings

PARTICIPANT	INCOME-GENERATING ACTIVITY	INCOME PER DAY	TOTAL INCOME LAST WEEK
FEMALE			
Almaz	Begging	About 2–3 birr	N/A
Aster	Begging	About 1–2 birr	5 birr
Belaynesh	Begging	About 2–3 birr	N/A
Fantu	Occasional housework Begging Collecting garbage	N/A	18 birr
Fatuma	Washing clothes for people Begging	N/A	60 birr
Genet	Begging	About 2–3 birr	20–30 birr
Kedega	Begging, but often sick Children selling tissues for 1 birr each and getting 10 cents for each packet. Children also selling sweets & gum to earn their lunch	1.50 birr	N/A
Samira	Begging	About 3–4 birr	10–15 birr
Yelfu	Washing clothes for people	N/A Not regular	15 birr
Zinash	Begging	About 3 birr	N/A

Befekadu	Carrying bags. Income depends on distance, 50 cents per short trip	3–4 birr	N/A
Bekele	Manual labourer	5–10 birr Not regular	N/A
Bizuayew	Manual labourer	20–30 birr Not regular	60 birr
Getachew	Manual labourer	10–15 birr Not regular	N/A
Kebede	Manual labourer	5–10 birr Not regular	50 birr
Mekuria	Manual labourer	10–15 birr Not regular	N/A
Melaku	Carrying bags for people	Not regular	10 birr
Mesganew	Manual labourer	Not regular	22 birr
Shewangezaw	Carrying bags	1–2 birr per day	10 birr
Tesfaye	Makes woollen hats for 12 birr each	Not regular	N/A

Figures given in birr are unlikely to be current due to the major price increases since the study was undertaken.

That income from begging is not enough to make a living is confirmed by all the other women. Genet, for instance, tries to save as much money as possible from 'the alms' she receives from begging, to provide food and clothes for her children. But often she cannot earn enough to make ends meet. Most women, like Aster, Almaz, Samira and Zinash, also suggested that begging is problematic, as it is not a steady source of income. Samira, for example, said that although she usually earns 3–4 birr per day, last week she only earned 15 birr, leaving her insufficient money to buy necessities.

Even those women who depend on casual work, like Yelfu, or on a combination of begging and casual work, like Fantu and Fatuma, do not fare much better than those relying solely on begging. As Yelfu stated: 'I have no regular job and depend on the little work I can find as a "servant", washing clothes for other people. My entire earning last week was 15 birr.'

The ability to beg is also sometimes hampered by illness for a small number of women such as Almaz, Genet and Zinash. Zinash, for example, a widow with two children (a 17-year-old girl and a 10-year-old boy), suffers from TB and is often sick, so her ability to beg is greatly limited, and whenever she cannot beg, her family has difficulty affording food. She pointed out that:

> I sometimes make about 3 birr per day from begging. But I often get sick which means I cannot do any begging. Then we have to rely on my daughter who earns 100 birr per month as a waitress. But this is often not enough to feed us.

The men

Just as the women could not make a living from begging and casual work, the men also struggled. None of the men interviewed had a stable job and income, most had trouble finding work in the first place, and the little work they found paid hardly enough to survive.

The kind of work the men found were casual jobs, either as daily labourers where they are hired by someone on demand, or carrying bags and other materials. According to some of the men, this work can be obtained at building sites, small businesses and local markets. Those who have to rely on 'carrying bags'—like Befekadu, Melaku, Shewangezaw and to some extent Bekele—earn less than a daily labourer. For instance, Bekele normally carries bags, but has, on occasion, managed to get work as a daily labourer at construction sites. Instead of the small amounts he earns by carrying bags, which may only add up to 3–4 birr per day, he can earn 5–10 birr per day as a daily labourer. Thus, he said:

> I am living by carrying bags for people on the road. I usually get paid 50 cents for a small distance and 3–4 birr for a longer way. But this work is never regular and I never know how much I will earn at any time. I really want to be a daily labourer—because I make more money but have not been able to get much work like this.

But Bekele, like all the other men, pointed out that there is sometimes no work and income at all. Then he cannot afford even food, and depends on the subsidised meals provided by Hope Enterprises. When things are really bad he cannot even afford the 60 cents per meal and has to find someone to buy him the meal ticket.

While most men depended on casual work, Tesfaye was the only man who earned his living by making woollen hats. He charges 12 birr per piece and thus estimates his monthly income as 40–50 birr if he works hard. But he stated that he is frequently ill and cannot make many hats anymore.

IMPLICATIONS OF LACK OF MONEY

Table 3.2 provides an overview of the items identified by the Poor, which they cannot afford. The table also makes clear the different needs of the women and men. The most salient of these differences is that many women have households to run and children to look after, while most of the men live by themselves.

TABLE 3.2 Poor participants' list of what they cannot afford

PARTICIPANT	CANNOT AFFORD
Female participants	• enough food for themselves and their children • a house and better accommodation • furniture like a sofa, table, chairs • beds for themselves and children • blankets • cooking materials and basic household goods such as cutlery, cups and plates • traditional food to cook, like *teff*,[1] red pepper, oil, *shiro* • tea, meat and quality food that is nutritious for the children • oil for hair, soap and toiletries • adequate clothing, including one pair of new clothes once per year • school uniforms and other things necessary for the schooling of children
Male participants	• to rent or buy a decent house • house equipment such as a mattress • to buy some more clothes and shoes • to buy enough food to eat or to cook • to have a family, a girlfriend • to go back to the countryside and resettle there • either to buy some land and animals and become a farmer, or to buy a shop/business to make good living and become independent • education or training

1   *Teff* is an indigenous cereal that grows mainly in the highlands and from which *injera* is made.

When the participants do not have enough money, they cannot buy their basic needs. While both women and men interviewed were greatly affected in this way, lack of money was of even greater concern to the women.

The women

Women interviewed in this study not only have to worry about themselves, they also constantly agonise over the well-being of their children. As Yelfu put it, 'women often live for their children—rather than for themselves'. Typical examples here are Belaynesh, Zinash, Yelfu, Samira, Fatuma, Fantu and Genet.

Belaynesh has resigned herself to her fate, musing that 'a person wants everything but can't have much'. Asked what she would need to have a better life, she lists only those necessities that would ensure that her daughter can continue to go to school. Thus, her list includes:

- a better house
- a bed
- *teff* and proper food so that her daughter can get good nutrition
- enough food so that her daughter can have food before and after school
- clothes and shoes for both herself and her daughter
- school materials for her daughter.

While Belaynesh stated that her current income generated through begging is 60–90 birr per month, she estimates that to care for her family adequately, she needs 600–1000 per month. Table 3.3 lists the items she considers absolutely necessary to cover her needs, and their costs per month.

TABLE 3.3 Belaynesh's estimated cost of basic living expenses

EXPENSE	COST IN BIRR PER MONTH
Accommodation	100–200
Clothes (second-hand)	100–200
Teff for *injera*	100–200
Onions, vegetables and other greens	200
Four pieces of soap	10–12
Other expenses	100–200
Total estimated expenses	600–1,000

Belaynesh lamented the few possessions she has with which to care for her children. These possessions include a small stove, one water bucket, a small wooden cupboard for their clothes, one mattress and one blanket for all of them. Asked what she lacks and cannot afford, she listed many things most women have and do (see Table 3.2), as well as:

- equipment to make her own coffee
- blankets
- shoes for her son and daughter
- trousers for her son
- a tape recorder to play 'spiritual music'
- a TV for the children.

The men

As most men lived by themselves, they highlighted their lack of companionship, with some men stating that their poverty prevented them from having friends and family, and others arguing that poverty meant lack of opportunities, education and a general lack of life experiences.

Some men, such as Bekele, Getachew, Melaku and Mesganew, complained bitterly about their lack of possessions and the things they could not afford. To illustrate their predicament, they pointed out that they have nothing apart from the clothes they wear. Bekele, for example, wears very old, dirty and shabby overalls with holes in them, and his shoes (sneakers) are torn at the sides. Bekele looks dishevelled and feels ashamed of his appearance. He stated that he would buy himself new clothes and shoes if he could afford it. Similarly, Getachew, Melaku and Mesganew all pointed to their old and worn-out clothes, lamenting the lack of belongings.

According to Getachew, he owns an old pot in which he can occasionally roast potatoes on charcoal, but this pot is so old and shabby that nobody would even want to steal it. While Getachew reiterated what he lacks and cannot afford, he also made another important point: the poor (and especially the homeless) lack storage facilities for their belongings (as further illustrated in the Substandard Accommodation section below). He thus stressed that:

> Because of my poverty I cannot afford any other clothes, decent food, a blanket, rent a flat or house. ... [And] even if I had any of those things—

like a blanket, for example, I would have no place to put it. Nothing is safe in the tent, and when I am out anyone can steal anything that would be worthwhile.[8]

Apart from what most participants cannot afford, as listed in Table 3.2, there was also a small number of respondents wanting something out of the ordinary. Zinash, for example, wanted a TV and tape recorder for her children. Melaku wanted a truck to set up a business and buy a car. He said that he always 'dreamt of getting a Toyota Pajero, one day', when he can afford it.

While Zinash and Melaku were concerned about the here and now, Fantu and Tesfaye already thought about their 'afterlives'. Both pointed out that while it is very important in Ethiopian culture to receive a burial, they cannot afford the membership fee to join an *iddir*,[9] an organisation that assists people with burials when they die. Thus, Fantu cannot stop thinking about it: 'When I die nobody will bury me. This worries me a lot.'

LACK OF FOOD

Lack of money and income often meant that the Poor had insufficient food, and therefore, heavily depended on the free or subsidised food handouts provided by Hope Enterprises, without which none of the interviewees would have been able to manage. However, participants all commented that food assistance was only provided at lunch time, and not on Sundays. Some also said that it was sometimes difficult to travel to Hope Enterprises to get the food. This limitation applied especially to the men, due to the transient nature of their work, and to the old, sick and disabled. In general, the amount of money available for food also depended on the other expenses to be covered by the Poor. While the women and their children were most at risk of going hungry, the men were also affected by hunger. Some women also depended on Hope Enterprises and similar organisations to help them with their children's school expenses, and were anxious about the possibility of this assistance being discontinued.

The Women

I am so lucky because both of my children go to school. The Christian Relief Fund pay for the children's school fees, uniforms and materials. But I often

48

struggle. When I don't earn enough for the food and rent through washing clothes and other housework, I have to go begging in the streets. ... I work hard to get food for us on most days and try to cook about every second day, depending on how much money I have. I cook mainly *injera* with *shiro wot* and potatoes. Since I have no refrigerator, I keep the leftovers in pots in a hole on the ground (Fantu).

Many women stated that occasionally they had nothing to eat for breakfast and/or dinner. For example, Samira reported having no breakfast 2–3 times per week, and Almaz, Kedega, Fatuma and Samira stated that they miss dinner 2–3 times per week. For people like Genet and Zinash, the availability of food was also highly dependent on their health, as they could not beg when they were sick. A small number of people, like Belaynesh and Genet, reported that at least once or twice a week they had nothing to eat at all.

Many women participants struggled to provide food for their families, make ends meet and support their children through school. A typical case is that of Samira. Like Fantu, Samira's children go to school with the help of a local NGO—which pays the children's school fees and some of the school materials. Nevertheless, Samira said that she finds it very difficult to manage and provide food for her family. To keep the children at school she always tries to provide breakfast consisting of bread and tea, and to save money for dinner by going to Hope Enterprises for the subsidised lunch. If she has enough money, Samira tries to cook as much as possible and manages the little money she has by paying her rent on a daily basis. This is to ensure that she does not run out of food for the children. However, as her earnings are highly irregular, she often cannot afford the family's breakfast or, sometimes, even the dinner. Whenever she does not make enough money by begging, she falls in arrears with her rent but still tries to feed the children and pay back the rent money later. Therefore, Samira is under constant pressure to provide for the family's basic needs.

Examples similar to those shown in Box 3.3 demonstrate how other women like Yelfu, Genet and Zinash try to prioritise their spending so they can feed themselves and their children. In most cases, the women and children rely on a small amount of food for breakfast, such as bread and tea, which have little nutritional value, but the women also report having difficulties providing dinner. Some typical responses were from Zinash:

I will try to buy tea and bread at least for my daughter so that she has something to eat before going to school. I then get my own lunch at Hope which is sometimes free. For dinner I will try to buy *injera* with the cheapest *shiro wot* if I have the money, but we normally go without proper dinner about 3–4 times per week. When we don't have enough money, we share a few pieces of bread and roasted barley. This is poor peoples' food.

Box 3.3 Female case examples of lack of income and food

GENET

Most of Genet's money goes on rent, with little left for food. She therefore depends on the lunch from Hope Enterprises and also begs in hotels/restaurants for food. Whenever she has money left, she will do some basic cooking at home. However, Genet has no friends or family in Addis Ababa, and no one to support her. So whenever she gets sick, as she did last week, she cannot come to Hope Enterprises and get her lunch or beg. Then she has nothing to eat and cannot feed her children.

YELFU

When Yelfu does not earn enough, she depends on food handouts from Hope Enterprises. She often lacks money to buy cooking oil, flour, *teff* and other basics, such as bread. To have more money for food, she buys only two sets of clothing per year, providing she saves enough money to afford that. Yelfu states that she 'lives for her [14-year-old] son' who goes to school, and she works hard to ensure that he can continue to study. Although the school is free, the school uniform and materials are not. These are paid for by Hope Enterprises, which is sponsoring the son's schooling.

ZINASH

When Zinash gets sick and cannot beg, there is not enough money for the entire family to eat regular meals. She tries to buy bread and tea for breakfast but can only afford *injera* with the cheapest sauce even at the best of times. When the family has no money or insufficient food, they share a few pieces of bread and roasted barley (poor people's food). To make ends meet she goes to Hope Enterprises to get the subsidised *injera*. She takes her son with her, but he feels uncomfortable standing in a queue amongst all the poor people. Her son also complains about being so poor, and is ashamed in school when he has no money and other students eat pasta for breakfast.

And from Kedega:

> For breakfast we simply have tea and bread and my daughters eat lunch
> from what they sell. I have my lunch at Hope Enterprises. If we have money
> we will buy *injera* with *shiro wot* for dinner. But we often don't have any
> money for dinner.

While all women were grateful to Hope Enterprises for the food assistance
provided, many were frustrated about having to depend on the daily food
handouts, and about eating the same kind of food every day. Thus, women
like Fatuma, Samira, Yelfu and Aster would rather cook for themselves at
home, but often do not have enough money to buy even basic foods. Box 3.4
lists some of the items requested by those women.

Box 3.4 Requested food items for cooking

FATUMA WOULD LIKE

- *injera* and other food items
- onions, tomatoes and pepper
- cooking oil
- fruits such as bananas and oranges.

YULFU WOULD LIKE

- cooking oil
- flour
- teff
- other basic necessities such as bread.

ASTER WOULD LIKE

- meat
- fruit
- *teff* instead of corn (now costs 600 birr per 100 kg)
- wheat, oats.

The Men

Like the women, most men depended on the food handouts from Hope Enterprises for their lunch. They too made the point that no lunch is provided on Sundays, and no dinner. Some men, therefore, struggled to have enough to eat, and sometimes went hungry. All the men considered food very important, since they often were working casually or looking for jobs.

Bizuayew, for example, makes food his first priority and tries not to go without it. If he has enough money he will have breakfast with bread and even pasta. He comes to have his lunch at Hope Enterprises every day and will try to buy *injera* for dinner at night, with assorted sauces.

While Bizuayew always had something to eat, he was the exception. Many men, like Bekele, Kebede, Mekuria, Mesganew and Shewangezaw, sometimes had difficulties buying their simple breakfasts of bread and tea. For example, Shewangezaw said that, on average, he can only afford breakfast 2–3 times per week, while Mesganew and Melaku said that they do not have enough money for breakfast on most days. Bekele, Kebede, Befekadu, Mekuria, Shewangezaw and Tesfaye all reported occasional difficulties affording dinner.

The importance of food and how the lack of it can affect the lives of the men is illustrated by Kebede, Bekele, Mesganew and Befekadu. According to Kebede, he normally has no money for breakfast and tries to save what he has for his dinner. He stated that dinner costs him about 3 birr and he can only afford it about 3–4 times per week, on average. But dinner is very important for him as he normally sleeps in shelters with other homeless men, where many men sleep on the ground on mattresses next to each other. He said that he dreads the night-time because these shelters are so dreadful (see the Substandard Accommodation section for more details). Dinner helps him to go to sleep more easily and endure these nights: 'Dinner is the most important meal of the day. Dinner makes it easier for me to sleep in the house next to all these strangers' (Kebede).

Whereas Tesfaye said that he saves the costs for food by fasting on Wednesday and Friday each week, Bekele reported eating what he can and also collecting food scraps from the garbage in the city, looking for leftovers in restaurants, and carrying a small water bottle which he fills up wherever he can. 'On a good day' he eats bread and tea for breakfast, *injera* with *shiro wot* for lunch at Hope Enterprises, and whatever he can find for dinner. If he has no money for food on Sundays, when Hope Enterprises is closed, he tries to sleep all day so that he does not feel hungry.

Like most of the other men, Mesganew stated that he depends on Hope Enterprises for his lunch and has not enough money for breakfast on most days. He said that he often misses out on dinner and sometimes begs for food in restaurants, where staff are getting increasingly hostile to people asking for food:

> I can only afford dinner occasionally and beg in restaurants for *bule* (leftover food). But begging in restaurants is getting harder. Some waiters and waitresses now refuse me food and even call me a thief and scoundrel (Mesganew).

Befekadu summed up the importance of food, not just in terms of meeting the most basic human need, but also as an important social and cultural activity: 'I want to cook, eat and be happy, especially during the festivity times, so that I can feel equal to those people who are not poor.'

SUBSTANDARD ACCOMMODATION

> A house to stay in is one of the most important things to have. It provides stability in life and hope. If it is one's own, no one will ask for rent and one is less dependent on others. Having a permanent house to live in is also an 'insurance' providing safety and security. ... [I]t is not safe on the streets for older people and women/girls especially, as young people often beat up the elderly and more vulnerable. These men also rape the women and girls on the streets, which I can sometimes hear from my shelter. ... [And] if someone gets into a fight and comes to the sisters (Missionaries of Charity) with blood over their clothes/body, the sisters will even refuse to assist them with health care (Shewangezaw).

For all participants, lack of suitable accommodation was a major part of their poverty experience. As Shewangezaw pointed out above, a house and home is one of the essentials in anyone's life, providing security and stability. While the living situations were worst for the homeless women and their children, most women participants had more stable housing than the men interviewed. The women usually 'rented a space' or corner in a dwelling, having to share their spaces with other people. This often led to uncomfortable and exposed living arrangements, with few sanitary and other facilities available for the women and their children. Most men largely depended on squalid overcrowded shelter-type accommodation, often sleeping on flea-infested mattresses hired for the night.

The Women

While the three homeless and semi-homeless women (Almaz, Kedega and Genet) were in the most difficult plight, six women and their children lived in more stable but still substandard conditions. Box 3.5 outlines some of the main accommodation problems identified by the women.

Box 3.5 Accommodation issues identified by the women

LACK OF

- decent, affordable and appropriate housing
- secure and stable tenure
- separate and private spaces to sleep, cook, eat, for personal hygiene and toiletries
- protection
- insulation against the cold and heat
- storage/safe keeping for belongings and documents
- amenities for the children
- furniture, cooking facilities, bedding
- sufficient electricity
- water for personal hygiene and to wash clothes
- toilet
- privacy, safety, dignity and self-respect.

Thus, the women's concerns include lack of security of tenure, lack of space and facilities, and lack of basic privacy and dignity. Only one woman, Fantu, had managed to rent a dwelling totally by herself.

Homeless women like Almaz and Kedega are hardest hit by having no accommodation, as they lack safety, are exposed to the weather, have no free access to sanitary facilities, and nowhere to store their few belongings. Homeless women with children find themselves in even more precarious predicaments, as illustrated by Kedega and Genet.

While Kedega and her two daughters normally live on the streets, they have recently found temporary shelter on a veranda, in front of a bar. During the day, Kedega begs and the children sell sweets to make a living. The children do not go to school, have no home to go to, and have to wait until after 10 pm (when the bar closes) before they can return to the veranda. They must be careful not to be seen by anyone, and make sure that all the patrons of the bar have left. Every night, they are anxious about their safety and check that no one is hiding and waiting for them. Only when they think it is safe do they prepare to settle for the night, eventually sleeping on cardboard boxes they have managed to get from a shop owner. Since there are no toilets or other sanitary facilities, they cannot wash, and have to relieve themselves in the open, hiding behind bushes. Again, they must be careful not to be seen, as the streets are dangerous at night. Kedega states that whenever they can they go to the river to wash themselves and their clothes. In the early morning, the family has to vacate the veranda, and Kedega carries all their possessions everywhere she goes, as she cannot leave anything behind.

Genet is renting a plastic *bet*[10] from someone who lives nearby and owns several such places. While she is not quite as desperate as Kedega, Genet indicated that the plastic sheets of this makeshift shelter barely help to keep the rain and wind at bay; neither does the shelter provide protection against the cold or heat, nor offer any security. Genet said she had TB about one year ago and finds it hard to keep warm during the cold nights: 'To protect myself and the children from the cold I cover the mud [floor] with cardboard boxes I collected off the streets. I sleep on one old mattress together with the children to keep warm.'

In Genet's hut, there is no electricity, water or toilet. She said she has to buy the water for 10 cents per bucket, which she uses to wash their clothes, herself and the children. They either use the public toilet, if there is enough money, or simply relieve themselves in the open nearby. There is very little space in this tent for anything or for the children; here they must sleep, eat, wash and play. Genet has few possessions, only a few clothes and some cooking utensils so that she can cook in the hut if possible.

Some of the other women interviewed may not be living on the streets, or in a makeshift plastic shelter like Genet, but also live in difficult and precarious situations. Depending on their available money, they often rent 'a space' or corner in a dwelling; this type of accommodation is invariably insufficient and substandard.

Typical scenarios are those of Fatuma, Zinash, Samira and Yelfu. Fatuma 'rents a space in a house' with her daughter for 60 birr per month. She stated that the room they use is part of the kitchen:

> The kitchen is covered with a lot of soot from all the cooking and it has a corrugated iron roof. The roof has many holes in it, where water leaks through during the rainy season. The walls of the house are made of mud and straw and the ground is also mud. ... My daughter and I sleep in the same room and we both sleep on old bags, covering ourselves with our *gabis* [because] we don't have any blankets. I have one old pot where I can prepare some basic meals on charcoal, if I can afford the food. I can also use the kitchen to bake bread for people if I have any orders (Fatuma).

Like all women (and all participants) interviewed, Fatuma said she lacks adequate sanitary facilities for herself and her daughter:

> But there is no water in the house and I really can't wash my body properly as we have no water here. ... I collect water in water bottles whenever I can and take them home, [so that] we can at least do some basic washing in the room. There is no toilet either and we have to use the public toilet and sometimes also relieve ourselves outside.

To wash her clothes, Fatuma reported taking the bus to a local river every two weeks. Paying 3 birr each time, she and her daughter get to the river at about 8 am, when there are already many other people washing clothes and themselves. Fatuma and her daughter do their washing on big rocks, with soap if they have any. They need to hurry to get everything dry, as they have to leave before it gets dark. While going to the river is also an opportunity to bathe, Fatuma is afraid and just washes her legs: 'Since I am old I don't want to be seen to wash in front of men. There are many young men there and it is not safe for a woman and I don't send my child there [the river] alone.'

Like most of the other women, Fatuma is very anxious about her housing situation. Finding it hard to keep paying the rent each month, she said: 'If I cannot pay the rent, the owners will just take whatever we have as compensation—and if there is not enough to cover the rent, we will get evicted.'

Her precarious housing situation makes Fatuma often depressed and she sometimes loses hope. Despite these conditions, she said that she tries to make sure that her daughter can continue her schooling, but is concerned about her welfare. She has difficulties affording the school fees[11] and cannot provide her daughter with all the things she needs.

For Zinash, things are difficult too. She reported that she rents a small space in a house with her two children for 50 birr per month. In this dwelling, they occupy a small space on a makeshift 'second level', which has been created below the ceiling. Describing their quarters and living situation, Zinash explained that:

> ... to get to our space we have to climb a wooden ladder through a small hole. Under the roof you cannot stand up. I find it difficult to climb the ladder to get up there and have fallen down a few times. The house is near a river and it is very cold at night under the corrugated iron roof [because] there is no insulation. The ground level is rented out to about ten men who sleep on mattresses. There is electricity in the house but no water which we need to buy for 10 cents per bucket.

Apart from the substandard nature of this shelter and its lack of facilities, Zinash is concerned about the lack of privacy and the embarrassment of having to share her living space with so many men. As she pointed out, not only is there is no toilet or water for drinking and washing, there is also nowhere they can wash themselves in private:

> We have to wait until evening when all the men are inside the house. Then we take the water bucket outside and wash ourselves in the dark. Because there is no toilet we use the communal toilet[12] for 2 birr per month, if we have the money (Zinash).

Like Zinash, Samira's lodgings are inadequate for her needs and those of her children. Samira and her daughters rent a small space on the ground of a one-bedroom brick house, for 60 birr per month. She stated that the small room is divided into an upper and lower part. A small space has been created under the roof, by erecting a wooden frame. This is where the two sons of the owner of the house live, while Samira and her daughters stay and sleep on the ground. Samira and the children all sleep on one straw mattress and share one sheet and one blanket between the three of them. There is free electricity in the house but they have to buy the water for 10 cents per bucket.

Similar to Zinash, Samira said she is often embarrassed by her living situation. She too complains about the indignity of having no privacy, and being constantly 'on display' and 'watched' by the two men. Nevertheless, while Samira is indignant about her living arrangements, she had to get used to it. She stated that since it is hard to find places to live, she is still lucky to be able to have stayed in this shelter for almost two years. Making the best of the situation, she explained:

> The children and I wash ourselves as well as we can from their water containers, out of sight of the two men. This is often not easy. ... But we are lucky we can at least use the public toilet in the neighbourhood for free (Samira).

Samira is also happy to have a few cooking utensils. Thus, apart from the few clothes, straw mattress, sheet and blanket, her meagre possessions include '... an old *yekesel midija*,[13] [which] someone gave to me, and a couple of water buckets'.

Whereas Yelfu and Belaynesh also rent a space in a corner of a house, they are better off than the other women. They have to share with only one other female, which makes it much easier for them and their children. Describing her arrangements, Yelfu explained:

> I am lucky [because] the owner took pity on us. Our house has only one room and is made from corrugated iron. My son and I sleep in one corner of the house and the owner in another. There is no furniture or toilet, but a small kitchen outside. I keep all my belongings in a plastic bag. If I have money for food, I can do some cooking inside the house. I am not allowed to use the kitchen and must ask the owner to lend me her *yekesel midija*. We are very lucky [because] there is one water tap with clean water for all of us. We use a water bucket to wash ourselves inside the house and use the public toilet outside which is shared by 4–5 other neighbours.

Similarly, Belaynesh and her daughter share with another woman from the same town she originally comes from Wello. She explained:

> Our house is made of mud with a corrugated iron roof. It is very small, maybe about 2–3 meters. We cover the mud with cardboard boxes and sleep on mattresses. We have some cooking utensils for some basic cooking and buy water for 10c per bucket. We use the public shower for 1 birr each and go to the public toilet or sometimes to the one near the local mosque.

Fantu is the only woman—and the only participant in the study—who has managed to rent a house by herself with her two children. She stated that after her husband died she had nowhere to go and moved into a plastic *bet* with some other people until it was dismantled by the local *kebele*. But she eventually found her current one-room house, which she now rents for 60 birr per month.

According to Fantu, her house is outside Addis Ababa and part of six other houses, located within a small compound. She described it as having one room of about 2–3 metres by 2 metres. It has mud and straw walls and a corrugated iron roof. The family cooks, washes and sleeps in this one room, covering the mud floor with mattresses to sleep on at night.

As they rent a house by themselves, their situation is better than that of the other women interviewed. They have more privacy, at least among themselves, and more safety. They can live in more a dignified way, without being observed by others inside their space. Fantu described their situation thus:

> I own some pots, a small *yekesel midija*, a blanket and a bag from Eritrea. There is one toilet for all the houses in the compound, which is not clean. We take out the mattresses and wash ourselves in the room with the water we get every 15 days in some water containers. This water is included in the rent, just like the electricity, as long as the light is switched off after 9 pm. Light after this time will cost extra. Because we don't have much water we can only wash our clothes in a bucket about every 15 days.

Although most of the women live in substandard lodgings, their shared living arrangements are still more tolerable than those experienced by most of the men.

The Men

Compared with the women, many men interviewed have unstable and transient lives. Instead of renting spaces in houses, they normally sleep in dormitory-type shelters, 'renting' a mattress on the ground. Sharing these places with other similar men, they spend the night in various degrees of discomfort and often under dismal conditions. This type of accommodation situation is reflected in Box 3.6, demonstrating some of the issues identified by the participants. While many are transient, three participants had lived in shelters for longer periods.

Box 3.6 Accommodation issues identified by the men

- being transient, depending on dormitory types of accommodation
- being unhygienic, smelly and without appropriate ventilation
- being overcrowded, with total strangers (often unwashed) sleeping next to each other, in very confined spaces
- having little or no insulation to protect against the cold or heat
- having dirty mattresses which are flea or lice infested
- being closed during daytime
- having no storage facilities for personal belongings/documents
- having few or any appropriate sanitary facilities, such as drinking water, water for personal hygiene and washing clothes, or toilets.

One example of dormitory type accommodation is provided by Kebede, and is similar to that experienced by others, such as Befekadu, Bekele, Melaku, Mesganew and Shewangezaw (as shown in Box 3.7).

Kebede said that he rents a straw mattress for 1 birr per night in a room he shares with about five other people. The type of shelter he described is typical:

> ... a small hut, which may be two by three metres big, with a small window and a wooden door. The roof is made from corrugated iron, [and] ... there is little insulation from the cold at night. The walls of the house are made of mud and straw and the ground is just mud (Kebede).

According to Kebede, the men in the house are usually strangers, finding shelter wherever they work during the day—or happen to be at night. Kebede finds it difficult to get any sleep there because:

> ... the straw mattresses are infested with fleas and bugs. Some men also have lice and there is no room to move on the ground [because] all the men have their plastic bags next to each other, to keep their belongings safe. The lack of space makes the men sometimes fight and the stronger ones try to dominate and create more room for themselves. There is also a strong stench in the hut [because] most men have not washed themselves for a long time. The house has no facilities and everybody must use the public toilet for 25c, each time they need it.

Since there are no facilities, he often relieves himself in the open, and manages his personal hygiene thus:

I normally shower at a private facility [hotel[14]] for 1 birr each week, paying another 1 birr for soap. I take the bus to a river about once per month to wash my clothes. But I have to take all my belongings to the river because I cannot leave anything behind in the house (Kebede).

Like many participants, Kebede reported having nowhere to store his things safely. All men must leave the shelter during the day, and Kebede cannot leave anything behind, as it would get stolen. He therefore has to take his plastic bag with him wherever he goes. This also creates problems when he finds work, in which case he will try to give his bag to a *zebegna* nearby to watch over.

While many of the men interviewed live in temporary shelters, a few men, such as Mekuria, Tesfaye and Bizuayew, lived in places more permanently. Getachew was the only male participant living in a plastic *bet*.

Thus, Mekuria, Tesfaye and Bizuayew are more fortunate than the others, having some stability in their living arrangements. They often share their shelter with people they know and are friendly with. Although their accommodation is not much better than those of the other men, the stability and friendships helped them to cope better with their plights. These three men have stayed at their places for a number of years. Mekuria, for example, has been in his house for six years, sharing it with seven other men who have also lived there for some time. He said he is also friendly with the owner, who sometimes works with him. Whereas the living conditions and practices in Mekuria's and Tesfaye's shelters are very similar to those discussed earlier, Bizuayew is in a better situation than all the other men.

Bizuayew explained that he lives in a compound of three or four small houses. The owner of the house is rich and lives there with his family. Although Bizuayew rents a mattress on the floor in one of these houses with 13 others, his housing facilities are much better than those of the other participants interviewed. As he described his situation:

There are eight men who sleep on the ground on mattresses and, like myself, pay 1.50 birr each. Another five men sleep in cot beds for the cost of 5 birr each. We all get blankets to keep warm and going to the toilet is free. There is also [a] small water allowance for cleaning and drinking. The ground of the house is covered with plastic flooring to stop the cold and the ceiling is also insulated with plywood. ... We all know each other and have been there for some time. ... Everyone also has a key to the house and we can stay

Box 3.7 Case examples of accommodation conditions

BEFEKADU
Rents a straw mattress on the floor for 1 birr per night, in a mud house with about ten strangers. The place is small, overcrowded and infested with fleas and other bugs. The rent of the mattress includes the electricity but not the water, which can be bought for 20 cents per bucket. There is a toilet but it costs 25 cents per use. He relieves himself in public areas and takes a bus to a river to wash his clothes once per month. To get to the river takes 30 minutes by bus, then a 20-minute walk.

BEKELE
Rents a mattress for 3 birr per night in Merkato, one of the poorest areas in Addis Ababa. The house is occupied by the owners who sleep in one corner on proper beds. The other corner has six wooden frames with mattresses stacked on top of each other. People can only stay overnight and have to leave during the day. There is electricity but no other facilities. There is a toilet outside, for the neighbours, but the men can only sometimes use this when it is unlocked. Bekele relieves himself wherever he can during the day and washes himself once per week in a creek, or sometimes with water coming from a storm-water pipe.

MELAKU
Rents a mattress on the floor of a small house with six to seven other people. It is difficult to sleep because there are many fleas and bed bugs. Most men have their belongings in plastic bags next to themselves to prevent them from being stolen. This makes the sleeping quarters even more crowded. There is a toilet the men can use for 25 cents per use. About every three weeks, Melaku takes a bus and a long walk to get to a river to wash himself and his clothes.

MESGANEW
Rents a mattress on the ground with up to 20 others; some men also sleep on wooden planks on the scaffolding. There is hardly any space to move and the men lie so close together that they cannot stretch their legs. This is made worse by the fact that each man has all his belongings with him, usually in a plastic bag. There are many fleas and bed bugs, which makes sleeping very difficult. The men can use a toilet which was recently sold to a private owner who now charges 25 cents per use. The floor of the toilet is made of cement and has a hole in the ground where a creek runs underneath. There are no other facilities.

SHEWANGEZAW
Rents a mattress for 4 birr per day sleeping with six to eight people. He gets a straw sack for less if he does not have 4 birr. The room is about 2 by 3 meters and the men sleep squashed together. There are fleas and other bugs in the mattresses so it is difficult to sleep. There is a toilet on the compound, which can be used for free. He has to pay for water for washing his feet and goes to a river to wash himself and his clothes once a week.

there during the day if we want to. [Because] we all know each other, we can leave our belongings in the house and they are safe. ... We try to clean the house as best as we can and pool our money for chemicals to disinfect the mattresses, to get rid of the fleas and other bugs.

This stability enables Bizuayew to look after himself better than the other men can. For example, he stated that he washes his clothes every Sunday at a river. Before he leaves, he buys soap for 1 birr and then takes a bus early in the morning. After washing is done, he waits about three hours for it to dry in the sun and then makes his way home.

Getachew said that he currently lives in a plastic tent near a bridge, 'where there is a big storm-water pipe underneath'. He felt that since he was homeless and could not find anywhere to live, he made the tent himself. Now, he and another man have at least somewhere to live. He explained his situation thus:

When I had nowhere to go I collected some wooden planks off the streets and bought some plastic sheets for 20 birr. Then I covered the wood with the sheets to make a roof. Now I share the tent with one older man to look after him but also to have some company. We try to protect ourselves from the cold coming from the ground by putting down cardboard boxes. Since the tent has no toilet or shower, I use the public toilet nearby, or just relieve myself at the bridge. Sometimes I will go to a public shower if I have the 1 birr or go to a river to wash myself and my clothes, maybe 1–2 times per month (Getachew).

SOCIAL ISOLATION

A friend is someone who helps you when you need support but [is] also [there] to share the happy times together (Befekadu).

As will be discussed in greater detail in Chapter Four, most of the participants originally came from the countryside. As they migrated to Addis Ababa, many of them were cut off from their families and friends. While the Poor, therefore, often lived lonely and isolated lives in the city, it seemed painful for most of them to talk about their past and about how they came to be in Addis Ababa. Many also felt ashamed about their current position and the fact that their families at home were sometimes not aware of their plight. In some cases, family ties had also been broken so that the participants could no longer connect with their families. In other cases, it was only pride that held people back from returning to their original homes. As the participants were quite uncomfortable speaking about their past and families at home, they gave only some indications about how they felt.

The Women

Typical comments from the women participants were made by Aster, Zinash, Fantu, Samira and Yelfu. They all lamented that they have no family and few friends to support them through the hard times. However, the women did have at least their children to keep them company, and their reasonably stable lives enabled them to make at least some connections with the people they lived with and their neighbours.

A typical situation is described by Aster:

> I am cut off from my family and don't have any friends. No one in my family supports me, like one of my daughters who is married to a rich man but does not want to know and help me. [Therefore] I feel alone and isolated. [But because] life on the streets is dangerous I depend on the company of other women and some men squatting nearby (Aster).

While Aster said that she looks to some squatters to support her, Zinash reported trying to make the best out of her situation by trusting in God to assist her, and by living for her children: 'I have no friends or family in Addis to support me. I have only God. But I try to be happy and don't want to show my sadness in front of my children' (Zinash).

Similarly, Yelfu stated that she does not go out much and has no friends apart from the owner of the house. Like Zinash, she does not wish to show how much she misses her family, and is trying to make her son happy: 'I don't want him to be too negative and depressed. I think this is what he expects of me' (Yelfu).

Poverty for Samira also means isolation and lack of family and friends' support. She has no one in Addis to turn to, and is anxious about her life and not being able to provide for her children:

> Sometimes I just want to commit suicide because of our miserable life and that I can't provide for my daughter properly. We have no friends or relatives in Addis and no one to help us. My daughter is always unhappy with our life (Samira).

While Fantu also lacks family and friends, she was the only participant who rented a house independently, and this stable accommodation connected her to the neighbours who sometimes invited her into their homes. However, as Fantu is poor, no one ever comes to visit her. Thus, the invitations by her neighbours shame and embarrass her, since she feels she depends entirely on the same neighbours for social contact. On occasion, this makes her feel even more isolated and cut off from her own family and other people:

> I often feel bad about my life, sad and depressed. Nobody visits us, but we are always the ones visiting them [the neighbours]. When I was still in Eritrea I had contact with my family but not now (Fantu).

The Men

Like the women, some of the men complained about the lack of family contact and friendships. Bizuayew, Melaku, Getachew and Mekuria all stated that they sometimes get very unhappy as a result.

Mekuria, for example, pointed out that his situation often makes him feel confused about his life. At times he feels angry and aggressive, although he tries not to take it out on other people. He explained his isolation thus: 'I have no contact with my family and have only a small number of friends in Addis Ababa. I have no community involvement as this costs money'.

While Bekele said that he used to have some good friends, many of them have died. He does not trust many of the people he now knows, as they often drink or use drugs. Bekele said: 'I feel alone and isolated and have no one for company. I only get small relief through some religious teaching from my church.'

Befekadu compared the life he now has in Addis with life in the countryside, where he still has friends and family. According to Befekadu, people in the countryside are more helpful than in the city, and the community as a whole is more supportive and caring about the people living there. However, he also pointed out that, in the countryside, begging is not really acceptable and people do not want to help with money, though they will help with food. For example, during the harvest season, farmers are happy to assist with food and cereal, and they give corn to the poor but not money.

Although Befekadu said that he experiences loneliness and isolation because many of his contacts are still in the countryside, he also suggested that the lack of money may lead to the lack of friends:

I am very lonely and isolated in the city. It is hard when you have nobody to be concerned about you and when people around you hate you. If you don't have anything you don't have friends, sometimes this involves money because for many people now, money is more important than people. In Addis, people just say hello (Befekadu).

EMOTIONAL AND PSYCHOLOGICAL ISSUES

I sometimes just dream of gold jewellery, and of eating and being healthy (Samira).

Despite the fact that many of the participants appeared to be quite unhappy about their poverty experiences and position in life, most did not want to talk about how they felt about their situation. Many participants were very religious, and some seemed to believe that their poverty must be 'God's will'. Nevertheless, there were some indications about how some of the Poor felt and suffered.

While most of the women were reasonably well groomed when interviewed, most of the men looked neglected. In many ways, the men seemed to have given up, losing hope to a much greater extent than the women. The fact that the women had their children gave them something to live for, but, on the other hand, it also made them worry about the children and their future.

The Women

Kedega, Fatuma, Samira and Fantu stated that, on occasion, they felt very depressed and hopeless about their lives. In the first instance, much of this unhappiness arose from their concern about their children.

Kedega, living on the streets with her two daughters, said that she is still distressed about the death of her husband and another child, but her main anxiety relates to the welfare of her surviving children: 'I have no one in the world but my two daughters. I am so anxious about their welfare. They don't go to school, and help me by being street vendors selling sweets and chewing gum.'

Like Kedega, Fantu and Samira were depressed and worried about their lives and children. Thus, Fantu worried about what should become of them if something should happen to her:

> I always pray to God that my children don't have my kind of life. My children are so important to me and I live for them. I hope they don't stop school or get ill and I often worry about them and who will help them if I die.

Samira, on the other hand said: 'I feel sad and disappointed about my life and my health. Often I am depressed and worried that I cannot feed my children. If I don't get any money today I am not sure what to do tomorrow.'

The Men

Typical responses by the men came from Kebede, Befekadu and Mesganew.

Mesganew stated that although he has some friends, he is often bored, lonely and depressed, especially if he has no work: 'Often, when I cannot find work, I feel so hopeless. Then I sit around, sometimes alone in a corner, or with acquaintances, being depressed.'

Kebede reported feeling inferior to other people, summing up his poverty and the way he feels about his life by saying: 'I cannot be like other [normal] people and I feel inferior because I don't have anything. … I have no education, no job or enough income. I don't have a family to look after me.'

Equally, Befekadu said he is often depressed and dejected, feels unworthy and desperate, and has lost hope. He has no formal education and missed out on all the opportunities other young men might have had. He said that he has no girlfriend because he is poor and has no knowledge about the world or life experiences, such as someone of his age would like to have had:

> I am unhappy because I am 23-years-old and have no experiences in life for [someone] my age. I don't even have a girl friend. I have not done anything and I have no education. I like football but have never seen a football match (Befekadu).

Summing up his feelings about his plight Befekadu said: 'I often quarrel with my God about this situation.'

3.2 THE PROVIDERS

Providers defined poverty in a number of different ways, bringing out the complexity of the problem. The data yielded four categories, as shown in Box 3.8; the material in each category is discussed below.

Definitions of Poverty

- multidimensional aspects
- lack of money and resources
- lack of opportunities and rights
- cultural and spiritual issues

MULTIDIMENSIONAL ASPECTS

> Poverty is when people lack the means of livelihood, both materially and
> non-materially (Provider 1).

The difficulty of defining poverty is shown in most of the interviews
conducted with the Providers, most of whom (Providers 1, 2, 3, 4 and 6) saw
poverty as complex and multidimensional.

For example, Provider 6 found it difficult to give a clear definition, stating
that income poverty, as the only measure of the problem, is not adequate.
For him, the poverty experience is a combination of a lack of basic needs and
factors which follow from this lack; thus, for Provider 6 poverty means:

- lack of food, shelter and medical services
- lack of running water/sanitation, including bathrooms and toilet facilities
- inadequate income
- lack of resources/essential materials
- lack of education
- bad living conditions
- lack of adequate room, where too many people have to live in one room
  and are exposed to many illnesses.

By contrast, Provider 3 set Ethiopian poverty into an international context,
pointing out that because the level of poverty in a country depends on its level
of development, poverty will vary between nations. Even so, for Provider 3
poverty is not just a matter of economic development, 'natural resources' and
'agriculture', but is also about the lack of basic needs and facilities and human
rights; he defined poverty as:

The deprivation of important things and items in someone's life, including internationally recognised human rights which should be adopted in any country. However, poverty is not the same in all nations and depends on the country's development. In Ethiopia poverty is particularly related to the lack of food, shelter, and inadequate education, health care/facilities. Despite of its natural resources and the fact that agriculture is the backbone of Ethiopia, the country cannot feed itself.

Provider 3 then added to that definition to include some social trends, such as the effects in Ethiopia of begging and marriage arrangements. He further pointed to the plight of specific groups:

Not only do poor people lack the basic necessities, their lives are undermined by having to beg for food in the streets. Poverty is worse for women and other vulnerable and marginalised groups. Most poor children lack adequate nutrition and health facilities and young people, especially in the rural areas, are unable to marry due to shortage of land and resources.[15]

For Provider 1, poverty also is multidimensional and includes:

- lack of means for survival, such as food and housing
- lack of money and property. When people lack money they cannot get what they need.

Provider 1 illustrates his definition of poverty by describing the lives of some of the poor:

Poor people might live in shanty towns and rundown areas without adequate services where they don't have enough to eat and are unable to afford the rent. The poor often have debts they cannot pay and once they are in arrears they might get evicted from the houses and end up living on the streets.

While Provider 1's definition of poverty consists of a fairly simple 'lack of basic necessities such as shelter, food and clothing, as well as the lack of money, resources, employment', Provider 4 defines poverty in much broader terms, to encompass the lack of:

Definitions of Poverty

- money, food, clothing and housing
- access to clean water
- income and employment, especially for young people under the age of 18
- adequate education
- necessary skills/training
- transportation, which means mules in the rural sector and vehicles in urban areas
- health services
- access to communication/information facilities such as telephone, mail/postal services and radio/mass media, including TV, so that people don't know what is happening in the world
- social networks
- access to societal/community-based organisations.

Another example of how the poverty experience can vary is given by Provider 5, who cites rural poverty as an example:

> [Poverty is] the lack of means of livelihood such as food, shelter, clothing, health care, education. This applies especially at the household level in the rural area where there is also inadequate physical infrastructure, lack of financial resources/institutions. Poverty in the rural setting also means the lack of appropriate knowledge and the inability to use the available resources locally.

Box 3.9 also demonstrates that rural poverty has some dimensions different from urban poverty. In rural areas, poverty also means having to make ends meet on small plots of land, so that men often have to leave their families for extended periods to look for income elsewhere. In difficult times, women might also have to assist the family and beg for additional income. Provider 5 points out that in such cases, where both parents are away, the elder children will have to care for the smaller ones. Poverty in rural areas often means little food, lack of facilities, and women and girls having to carry precious water for great distances. But poverty can also be dangerous for the girls carrying water, some of whom will be abducted by other tribes and forced into marriage.

As this section has shown, poverty is not simply a matter of lack of money and resources, although a number of Providers saw money as a very important factor, affecting the daily lives of the poor.

Box 3.9 Case example of rural poverty

Poor families have to survive on very small plots of land where they try and grow a crop such as maize. They might only have one cow and in a good year, when there is a decent harvest, they might have enough food to live on for six months. The rest of the time they will depend on using their labour to work on other bigger farms or go to the nearby townships to earn extra money. Thus, many men, as young as 14–15, will leave their families for many months, looking for work to support their families. During this time the women will stay home to look after the children. Before the man leaves he will try and make sure that there is enough food for the family while he is away. If there is not enough food the woman will also have to leave and beg for food in the local area. In this case, the older children will look after the animals and their smaller brothers and sisters.

Poor farmers will mainly eat maize with boiled cabbages. If available, they will also boil some milk with a few coffee beans. Many rural families have to walk for 5–6 hours to fetch their water. Whereas wealthier peasants have donkeys to carry the water, in poorer families bigger girls (12 years and older) and women have to walk for miles to get it. Thus, they will leave very early in the morning to carry often 20 litres all the way back home. Poverty is also dangerous. While richer farmers have donkeys and servants to protect them on the way, poor girls carrying the water by themselves are defenceless. Many girls are thus abducted by men in the bush who force them into marriage.

LACK OF MONEY AND RESOURCES

Poverty is also expensive because the poor peasant can only buy goods in small quantities for their daily use, instead of buying [in] bulk, which is cheaper. The poor often have nothing to live on for the next day/next morning and never know what is going to happen. They live by chance and cannot plan their lives like the wealthy farmer who can plan ahead to save and even invest money (Provider 5).

While Provider 5 makes clear how income poverty in the rural sector puts people into a disadvantaged position from which they often do not recover, Provider 2 looks at the implications of lack of money even for those who have casual jobs in the city. Provider 2 makes the important connection between low levels of education of the poor and their low incomes, arguing that lack of education means the poor have little choice but to look for the lowest paid jobs, such as daily labouring. However, the incomes from these kinds of jobs are unlikely to be adequate to pay rent on a house and for the living expenses of a family.

According to Provider 2, even the cheaper houses (two rooms) cost about 600 birr per month, while the manual labourer can only earn about 15–20 birr per day (100–120 birr per week, or 400–480 birr per month). He also points out that labouring work is highly casual and its income very unpredictable, a situation which does not guarantee a stable income for the poor:

> Since this kind of work is requested on building sites on demand, the income is very unpredictable and unstable. Thus, sometimes there is no work on construction sites, especially of late where the industry suffered delays because of shortages of steel, cement and other materials. Until the material arrives people have no work at all and have no support from anyone (Provider 2).

However, Provider 2 also makes the point that it is not only those with casual labouring jobs who are struggling. He draws attention to another related group of people he calls the 'working poor', who have stable jobs but earn barely enough to meet the needs of a family. Using the example of a low-paid public servant, Provider 2 states:

> A lower paid public servant, for example, earns only about 320 birr per week. This amount barely covers the rent and the basic necessities such as food, especially if there is only one person working in the family, often with many dependents.

Provider 2's account of the struggles of low-paid public servants and people with manual labour jobs reinforces the fact that those who do not have even this kind of work are even more deprived and impoverished. Thus, it is very unlikely that such people will be able to meet their basic needs.

Providers 3, 4 and 6 pointed out that, apart from the poor lacking the means to buy goods and services to meet their needs, lack of money also has social consequences. For example, Providers 3 and 4 argued that lack of money affects people's ability to marry, as young people do not have enough income to leave their parents and establish an independent household. This situation puts extra pressure on their existing families which have to continue to support them. However, by not being able to have their own family, young people cannot fulfil one of the most fundamental human needs of a person:

Lack of money also means that young people have to stay at home with their parents or other family members, like a brother for example, who will have the responsibility to look after them. Without money a young person has no resources to keep a separate household and therefore cannot get married, have children and have their own life. But having a family and children is one of the most fundamental human needs which can often not be met by poor young people (Provider 3).

Similarly, Provider 4 argued that while weddings are very important in people's lives, 'they very are expensive'. Accordingly:

Especially poor people are unable to marry until they are in their 30s–40s because they lack the necessary income to be able to save enough money. Since there are no social security payments, young people are forced to depend on themselves. Even some of poorer middle class students, struggling through university, cannot marry early as they have to save some money for a house first, unless they have wealthy parents (Provider 4).

For Provider 6, lack of money also means lack of status in the community, because 'without money the person concerned is considered a "nobody"'.

At the same time, lack of money also means that the poor cannot afford the membership fees necessary to join membership-based community organisations such as *iddirs*, which are set up to assist families in need. Referring to the plight of 'the sick and the disabled' in particular, Provider 6 states that:

People with disabilities and illnesses such as leprosy, for example, often find themselves isolated and ostracised by the community, without any assistance. Some of these desperate people were in the end forced to set up their own community near the old airport.

Provider 6 argued that in addition to these issues, without money the poor are unable to participate in the political process and, since they do not have access to modern technology, they cannot participate in the modern world. A poor person, therefore, cannot:

- hold a political office, since one requires money to lobby. A poor person can therefore never be elected to be a politician

73

- buy and obtain modern technology. Poor people don't have computers, mobile phones and other electronic devices. They are totally cut off from the modern world (Provider 6).

LACK OF OPPORTUNITIES AND RIGHTS

> In fact, as poor people lack opportunities to have a better life, they might sometimes get involved in criminal behaviour. If you put someone in the corner, they might have no other choice (Provider 1).

For Providers 1, 2, 3, 5 and 7 poverty was also related to lack of opportunities and rights. According to Provider 1, poor people often have few choices and opportunities in life, as they cannot get into the educational system, accumulate knowledge, or develop the necessary understanding to succeed in society. Thus, the poor are powerless and marginalised, and do not have access to health care and other services, even though they might be entitled to some of these via their local *kebeles*. Provider 1 argued that 'poor people have little to bargain with' and are under constant pressure by society. In many ways, they are disadvantaged and treated with suspicion by both the wealthy and by the authorities. Thus, the poor:

> ... are often suspected of deviant behaviour by mainstream society because they 'might steal something, or get drunk' and are under constant scrutiny by the rich and wealthy. One example of this negative thinking about the poor is the recent trend to force out beggars from the cities. Thus, some beggars were forcefully removed from Addis Ababa, where the authorities made no prior arrangements for them to be settled elsewhere (Provider 1).

Other comments by a small number of Providers related to the lack of opportunities for women, the inability of the poor to go to school and the lack of basic rights of the poor. In addition, there is an example relating to the rural setting, giving a very different perspective from those provided from the city.

Providers 1 and 7 stated that women are particularly vulnerable in society and have fewer opportunities than men to develop themselves. According to Provider 1, while women have many responsibilities heading households and often have many dependents to look after, they hardly have time to leave the house. He related this situation to the continuation of 'traditional values' which persist in Ethiopian society. Provider 7 argued in similar fashion: 'Women are particularly vulnerable to poverty as the tradition still demands of them to stay home and do the housework, thus depending on their husbands to provide for them and their children.'

For Provider 2, poor families have few opportunities to advance in society. With few resources and no assistance, they have trouble sending their children to school, and are often unable to afford school fees and exercise books. According to Provider 2, poor parents not only lack support to keep children at school, but many schools are also inadequate:

> Schools in poorer areas are often overcrowded with up to 70 students in one class and there is a high drop-out rate among the students. Poorer parents don't get any assistance or guidance to make it easier for their children to attend school. Given the lack of resources of their parents, poor children face uncertain futures with little opportunities to advance in society (Provider 2).

For Providers 3 and 6, poverty also relates to the denial of basic rights and freedoms. Provider 3, in particular, felt that the poor lacked political participation, which resulted in their loss of dignity as human beings. Thus, she stated that:

> Poor people are also denied the right to express their views and feelings freely by those in power. They, therefore, cannot exercise their right to develop ideas and lack participation in the social and cultural fabric of society (Provider 3).

Similarly, Provider 6 suggested that the poor lack the opportunity to have their voices heard in society, and as a result '… are not able to change their living conditions and lose hope and courage. This is why they feel inferior and fearful of having no future.'

While all the other comments by the Providers related to the poor in the capital city, Provider 5 gave an example of poor farmers in the countryside. The extent of the lack of opportunity and related lack of access to facilities here takes on a different meaning and describes a different kind of deprivation. Using a typical situation of a poor farming family, Provider 5 suggested that such a family lacks the opportunities and facilities that many people in the city enjoy.

To illustrate this, he first described a typical poor farmer's dwelling, and then the living conditions and 'facilities' inside such a hut:

> A typical local *tukul* is a hut made from straw. It will only be 3–4 meters in diameter. It will be built on mud and is just about 1.50–2 meters high. Everything the family owns will be placed inside this hut, such as cooking utensils made from clay. The hut will be divided with a basic partition where as many as 5–8 people sleep on the ground on straw. The family's animals stay near the door and cooking will be done in another corner of the hut. If the family is very poor they will use the woman's *gabi*, a traditional hand-woven shawl made from thick cotton, as blanket at night. The hut has no windows and only a small door that is made by tying tree branches together with straw (Provider 5).

Life inside the hut and its conditions were described in the following way:

> Inside it will be very dark, smoky and smelling of cow dung. There will be many lice and bed bugs. There is no toilet or shower. Because water is so scarce families cannot wash themselves often and relieve themselves under bushes. In these circumstances it is also difficult to make love since there is no water to wash. Poor farmers have no shoes and wear no underpants. The clothes they have they wear every day, patching-up the wear and tear (Provider 5).

CULTURAL AND SPIRITUAL ISSUES

> Some people are trying to escape poverty by begging, which demonstrates the dying values of our country (Provider 6).

A number of informants, such as Providers 7, 4, 5 and 6, suggested that there is a relationship between cultural attitudes/practices and spiritual values and poverty. For Provider 7 'poverty is the consequence of the selfishness of human beings [who are not willing] to share what they have'.

Provider 5, meanwhile, stated that '… it's interesting … that the poorer you are the more children you will have'.

Whether the attitudes and behaviours of the poor are the result of poverty itself or of traditional culture was a point of disagreement amongst the Providers. Provider 1 felt that some traditions and ways of thinking keep the poor 'ignorant', making it difficult for them to look at alternative positions in life or expect better outcomes. This ignorance in turn influences the way poor people feel about their situation, and ultimately results in their failure to look after themselves:

> Their general outlook in life might therefore be narrow and their thinking patterns might prevent them from imagining a better life and outcomes. It could also result in the inability to look after oneself, feeling inferior and psychologically deprived (Provider 1).

By contrast, Provider 6 thought that poor people often develop self-defeating and negative attitudes because of their dire situations. Since they cannot change their lives, many of the poor and homeless have come to accept their plight as 'normal'. Provider 6 expanded on this argument:

> We, as a society as a whole, have now accepted poverty and think it is God given. In this way society has become impoverished in its thinking and the value system needs to be changed. We actually no longer know what a better society/life should look like. [As a result] poverty is now overwhelming our whole community, where begging has become an acceptable norm and means of income (Provider 6).

In contrast to Provider 6's view that poverty has become an unfortunate norm, generalised throughout society, Provider 4's focus was on the role of tradition; he stated that the reason so many young people from the countryside come to Addis and end up poor is rooted in cultural traditions such as patriarchy. As Provider 4 explained:

> Young people in the rural area have to leave their parents as early as possible. This is dictated by cultural tradition where young men should have their own life, land to till, have their own animals and become a full member of their tribe/clan. This is part of the patriarchal society where men take care of themselves. Rural parents also often encourage their children to move to urban areas to generate as much income as possible and send it back home to their relatives. Many end up in towns begging or trying to sustain families as *listros*[16] or working for small businesses such as kiosks and taxis.

While the other Providers focused mainly on cultural traditions and thinking patterns, Provider 7 saw poverty as very much related to the 'lack of consciousness' of human kind and to spiritual matters. She acknowledged that poverty means 'the enormous suffering for a great number of people', and argued that poverty is also a spiritual matter. She conceded that poverty is still the 'hard reality' where people lack the essentials of life such as food, shelter, clothing and education, and that these needs have to be met with adequate income and resources. However, she also pointed out that needs can change over time and are not fixed, and have to be balanced with spiritual needs. Thus:

> One can be rich in spirit but be materially poor. Or one can be poor in spirit but rich in material wealth. Human consciousness, for example, is one of the most fundamental human needs and should not be forgotten. Spiritual poverty thus exists when people have lost their conscience and cannot blossom as human beings as a result. People who forget this have meaningless lives and cannot be fulfilled as people (Provider 7).

Provider 7, therefore, felt strongly that the 'lack of consciousness' in the world leads to a divided world of winners and losers. Accordingly:

> Winners are those who don't share what they have and the losers are the poor. The world runs at a pace where the winners win more and the losers lose more. If people forget what it is to be a human being then they put themselves at the centre of the universe and forget to share with others. The fact that the world allows poverty to happen is therefore a sign of a sickness of the heart and the mind. This is why poverty is a scandal for anyone who has a 'clean mind' and is conscious of being a [real] human being.

Poverty in this sense, therefore, cannot be defined just from the 'outside of a person', but has to also involve the 'inside'. According to Provider 7, once this is realised, a person can think and act differently and make important changes in their own life and those of others. Using this example, Provider 7 argued that through 'the change of human consciousness' it is possible to change societal attitudes towards the poor. By supporting and giving them what they need, for instance, we can thus receive much in return.

3.3 THE ADVOCATES

Like the Poor and the Providers, the Advocates defined poverty as complex rather than uni-dimensional, to the extent that they paid little attention to income poverty, focusing instead on the multifaceted nature of the problem. As Box 3.10 shows, the material contributed by the Advocates falls into four main categories, each discussed below.

Box 3.10 Poverty categories identified by the Advocates

- multidimensional aspects
- basic needs
- lack of participation
- attitudes and cultural issues

MULTIDIMENSIONAL ASPECTS

Although Advocates 1, 2, 3, 6 and 7 found the poverty experience difficult to define, all agreed that poverty does not relate only to money, thus reiterating poverty's multidimensional nature:

> There are many ways to define poverty. However, it mainly means being deprived of all essential needs on earth, namely economically, socially, and culturally (Advocate 3).

> Poverty relates to the lack of skills, knowledge, rights and the inability to live life according to one's preferences. Poverty is also lack of peoples' capabilities in many areas (Advocate 7).

For Advocate 1, poverty is a very complex phenomenon that affects all mankind, especially women, children and the elderly. Her definition includes the notion that poverty should be viewed as a relative concept, affecting the poor differently in various countries:

Definitions of Poverty

The problem of poverty does not only refer to money. In the first instance, it should be seen in relative terms, between poor and rich countries or societies. Poverty thus affects societies differently but all their people negatively, especially the children, women, and the elderly (Advocate 1).

Advocate 1 also drew attention to the existing wealth and inequality in a society:

[When looking at poverty] we should take into consideration the way people live, the distribution of resources and wealth in society, and whether society is structured to ensure equality between people. Since a country's wealth includes land and many other resources, the meaning of real wealth should also relate to how humans live. So poverty then is where poor people are voiceless, cannot participate or belong and are excluded from society. They are helpless and the rich in society don't think and care about them.

Thus Advocate 1's view of poverty has several layers: poverty relates to structural issues and the way a society is organised; poverty results from the unequal distribution of wealth in a given nation; in such a nation there is a lack of concern for the poor, which in turn helps to marginalise and exclude the poor.

Advocate 1 argued further that poverty often means little safety, security and protection for the poor. Particularly women, girls and smaller boys are very vulnerable and unsafe, and often suffer sexual and other abuses, including rape. Women also have the additional burden and responsibilities of child rearing, which makes their lives more complicated and difficult.

Advocates 2 and 6 also found poverty complex and multifaceted:

Poverty can be defined in different ways, for instance it can be seen in economic, cultural, political and social terms. Poverty also includes things like social and political capital as well as low participation in society. There are also different levels of poverty where the poor cannot easily be identified by the way they look and behave, i.e. begging (Advocate 2).

Advocate 2 also made the important points that it is not only people who beg who are poor, as many other people, whom he calls 'the working poor', are also deprived. Thus, poverty for Advocate 2 means that the poor:

- cannot live with their available resources in dignity
- are deprived of basic needs such as food, shelter, health, education
- cannot predict their future
- do not have access to all kinds of services to satisfy their needs, including those advocated by international conventions
- lack opportunities for political participation.

Advocate 6 argued that the so-called poverty experts do not readily agree about the meaning of poverty, so that there are many different ways to conceptualise it:

> Some people, for instance, want to measure poverty solely in terms of income, i.e. people have only $1 or $2 per day to live on. Others think that income poverty is more relevant in urban areas than in rural districts. … But there are other factors more important than income when considering poverty and it has to be seen holistically—where the poor find themselves in a hopeless situation, being disadvantaged within mainstream society.

According to Advocate 6 poverty exists when a person:

- is dying because of famine
- is hungry because they don't have enough to eat
- has inadequate income
- lacks access to a decent livelihood
- lacks access to education
- has no power and influence in society
- is denied participation in their community.

Thus, the Advocates saw poverty as being complex and multifaceted; indeed, across these informants, more than 20 components appeared within the multidimensional aspect of poverty.

BASIC NEEDS

While most Advocates suggested poverty means that peoples' basic needs are not met, the needs identified by this group ranged from the concrete to the abstract to the spiritual. Thus, for Advocate 3, basic needs relate to: 'Subsistence needs–adequate nourishment twice per day for every member of a family, good education, continuous employment in whatever way.'

Advocate 7, on the other hand, thought that:

> Part of poverty is also the lack of health, adequate sanitation and the fact that the poor no longer belong anywhere. As poor peoples' needs are not fulfilled, they are marginalised and pushed away from mainstream society.

More concrete examples of the needs are listed by Advocates 1 and 4. However, while Advocate 1's list applies to everyone, regardless of age and health status, Advocate 4 contended that the only real poor are the old and the sick (see also the Attitudes and Cultural Issues section below).

Thus, for Advocate 1, poverty is the lack of:

- shelter
- clothing
- food
- water, sanitation
- good health; the poor often die of illnesses
- security and safety; sometimes the poor die of beatings/violence and no one knows who killed them
- education
- chances and opportunities
- job prospects/opportunities.

For Advocate 4, poverty only really inflicts the old and sick who lack:

- food
- clothes
- shelter/a clean house
- assistance and support in their daily living arrangements
- adequate medical care
- moral support.

Advocate 5 took a different approach, and divided needs into two main categories: material needs and spiritual needs. Material needs correspond to:

> ... the lack of food, drink, shelter, and involve the general destitution of people and families. When one is in poverty, a person cannot keep a family together and loses their status in society. Poverty also means the lack of money. However, it is difficult to measure the minimum income required for the maintenance of a family by a poverty line (Advocate 5).

In terms of the spiritual needs, Advocate 5 talked about the rich Ethiopian cultural traditions which value faith and spirituality. As further elaborated in the Attitudes and Cultural Issues section below, he argued that these traditions offer significant levels of faith to the community and, in turn, much kindness and sharing between people. If these spiritual aspects are missing in the community, people experience spiritual poverty: 'If people don't have this spiritual richness and "dignity of God" then they can be considered as impoverished and poor' (Advocate 5).

LACK OF PARTICIPATION

Almost all Advocates suggested that poverty involves the lack of participation in society. While for some this takes the form of active exclusion, for others it means passive exclusion, where the poor cannot participate because of lack opportunity and freedom.

Advocate 3, for example, thought that '... the marginalisation and lack of participation of the poor is one of the worst aspects of poverty'. As the poor are marginalised and excluded from society, they have no way of 'developing their intellects' and cannot fulfil their potential: '... while human beings differ from animals in that they are intelligent, the poor are not promoted to fulfil their intellectual potentials' (Advocate 3).

Similarly, Advocate 1 suggested that the poor cannot take part of the normal activities in the community:

> Poor people are relegated to an observer role where they see the rich drive around in cars, go to restaurants and eat etc., but they themselves cannot participate in any of these 'normal' activities (Advocate 1).

Advocate 1 also felt strongly that society as a whole had decided that the poor are deviant and dangerous; while the poor are in fact the victims, the community victimises and discriminates against them. Hence, the disadvantaged are not consulted, have no voice and do not participate in the public discourse. Being at the mercy of society without any input, the poor have to accept whatever happens to them:

> The poor are categorised as criminals and people are afraid of them. They are seen as dangerous, sick, dishonest no matter if they are young or old. People don't actually talk to the poor. They [the poor] don't have the opportunity to give their opinion about anything and simply have to accept whatever happens and that is given to them. (Advocate 1).

Advocates 7, 4 and 6 broadened the discussion to the national Ethiopian and international levels. Advocate 7 saw lack of participation mainly in terms of a country's economic development, Advocate 4 looked at lack of political freedom, and Advocate 6 considered the powerlessness of people in the rural areas through their lack of knowledge.

Advocate 7 stated that in many developing nations the lack of participation experienced by the poor stems from the fact that:

> Poor people have no significant connections to the influential and powerful in society. This means that their needs are not enshrined in regulation and their interests are often ignored and unprotected. While the poor are increasingly disempowered, the rich are well connected and have access to the country's wealth and resources. Rather than serving the needs of poor people, politicians in developing countries simply use the poor to stay in power (Advocate 7).

According to Advocate 4, poverty has to do with the lack of freedom of the population—people without freedom of movement and without peace are impoverished. Using the history of Jerusalem as an example he suggested that: 'When people are not free they lack control and our strengths to help each other depends on how much freedom we have' (Advocate 4).

For Advocate 6, lack of participation of the poor in society is relative, as is the whole concept of poverty. In the first instance, participation can be seen in a number of sectors, including the economy and the political and social systems. As the poor are often marginalised and lose their voice in society, the degree and level of participation depend on the 'setting'. Advocate 6 drew particular attention here to the regional setting, especially to differences between rural and urban areas. For him, lack of participation involves environmental issues, powerlessness and the differential lack of knowledge between the poor and the rich. Thus, participation depends on:

> ... the specific setting, and can involve unequal power relationships, environmental issues, and the lack of knowledge of wealth (by the poor) and the lack of knowledge about poverty (by the rich). ... In this context a person from the rural area does not know the kind of life someone might have in a rich suburb in the city, and the kind of things he/she is actually missing out on. Equally, people living in urban and affluent circumstances cannot imagine the depths of poverty faced by many others, especially in rural areas (Advocate 7).

For Advocate 6, when people lack knowledge of the lives of those in circumstances different from their own, there are two fundamental and negative consequences: first, if the poor do not know what they are missing, they are less likely to demand better lives, participation and services; second, if the wealthy do not realise the depths of poverty of the deprived, they will not understand the plight of the poor or the issues involved, and so are less likely and less willing to assist the poor.

Knowledge of and understanding about the plight of the disadvantaged, as described by Advocate 7, also relates to societal perceptions and the way the poor are perceived by society. This issue is briefly discussed in the next section.

ATTITUDES AND CULTURAL ISSUES

> If someone is healthy but lacks money they cannot be called poor; it simply means that they are short of money. For this reason poverty involves old age, mental illnesses and various physical disabilities. [This] prevents people from being able to work [who] then find themselves in poverty. Thus poverty means that someone might have no legs, or hands, or lost their mental or physical abilities. They may have no assistance and be old and bedridden (Advocate 4).

As well illustrated by Advocate 4 above, poverty relates to the societal perceptions about poverty; such perceptions often involve value judgements about the poor. While most Advocates saw these perceptions as negative, others believed that they can be positive.

To illustrate the negative and exploitative aspects of societal and cultural attitudes towards the poor, Advocate 6 looked at the tourist industry and the way it portrays an indigenous person living in rural Ethiopia. He stated that in many ways, the indigenous person comes across 'as living in the dark ages' and that this picture of native people is deliberately used by the industry to generate income. Advocate 6 suggested that 'while this may help to preserve local cultures … it is an unacceptable situation where many people living in rural areas lack basic services and resources, basic rights, education, appropriate infrastructure and development' (Advocate 6).

Advocate 6 also felt strongly that:

> … the farmer's life always needs to be compared with the best of human development which includes the provision of basic services and rights such as having food. This must apply regardless [of] whether the person in question considers themselves happy and in poverty or not. This is the case because the poor in Ethiopia might be happy today but have no knowledge and conception of their collective entitlements and government structures.

Advocate 6's view here is interesting as he queries the attitudes, judgements and traditions of the poor themselves. In one sense, this thinking undermines notions of empowerment and self-determination, which are often seen as part of human development. Similarly, Advocate 4 questioned the 'wisdom', 'culture' and 'attitudes to farming' of some rural communities. As one example, he used the recent flooding in southern Ethiopia, which devastated local livelihoods. Advocate 4 claimed that local people were flooded because their actions were based on their old traditions and 'outmoded thinking', and suggested that these traditions have continued because local people lacked access to education and relevant knowledge: 'Peoples' knowledge was inadequate about the world and their surroundings. They were flooded because they had no education and made the wrong decisions' (Advocate 4).

Whereas both Advocates 6 and 4 questioned some of the traditions and attitudes of the poor, Advocate 7 looked critically at mainstream society's values.

According to Advocate 7, certain cultural beliefs, behaviours and attitudes are considered the 'norm' in the community. Society perpetuates 'these common values' from birth to old age, and people are expected to adhere to them. If someone's behaviours and attitudes differ from what is believed to be 'normal', that person is often called 'deviant' or 'abnormal'. The poor are in this latter category, as they cannot meet society's expectations or function within common and accepted societal denominators. Advocate 7, therefore, argued that since the poor do not have the necessary opportunities, they cannot meet society's cultural expectations and conventions, and so are caught in a vicious circle which involves lack of opportunities, not being able to conform, being discriminated against, and being marginalised:

> Poor people cannot meet the expectations of society and are discriminated against in many ways. For example, poor people lack many of the opportunities other people have, including education and jobs. Poor people are frequently marginalised and their lives are lived in vicious circles of unmet needs, lack of opportunities and marginalisation (Advocate 7).

By contrast, Advocate 5 saw societal attitudes to and traditions about poverty in a different light: 'People in Ethiopia have a lot of belief and faith in spirituality. This sustains them and their families.'

A social contract emerges from these values, a contract from which both society and the poor benefit. First, there is society's tradition and the culture of giving alms to the needy. The act of giving to the poor here 'is a sign of the faith in God and demonstrates kindness between people' and the people's willingness to share among themselves. If this kindness is lacking in the community, then a poverty of values and morality appears. Second, in Ethiopia, traditional belief systems are based on faith and spirituality, giving the poor value and an inner power. It also 'makes them content with what they have', enabling them to continue their struggle with their daily lives:

> This sharing can be an example to wealthy countries. Being part of this spiritual richness, the poor are also contend with what they have and accept their situation. The spiritual richness keeps them going and they have no sleepless nights because of materialism or envy. Therefore being a son of Allah or God does not mean a poor person is valueless, because an inner power enables people with faith to continue to struggle. Also, if people

87

don't share among themselves and are greedy in society it ultimately means poverty of community values and morality (Advocate 5).

Summary

This chapter dealt with the way in which three groups—the Poor, the Providers and the Advocates—defined poverty. The material presented an insight into the variety of views around the notions of deprivation and human need. While the definitions between the groups are diverse, they clearly articulate the complex and multidimensional nature of poverty and its associated experiences.

Interviews with the Poor highlight the great importance of listening to their voices, as they are the real experts in the poverty experience. The data provided by the Poor show that even their most basic needs are often not met, and they suffer great deprivation as a result. Although the data analysis demonstrates that women are more vulnerable and insecure than their male counterparts, all the Poor are affected by lack of money, food, appropriate housing and sanitation, and by the suffering caused by their emotional scars. In this way, the lives of all the poor participants are a constant struggle for survival. Feeling ashamed, humiliated and isolated in the community, they often live a lonely existence without family ties, friendships and little societal support.

Interviews with the Providers demonstrated that these participants are one step removed from the actual poverty experience. While this group had some initial difficulty in conceptualising poverty, their views show awareness and understanding of the extent of the deprivation experienced by the poor. Thus, the Providers brought out the multidimensional aspects of poverty and the effects of lack of money and resources. At the same time, they made important connections between the notion of poverty, differences and variations between the urban and rural sectors, and the lack of opportunities and rights, as well as cultural and spiritual issues.

Interviews with the Advocates demonstrated that their understandings of poverty were the furthest from actual poverty experience and the most highly conceptualised. Although the interviewees in this group paid scant attention to the effects of income poverty, perhaps assuming them, they reiterated the multifaceted nature of the problem. Some Advocates looked at the international, national and local contexts of development, identifying some of the structural issues behind poverty. Some Advocates acknowledged that the basic needs of the poor were not met, although their accounts of those needs were not as detailed as the accounts of the other two groups. The Advocates made also important observations about the poor's lack of participation in society, and presented interesting views about how societal and cultural attitudes towards the poor can differ.

Chapter Four

CAUSES OF POVERTY

This chapter explores the causes of poverty as articulated by the Poor, the Providers, and the Advocates. Causes described by the Poor relate closely to their personal experience and demonstrate little awareness of more abstract and structural issues. While both female and male participants present interrelated poverty cycles, their views differ in many respects due to their different life patterns. By contrast to the Poor, the Providers and Advocates are more financially secure, educated, and well-connected professionals, and present a less complex but more coherent picture of poverty causes. While Providers seem to draw their insights, at least in part, from working directly with their clients, the Advocates present far more abstract and general factors of poverty than the other two groups, commenting on such matters as economic principles, society's structures, government policies, and human nature.

4.1 THE POOR

As can be seen from Box 4.1, causes of poverty identified by the Poor cover a wide spectrum, ranging from social attitudes and lack of community support to family and personal matters. Issues thus articulated are based on the acute levels of deprivation experienced by the Poor and sustained over long periods of time. Steeped in their daily struggles to survive, respondents presented a complex and often cyclical picture of poverty, where their experiences and life stories are interrelated and enmeshed. As life experiences differ between females and males, the two groups also articulated causes of poverty in various ways, as is shown in Box 4.1 below.

Box 4.1 Overview of causes of poverty identified by the Poor

THE WOMEN

- negative social attitudes about the poor
- lack of community support
- rising cost of living
- poor family backgrounds
- being pressured into marriage and having children
- limited life chances
- family breakdown and conflict
- migration to the city
- lack of services
- health issues
- life choices and individual responsibility
- unemployment

THE MEN

- unemployment in general
- not enough job opportunities
- absence of permanent work
- inadequate incomes for low-level jobs
- lack of money in general
- rising cost of living
- lack of societal influence and connections
- lack of opportunities due to family background and upbringing
- family breakdown
- no formal education and training
- inability to read and write
- lack of housing
- lack of family support
- lack of community and government support
- lack of government pension
- inability to join a community association to get support from its members
- lack of opportunity to be with people, socialise and share resources
- lack of belonging to the community
- inability to get an ID from the kebele

Based on the analysis of the material provided by the Poor, four main categories emerged to guide the discussion of the material, as shown in Box 4.2 below.

Box 4.2 Causes of poverty identified by the Poor

- societal issues
- family issues
- displacement and migration to Addis Ababa
- personal issues and choices

SOCIETAL ISSUES

In relation to societal issues, the Poor generally demonstrated little awareness of structural causes of poverty, such as economic trends and their impact on unemployment and the rising cost of living. Although they did not articulate clearly or appear to have deeper understanding of such ideas, participants revealed some nascent notions of inequality, especially in relation to inequitable distribution of wealth and resources. While noticing the growing division between the rich and the poor, most participants felt unsupported by the community. These issues are therefore discussed under two sections below: society and community, and cost of living.

Society and Community

The women mainly commented on negative social attitudes towards the poor, attitudes which explained to some extent the lack of support provided to them by the community. The men articulated a wider range of causes, a range which included those causes mentioned by the women, plus concerns such as lack of educational and employment opportunities. The men also had some inkling about a class structure which left them powerless, unemployed and worse off than the wealthy in their society.

The women

The women's articulation of social and community-related causes of poverty was less sophisticated and extensive than that of the males. Thus, only half of the participants responded here, and those respondents were mainly concerned with unhelpful community opinion towards the poor and the lack of support they received from society.

Only three women—Almaz, Fatuma and Aster—commented more generally on societal causes of poverty. Almaz argued that most members of society are simply not interested in the plight of the poor and do not want to help them:

> … most people in society don't think about poor people and they don't want to share with them what they have. There are only a few people who want to help and that makes me angry. People look at me and think that I am able … but I don't have any work and can't work (Almaz).

Fatuma and Aster agreed that there is a lack of interest and community support for the poor, but also think that the current government is not doing enough for them. Fatuma also compared current government assistance with a previous period:

> There is not much community support for the poor and no one visits them to help. The current government is [also] not interested in helping the poor. … Even during the Derg[1] period when there was hunger, the politicians sent aeroplanes with food to help the poor (Fatuma).

Aster also pointed out that those members in society 'who can and are able to help' do not assist the poor enough, and do not advise the poor about how to get out of poverty. She also thought that 'the government is ignorant about poverty and does not take any initiative [to solve the problem]'.

Almaz agreed, arguing that negative societal attitudes persist as people have very little regard for someone with low socio-economic status. Since this negative attitude is pervasive in a society where influence, money, and power are of prime importance, neither individuals nor government is interested in helping the powerless poor.

Other female respondents stressed immediate and concrete notions of the causes of poverty. Fantu complained about the difficulties in getting free health services. Outlining the process, she stated that the first step she has to make is to take her identification card (ID) to the local *kebele* and make a written application. She must also bring two witnesses who will testify that she is poor.

93

The *kebele* will then write a letter to the clinic certifying that she is poor, and thus entitled to free health care. However, this certification is only valid for three months, after which she has to go through the same process again.

While most of the women looked for the causes of poverty in the shortcomings of society, Belaynesh presented a minority view. In her opinion, poverty is very much God's decision and not related to society or individuals: 'People are not responsible for poverty. God makes people poor and He decides everything [that happens].'

The men

> When one is living in poverty and dirty conditions, one cannot keep clean. Thus people are less likely to employ poor people because of their appearance, which makes it hard to find employment or get into job training (Mesganew).

While the men saw unemployment, lack of income, and the rising cost of living as the major causes of poverty, like the women, they demonstrated little understanding of the wider socio-economic context of the poverty problem, and did not make any structural links between the economy and unemployment. The only man to comment on this factor was Shewangezaw, who thought that poverty is somehow caused by economic forces. But when asked what these forces were and how they worked, Shewangezaw did not know. He simply speculated that it related to the inequality between the rich and poor in society.

Instead, issues such as unemployment were mainly seen by the participants as the result of having a disadvantaged family background. The resulting low socio-economic status was then associated with the lack of opportunities, such as education, limiting the men's life chances and social engagement. Thus, amongst the poor men, there was a strong feeling that poor families lack the influence and societal connections necessary to gain employment and the support of society and government.

Social background and lack of opportunity

Most men, like Befekadu, Bekele, Bizuayew Getachew, Mesganew, Melaku and Shewangezaw, believed that family background shapes peoples' opportunities and life chances. They argued that the wealthy have money, power and influence, giving them important connections and the support of society as a whole. By contrast, the poor have no money, power or connections; therefore they lack both support in the community and the services they need.

As the poor are powerless to change their position, and have no education or positive status in society, they have been relegated to badly paid jobs, such as carrying bags and daily labouring. Since this work is always temporary and casual, they can never make an adequate living. Poverty then becomes a chronic experience the poor simply cannot escape. While Kebede, for example, did not blame society, he thought that finding work without societal influence and family connections is difficult:

> I do not blame society for poverty or say [that] people want the poor to be poor. But I think [that] there is not enough employment for all the people needing it. Poor people have a poor family background. They have no influence and connections like the rich in society (Kebede).

Getachew, like most others, agreed and said that he has been without a stable job for more than 17 years. As so many people are unemployed, getting a job is increasingly difficult: 'Even if you want a job as a daily labourer today you need to have some connections' (Getachew).

However, the ability to get jobs depends on more than status and family connections.[2] Other factors include lack of education, age, health and the ability to obtain an ID, as discussed in the following section.

Most participants also pointed out that poor family background leads to low or no educational attainment. Poor children are less likely to go to school than wealthy children. For Kebede and Befekadu, this is part of an intergenerational cycle of poverty where: 'Poor parents are less likely to send their children to school. That is why the children have no influence and connections they can use later' (Kebede).

Befekadu illustrated this cyclical nature of poverty further when he suggested that the poverty cycle starts with being born into a poor family. As shown in Box 4.3, being born into poverty inevitably limits life chances. For example, Befekadu pointed out that while the poor find it difficult to afford to send their children to school, education 'has also a time factor', as poor people and their children are often so occupied with trying to survive that they might not have time to go to school. As a result, Befekadu and many of the other men cannot read or write, and they have no qualifications or training that could help them to gain a better position in society. With little support from the community, they are left to fend for themselves by doing the least desirable and lowest-paid work.

Box 4.3 Befekadu's cycle of poverty

- his poor family background limited his life chances and opportunities; his mother was so poor that she worked while carrying a baby on her back
- lack of opportunities to go to school, since the poor cannot afford: 1) the time, as they constantly need to look around for work and food, and 2) the school fees and materials
- being illiterate
- lack of family influence/connections
- unemployment, low-level casual work
- lack of adequate income
- lack of societal support.

While most of the men think that low family background and education play a part in unemployment, Tesfaye and Shewangezaw also gave ill health and old age as reasons for it. Shewangezaw, for instance, is 66 years old and has no pension. He stated that, apart from the occasional offer to carry bags for people, his age prevents him now from getting the casual jobs he used to get, because he is no longer strong enough. This limits his income and increases his dependence of food handouts: 'I can only now make 1–2 birr per day, but often don't get any work for 2–3 days. Most weeks I only earn 5–10 birr per week on average. That is why I depend on the food handouts provided by Hope' (Shewangezaw).

Lack of support

Apart from broadly commenting on lack of service provision in areas such as income support, education and training, housing, and food subsidies, the men used their difficulties in obtaining an ID to illustrate this lack of support by local government (*kebele*). Like the women, they argued that since they were not able to get an ID, they were precluded from accessing some of the basic entitlements provided by the community.

Eight of the ten men had no ID, saying that the process of obtaining one was far too bureaucratic. Befekadu described the process: to get an ID one must register in a local *kebele*, but to be able to register one needs to have a permanent address. Since most poor people do not have a permanent address or know anyone who can help them to get one, they cannot register and get an ID. As the examples in Box 4.4 show, without an ID people find it difficult to get jobs, do not have access to local services such as free health care in hospitals and housing, can have problems getting into training, and have difficulties with the authorities when stopped and questioned.

Box 4.4 Lack of identification card

BEFEKADU

Since he has no relatives, friends or a permanent residence where he could live with someone who could help him register, it is not possible to get an ID from any *kebele*. Without an ID, it is difficult for him to get a job, get into school or training, or receive health care assistance. Respectable employers are unlikely to offer work to people without IDs, since there is no proof of who the person is. Thus, it would be very difficult to find work in a household, as a *zebegna*, for example, where families need to be able to trust someone.

MEKURIA

The owner of his house is not happy for the men (who live there) to register themselves with the kebele under his address. Since they don't have relatives in the vicinity who could help them instead, they cannot get an ID. This then makes it difficult to get decent employment. In Mekuria's experience, employers don't believe anyone without identification, and not having an ID has cost him a number of jobs. For example, he found jobs as a gardener and as a metal worker, but on both occasions the employers asked for the ID.

MESGANEW

As a result of not having an ID, Mesganew has missed out on a number of job opportunities in the past. For example, he was refused work as security guard, as he was unable to produce identification. Without ID, one can also be picked up by the police if found sleeping on the streets and put into jail for one day.

Causes of Poverty

While the male participants commented on the lack of support provided by the government, they did not blame society directly for their plight. In this regard, except for Befekadu and Shewangezaw, the men were generally less critical than the women. Befekadu believed that government dislikes and is reluctant to support poor people: '… if we have foreign visitors we have to move aside. Our government does not like us.'

Shewangezaw argued that the actions of politicians are influenced by the 'few' wealthy who despise the poor: '… there are only a few rich but many poor people. I often think that the rich want the poor people just to die.'

Another minority view was that of Bizuayew, who, rather than being critical of government, the wealthy, or the poor themselves, was philosophical about his own poverty: 'People are not responsible for their own poverty, it's just about luck. In my case God has decided that I should be poor, so I am poor. … But I still hope He will change his mind one day' (Bizuayew).

Cost of Living[3]

All participants suffered from the continual rise in the cost of living in Ethiopia, making it increasingly difficult for them to survive. Women here commented much more fully than the men: not only did they have to care for themselves and their children, many of them also tried to run a household. Men, on the other hand, lived more transient lives, often without stable lodgings and lack of opportunities to prepare meals.

The women

Most of the women, like Kedega, Almaz, Fatuma, Belaynesh, Fantu and Yelfu, stressed that the rising cost of living makes it increasingly difficult for families and individuals to meet their needs. A typical comment is: 'The rising cost of living has affected the living standards of poor people especially. Many of them cannot meet their basic needs, even if they are working' (Belaynesh).

Kedega illustrated this situation by comparing the amount of money she would currently need to feed and house her family with the amount required about one year ago. As shown below, she estimates that to meet her needs, she would have to spend as follows:

- food: 455 birr per month (15 birr per day)

- accommodation: 90–100 birr per month (3.3 birr per day)
- clothes and other necessities: 100–200 birr per month (3.3–6.6 birr per day)
- total: 645–755 birr per month (21.5–25 birr per day).

According to Kedega, a year ago these costs would have been 500–550 birr, or 33% on average less than today.

While all women agree that the cost of living has increased, they display concern about different aspects of this rise. For instance, Fatuma stated that rising prices make it more difficult for a poor family to have children, and make life more difficult in poor communities, since there is less money to employ people, especially in small businesses:

> Having children can cause more poverty because they are expensive and need good food, housing, clothes and shoes and a good life to grow up properly. Higher prices makes living in a poorer community harder … no one has the money to employ people anymore (Fatuma).

For Yelfu and Almaz cost of living is also a cause of poverty, but to the problem of rising prices they add lack of income and lack of employment. These problems, in turn, lead to:

Yelfu:
- lack of permanent housing
- lack of house equipment/furniture
- unstable family life
- increases in dependence on other people and inability to look after oneself
- inability to be part of a community association (*iddir*), which provides a lot of support for its members.

Almaz:
- housing problems
- lack of food and drink
- being unable to cure her illness
- disagreements with her family and relatives at home.

While the women's responses on the cost of living provided good detail, relatively little information was given by the male participants.

The men

Like the women, the male participants also struggle to survive. As they earn little from their casual labouring jobs, their situation constantly deteriorates as prices rise and the cost of living increases. Bizuayew, Getachew Mekuria, Melaku, Mesganew and Bekele, like most men, commented that the prices for goods and services are steadily rising, leaving them increasingly unable to afford necessities. A typical response on this issue is:

> Everything is now very expensive, like flour, pepper and *teff*. ... The price of *teff* alone has increased substantially so that it now costs 500 birr per sack (Bekele).

Bekele also said that renting a house is impossible for him and most of the poor:

> I estimate that renting a house (with one room only) would cost about 300 birr per month, but there may be cheaper ones. To get such a house one would also need a deposit amounting to the equivalent of three months rent; [and] one would not be able to get a house without having stable work, being well dressed and presented.

Given these kinds of expenses, Bekele thought that an income of even 1,000 birr per month is no longer enough to live on, and this income is impossible to achieve by working as a daily labourer.

While this section looked at societal issues and how participants were affected by community attitudes, lack of support and rising costs of living, the next part discusses how peoples' lives have been influenced by family matters.

FAMILY ISSUES

While family situations are embedded within the wider social system, causes of poverty attributed to broader societal issues inevitably connect and overlap with family issues (see, for instance, Box 4.3: Befekadu's Cycle of Poverty).

Indeed, for most respondents, early family experiences had particularly strong and pervasive influences on their future lives; in many cases these experiences had, at least initially, a more direct impact than those relating to the wider society. Thus, participants talked extensively about family issues, linking these with causes of poverty as discussed in the following three subsections: life situations, marriage and separation, and family conflict.

Life Situations

Most participants saw causes of poverty in terms of poor family background and entanglement in various family matters. Having insufficient means and land for subsistence farming, poor families often found it difficult to stay together. For the women, poor family background invariably meant having to get married, often through arranged marriages, to find a livelihood outside their families. Such marriages often failed, thus perpetuating the women's disadvantaged position in society. For the male participants, this situation frequently meant having to leave home to find work elsewhere. Thus, to some extent, both men and women entered an intergenerational cycle of poverty; however, after leaving home, the women found themselves in a much more vulnerable position than the men. In many ways, being born female in a patriarchal society greatly limits the women's choices, where marriage is often seen by society as the only option in an uncertain future.

The women

Seven of the ten women interviewed stated that they were born into a poor family; typically, they lived on small plots of land, too small for the family to make an adequate living. The three exceptions were Fatuma and Samira, who said that their families had been quite well off, and Yelfu, who indicated that while her family originally owned much land, it had been confiscated by an earlier government.

That poor circumstances through family background can affect someone's life is illustrated by Almaz, Belaynesh, Genet, Kedega and Zinash, whose parents were poor farmers unable to support themselves and their children on the land available. Consequently, the women had to leave their homes, marry, find work and support themselves outside their original families and communities. Eventually becoming displaced, all of them migrated to Addis

Ababa to look for a better life and more opportunities (see the Displacement and Migration to Addis Ababa section below for more details).

While poor family background was at the beginning of many women's poverty, being pressured by parents into marriage (and invariably to have children) also limited greatly their opportunities in life. In many ways, marriage seems to perpetuate what appears to be a vicious cycle that keeps many women in extreme deprivation, potentially for the rest of their lives. Table 4.1 demonstrates further both the complexity and the poverty of the women's lives.

TABLE 4.1: Women's life situations

PARTICIPANT	FAMILY BACKGROUND	HISTORY
Almaz	• parents very poor farmers • 8th grade schooling • arranged marriage at 19 • one child	• husband drafted into army • separation • brothers and sisters left for Addis to make a living • lived with brother; arguments with sister-in-law
Aster	• parents poor farmers • 7th grade schooling • father died; mother left for Italy	• was brought up by an aunt in Addis; arguments with aunt and left to find work • had five children • husband died (uncertain whether she was married)
Belaynesh	• parents poor farmers • no formal education • orphaned as a child	• married had two children • husband died
Fantu	• parents poor farmers • no formal education • arranged marriage at eight	• fled first marriage due to problems at 13 • joined army to work • good marriage in Addis; two children • death of second husband dislocated family

Fatuma	• parents rich • no formal education • arranged marriage at eight • orphaned at 10	• two children; husband died • allocated piece of land by family; left because land was too small to survive on
Genet	• parents poor farmers • 6th grade schooling	• neighbour offered to raise her in Addis • left neighbour after arguments as teenager; was raped on the streets and got pregnant • became pregnant and abandoned by another man
Kedega	• parents poor farmers • no formal education • orphaned when six	• argument with aunt • marriage in Addis; two children • husband died
Samira	• parents not poor • no formal education	• married soldier who abandoned her with children
Yelfu	• parents had land which was taken by government • no formal education • arranged marriage at 16	• many arguments with husband, one child • separation
Zinash	• parents poor farmers • no formal education • orphaned • arranged marriage at 14	• two children • left husband after many arguments with mother-in-law

Causes of Poverty

Only three of the ten women received any formal education or training, and early and arranged unsuccessful marriages were common, as were early deaths of parents and partners. Although the women had made some life decisions, such as leaving their husbands, these decisions seem mostly limited to escaping intolerable situations and have to be seen within the larger context of their histories, lack of opportunities and life chances. Thus, the women's poor background are inextricable from subsequent poor marriages, having children and their separation from husbands, all of which contribute to the poverty they ultimately experience.

The men

Although the male participants also struggled, their life situations were not as desperate as those of the female interviewees. Almost all of them were single and did not have to deal with arranged marriages, nor did they have to worry about having and caring for children.

As Table 4.2 shows, the men's life chances were also affected by their origins, as half of them came from poor family backgrounds. Six male participants had no schooling and, like the women, family conflicts and separations influenced their lives. Some of these factors led to their dislocation and ultimately brought them to Addis Ababa.

Table 4.2 also demonstrates the complexity of the participants' lives and how their life situations were intricately interrelated.

Marriage and Separation

While family background discussed in the previous section was seen as important, marriages and family separation were also identified as significant causes of poverty. However, as the following discussion makes clear, marriage as a factor in the cause of poverty was mainly cited by the women, whereas family separation applied to both groups.

The women

Most female participants stated that in the countryside they had little or no choice but to marry, and that the end of their marriages was precipitated most commonly by conflict (seven women) and sometimes by the partner's death (three women). All women participants had children, making their lives more difficult than those of the male participants in this study:

One of the main causes of poverty in my life was that I got married and had children. … When a woman gets married she has no control over her life and how many children she will have (Samira).

TABLE 4.2 Men's life situations

PARTICIPANT	FAMILY BACKGROUND	HISTORY
Befekadu	• parents very poor farmers • no formal education • eight siblings • farmer on parents' land • land can't support everyone	• left to escape poverty • heard that there are jobs in Addis
Bekele	• parents owned land • no formal education • worked as farmer • married with two children	• was conscripted into army • after war parents had died • went to Addis and never back to countryside
Bizuayew	• parents poor farmers • 4th grade education • two brothers and one sister	• stayed with uncle in Addis • arguments with uncle's wife • moved to grandmother; left her then lived on the street
Getachew	• parents poor • 6th grade schooling • mother died young and father sick; dying in Addis	• joined brother's family in Addis • had many arguments with brother's family • worked as *listro* until conscripted into army • after army went back to Addis
Kebede	• parents had land and not poor • no formal education • three brothers and three sisters • became farmer	• heard that life is good in Addis • decided to leave countryside

Causes of Poverty

Mekuria	• parents not poor • no formal education • two brothers and two sisters	• because mother separated from husband much family conflict • family separation
Melaku	• parents very poor • father died early • no formal education • one sister and three brothers • land could not support family • worked as shepherd and farmer	• heard that there are jobs in Addis • left countryside to make a living in Addis
Mesganew	• parents not poor but died • early orphan • no formal education • raised by wealthy aunt • worked as farmer on aunt's land	• cheated out of inheritance by aunt • family conflict; left for Addis • found job in Wollega but got sick; spending savings on doctors • went to hospital in Addis
Shewangezaw	• parents poor • 6th grade schooling • worked as farmer with parents	• conscripted into the army; serving 24 years • in 1983 was taken to Addis • accommodated in rehabilitation centre; given small pension for two years only
Tesfaye	• parents had land father died early • 6th grade schooling • farmer until death of mother • could no longer afford to pay land tax and lost his land	• worked on coffee farm for three years but contracted malaria • worked on flour mill for two years until hearing and memory loss • went to Addis for free health care

Arranged marriages

Five of the ten women had marriages arranged[4] by parents, often without the brides' knowledge and consent; of these arranged marriages, four were unsuccessful (Almaz, Fantu, Yelfu and Zinash) and only Fatuma stayed with her husband until his death.

The story of Fantu, shown in Box 4.5, is one example of how an arranged child marriage can have negative consequences for a woman whose wedding had been organised without her knowledge and consent. When Fantu later found her married life unbearable, she faced an enormous dilemma by the early age of 13.

Box 4.5 Fantu's story

Fantu was born in Gondar in northwest Ethiopia, about 700 km from Addis Ababa. Her parents arranged a marriage for her when she was eight. She did not know she was getting married until the wedding day. She only realised it when she was being dressed in special bridal clothes, and wedding and food preparations were made at her home. Finally, she was covered in a shawl, put on a horse and taken to her new husband's home where there was a ceremony. She then had to stay at her mother-in-law's home for 15 days while they built a traditional house for the newly wedded couple. Fantu hated her life from the beginning, being forced to marry at such a young age to a young man of 16. No longer able to bear her existence and the sexual advances of her husband, she fled at 13 and joined the Ethiopian soldiers going to war in Eritrea. There she found a job with the army where she worked as a cook for the next ten years. After the war Fantu decided to go to Addis Ababa.

Fantu saw her decision to leave her husband as a choice between a life without rights and dignity, and an uncertain but self-determined future; this future ultimately became a life of poverty:

> I could no longer bear my existence. … There were sexual reasons for why I left and not having any rights and that I had to follow a man who was 16 years old. But the moment I left from home I was poor (Fantu).

Separation

> The main cause of my poverty is the death of my husband. Since then I can no longer afford to keep my house and find it difficult to support myself

[and children]. I feel dejected … [and] since we live on the streets I lost my
strength and can hardly work (Kedega)

Four women stated that their poverty in Addis was, to some extent, related
to separation, either through death of their husbands (Fantu and Kedega) or
being abandoned by a man (Genet and Zinash).

For example, Kedega stated that after she arrived in Addis Ababa
from the countryside, she initially got some casual jobs. Eventually she
met her husband with whom she had three children. The family lived in
a house together until the husband had an accident at work, where heavy
freight fell onto him. He was then admitted into care, organised through
the Missionaries of Charity, where he stayed for two months; he died five
months ago as a result of his injuries. According to Kedega she received no
compensation and had no means of keeping the house the family was renting.
Consequently, they lost their home and Kedega's life ended up even worse
than the life she had left behind in the countryside:

> … we all became homeless and ended up living on the streets. After 15 days
> one of my daughters died because of the cold. Now I am trying to support
> myself and other two children by begging and selling tissue paper. My
> daughters can't go to school and help by selling sweets and gum to earn
> their lunch (Kedega).

Fantu remarried in Addis after she left her first marriage in the
countryside. She stated that she had two children with her second husband
who used to be a printer, earning a good income of 400 birr a month.
According to Fantu, then the family could live quite well and afford to rent
a house for 100 birr per month. However, everything changed when her
husband died:

> My husband died six years ago and the printing centre where he had worked
> refused to give me a pension. Instead they only gave me 2,000 birr as a way of
> compensation. Since I had no job and income of my own, I had to leave the
> house with the children and move to another area. Since then I am poor (Fantu).

Both Genet and Zinash were abandoned by men. While Genet was
deserted by her husband, Zinash reported that she was deceived and cast

off by her boyfriend. Life for Genet in Addis has been particularly hard; she summed it up thus:

> … I was living on the streets for some time; then I was raped [and] I had my first child on the streets, without any help from anyone. About two years ago I met a man who promised to look after me and so we married. But this man abandoned me soon after I told him that I was pregnant [with his child]. After the birth of my second child I got very sick with TB, about a year ago (Genet).

Life in the capital started out quite well for Zinash, where she met an 'employment broker'. According to Zinash, this man found her work as a housemaid. Having worked in Addis for two years, Zinash met a man she liked and started living with him. While things looked very promising at the beginning, they did not end well for her:

> The man was well off and worked as a merchant. …. [But] when I got pregnant, the man announced that he actually had a fiancée, someone he would like to marry. He then asked me if I would organise their wedding for them. I then separated from him. … Now I am living on the streets begging for my daily food (Zinash).

The men

Like the women, a number of men saw poverty as related to family breakdown and separation from their families. (Material provided by the men also relates to other sections in this chapter, such as Family Conflict, and Displacement and Migration to Addis Ababa.)

Three of the men became separated from their families when their parents died. Shewangezaw, for example, stated that after his father and mother died when he was young, he did not have the opportunity to further his education and make something of himself. He therefore thinks that family breakdown is a key factor in people finding themselves in poverty: '… family break-up is an important factor in someone's poverty in early life and this is why I did not mind joining the army'.

When Getachew was in primary school, his mother died. Since the health of his father was poor, Getachew was brought up by a stepmother. His father had to seek medical attention in Addis Ababa where he later died. While

Getachew found a home with his brother's family, his situation subsequently deteriorated, as discussed in the Family Conflict section below.

Although Tesfaye was almost an adult when his mother died, he still feels that it affected his life very negatively:

> I was born in Kaffa, Southwest of Ethiopia, where I worked as a farmer on my mother's land, until she died when I was 20 years old. My life changed after my mother died because I could no longer afford to pay the land tax required by the government, something my mother always managed to pay while she was alive. Thus I lost the land and had to find a job on a coffee farm run by the government.

Separation from family also resulted from parental re-partnering. For example, Mekuria said that his family broke apart after his mother found another man, a shameful situation that he did not know how to deal with. Therefore, he left the countryside: '[My] family lived well and happy until my mother separated from our father to live with another man. This situation caused me [so] much distress that I decided to go to Addis, where I expected to live a good life.'

Although Mekuria had heard that it would be easy to get a job in Addis 'and make good money there', he found life very difficult. As will be discussed later, he found no work at first and lived on the streets until, eventually, he found some work as a daily labourer, work he still does to make a living.

Family Conflict

Feeding into the issues of marriage and family separation discussed above, family conflict was also reported by a number of participants as having affected their lives negatively and subsequently leading to poverty.

The women

Like Fantu, Yelfu's and Zinash's marriages were arranged without their consent, and both these women also left their husbands after many disagreements at home. Whereas Yelfu mainly argued with her husband, Zinash often quarrelled with the mother-in-law:

> I had to marry at the age of 16 [and] had a daughter who is now 20 by my husband. After our marriage I had many disagreements with my husband and lived in conflict with him. This led to our separation and I left him for Addis Ababa (Yelfu).

> I had to get married at 14 after my family arranged a marriage for me. I had my first child at 15. But I could not get on with my mother-in-law and after many quarrels with her decided to take my daughter and leave my home and husband for Addis Ababa (Zinash).

Family conflict of a different kind played a role in the lives of Kedega and Genet. Kedega was orphaned at six, then brought up by an aunt in Debre Zeit, but:

> I had many arguments with my aunt. One day after a big quarrel I ran away to the local church where I was found by a woman who offered me work as a babysitter. I went with this woman and stayed with her family for five years. I looked after their children but never got paid. One day I decided to leave the family and went to Addis Ababa. There I found work as a daily labourer.

Genet's mother died when she was seven. As her family had only a small plot of land and were very poor, a neighbour offered to take Genet with him to Addis Ababa, to bring her up in his own family. Genet, therefore, stayed with the neighbour's family for about ten years and went to school. But as time went on she increasingly had disagreements with the neighbour's family and started to run away. Genet said that as life on the streets was quite hard, she returned to the neighbour's home three or four times. But because their argument continued every time she stayed with them, she eventually left them permanently, saying that their differences had become irreconcilable. However, Genet's life on the streets soon became much worse, as she was eventually raped and abandoned.

Whereas family separation in the examples above was influenced by conflict, family tension also occurred as a result of the death of husbands. This is illustrated by Fatuma and by Kedega's second marriage. As Box 4.6 shows, Fatuma became poor despite coming from a very wealthy family when her family took over her estate after her husband had died.

111

Fatuma was born into a very rich family near Wello, about 450 km north of Addis Ababa. She has three sisters and four brothers. The family was related to a local lord and were called 'feudals' by other people. They had lots of land, cattle and other livestock such as sheep, goats and donkeys. When Fatuma was eight years old she was married as a result of an arranged marriage. Her parents died one year later and she had two children with her husband who died after their firstborn turned four. After her husband's death, her brothers and sisters said that since her farm and land was much too big for her to manage, they would take over and give her a small plot of land to farm. But Fatuma found it difficult to survive on this small plot where she could only harvest twice a year. Feeling that she had no choice she left the land and came first to Wello and then later to Addis, where she heard that people could get work easily and make a good living. She has been living in Addis for about two decades, and started to make a living here by baking bread for people, washing clothes and whenever there is not enough money, by begging around the churches.

The men

About half of the men cited family conflict as one reason they got into difficulties in their lives. When Bizuayew, for example, was invited by his brother and wife to stay in Addis in 1995, he agreed to move into their house and work as a *zebegna*. But soon he found himself arguing with his brother's wife and eventually had to leave the family. From there he moved into his grandmother's home, but again became unhappy, ending up living on the streets for two months.

Similarly, Getachew relocated to Addis Ababa after his elder brother asked him to live with him when he was 16, but: 'My brother had many children I was always fighting [with]. So eventually I decided to [leave and] become a *listro* when I was 17 [and] to become independent of my brother.'

While Bizuayew's and Getachew's family arguments occurred in Addis Ababa, Mesganew's disagreements took place in the countryside, precipitating his move to Addis Ababa. As shown in Box 4.7 below, events eventually led to major family conflict and, ultimately, separation; a situation Mesganew is still bitter about, feeling betrayed and victimised.

Despite his anger, Mesganew said that he greatly regrets not having a family and the support that one could get from it: '[I wished] it had been possible to live in harmony at home among my people, because I would not be in poverty today; my aunt is very rich.'

Mesganew was born in Debre Markos in northeast Ethiopia, about 230 km from Addis Ababa. He never knew his parents who died early. He was raised by his aunt, a wealthy hotel and land owner, who owns many cattle and other animals. Mesganew was never on good terms with the aunt's husband who, with his aunt, pressured Mesganew to work on their land as a farmer. He had to work hard but got little to eat. While his parents originally owned land that he inherited from them, his aunt asked him to sign a document one day, on false pretences. Since he could not read or write, he made his mark on the paper, not realising that he had signed his inherited land over to her. After he realised what happened he was very upset and argued with his aunt. But she did not want to give back the land to him and there was nothing he could do to get his property back. Thus, they fell out with each other and he left his home for Addis Ababa.

DISPLACEMENT AND MIGRATION TO ADDIS ABABA

Almost all participants settling in Addis Ababa came from the countryside where family issues such as marriage, family breakdown/ separation and family conflict increased the likelihood of their displacement from their places of origin. For the women, combinations of poor family background, losing one or both parents, getting married and having children, family conflict and separation explain why they came to Addis Ababa. Similarly, reasons for the men's migration include poor family background, small land holdings, family separation and conflict, personal difficulties and, in a small number of cases, conscription. Some participants had also been given the impression by others that work could be found in Addis Ababa and that life in the city was better than in the countryside. Thus, while many came to the capital to seek a better life, all respondents ended up in poverty.[5]

The Women

As Table 4.3 shows, and as discussed in earlier sections, the reasons most women left their homes are complex; their subsequent displacement is rooted in combinations of poor family of origin, losing one or both parents, getting married and having children, family conflict and separation. While most women originally came from the countryside to find better life and work opportunities in the city, their migration did not alleviate their poverty, but, in many ways, perpetuated it. Thus, almost all participants are now begging on the streets of Addis Ababa, finding it difficult to sustain themselves and their children.

TABLE 4.3 Women's reasons for and context of migration

PLACE OF ORIGIN	BACKGROUND AND CONTRIBUTING FACTORS OF MIGRATION	LIFE IN ADDIS ABABA
• Addis Ababa, but grew up in Tigray (Aster) • Debre Berhan ~ 130 km north of Addis Ababa (Almaz) • Gondar ~ 700 km north of Addis Ababa (Fantu, Samira) • Gurage ~ 155 km south of Addis Ababa (Zinash) • Tigray ~ 700 km north of Addis Ababa (Yelfu) • Wello ~ 300 km north of Addis Ababa (Belaynesh, Fatuma, Kedega, Genet)	• parents poor farmers with small land holdings • no formal education • losing one or both parents • arranged marriages • family conflict • separation, divorces • husbands drafted into army • husbands' death • insufficient livelihoods in other towns • finding work and better opportunities	• begging (all) • occasional housework (Fantu, Fatuma)

Thus, an early trigger of women's displacement is rural poverty; most of their families tried to make ends meet on plots of land too small to support them. Insufficient land was therefore seen by many female participants as one of the major causes of rural poverty. Some, like Belaynesh, Genet and Almaz, cited this as the reason they came to Addis. As Belaynesh stated: '[My] parents were very poor farmers with a small plot of land so that it could not support the family ... this is why I and many others end up coming to Addis Ababa [to look] for better lives.'

Box 4.8 Examples of women's background and subsequent dislocation

ALMAZ

Has three brothers and two sisters. Her father died three years ago and her mother last June. Her parents were very poor and could not make a living on their small plot of land with their children. Thus, Almaz's brothers and sisters left for Addis Ababa to find work and live with an aunt who had a shop. One brother then became a police officer and invited Almaz to stay with him when she was 12 years old.

GENET

Has one brother and one sister. Her mother died when she was seven but her father is still alive. When she grew up, her family had only a small plot of land and was very poor, so they had difficulty surviving. One of their neighbours offered to take Genet with him to Addis Ababa and bring her up there since her own family could not support her.

KEDEGA

An only child, her parents were poor farmers but both died when she was about six years old. Thus, she was brought up by an aunt in Debre Zeit for sometime, until she did not get on with her.

ZINASH

Has three brothers and three sisters of whom one has already died. Her mother passed away when Zinash was only two years old and her father also died when she was still a child. The parents were poor farmers with a small plot of land where they struggled to make a living. Zinash had to get married when she was 14 due to an arranged family marriage.

While other examples shown in Box 4.8 demonstrate that small land holdings contributed to poverty and the displacement of women, other issues compound their situation. For example, in cases like those of Genet, Kedega, Zinash and Aster, the loss of one or more parent played a part in the participant's dislocation.

That the loss of parents is significant is borne out by Aster, whose father died early and whose mother effectively abandoned her:

Causes of Poverty

I was born in Addis and have two brothers and one sister. My father died about 30 years ago [after which] my mother took me to Tigray to live as a young child. There we stayed for about two years until she immigrated to Italy where she found work as a cook; I returned to Addis and was brought up by an aunt but did not get on well with her. So I left home when still young and found a job in Wollega as a housemaid, working there for about 25 years. … I returned to Addis about seven months ago and now live on the streets.

As already discussed in the Family Issues section of this chapter, the plight of the women was not only affected by family poverty and missed opportunities, but also through enormous societal pressure to leave home, to get married and have children. As Belaynesh, Fantu, Almaz, Samira, Zinash and others suggested, marriage was also a major contributor in displacing women. Fantu put it thus: 'Poverty has a lot to do with being born into a poor family, having no education and knowledge and, in my case, the displacement from my home and family because of an arranged marriage.'

While Almaz originally came to Addis Ababa to join her siblings because of her parents' poverty, further dislocation followed, as in Fantu's case, through an arranged marriage:

When I was about 19 I visited my parents back in the countryside. There I was told that a marriage had been arranged for me. I had no choice and married the man with whom I had one daughter. … But we lived in very poor circumstances until the army conscripted my husband three years later. Not being able to survive by myself in the countryside, I went back to Addis to again live with my brother. But I could not get on with my sister-in-law and left their house about one year ago to stay at a church (Almaz).

Both Belaynesh and Samira were similarly affected. According to Belaynesh: 'My situation became worse after I got married and had two children. When my husband died I could no longer support myself and the children. So I went to Addis Ababa.'

Despite the fact that Samira came from a wealthy family, her marriage also led to her displacement. As Box 4.9 shows, after she was abandoned by her husband, her life became one of poverty.

Box 4.9 Samira's story

Samira was born in Gondar in the north of Ethiopia, about 700 km from Addis. She has one brother and one sister. Her father died when she was a child and her mother died about two years ago. Samira's parents were not poor and had enough land to get a good harvest every year. Her family still farms this land today. Samira married a soldier at an early age and had two children (twins) with him. But the soldier abandoned her after the birth of the twins and she had to find work in a small town near Gondar to raise her children. When, two years ago, Samira could not support them by doing daily labour work on construction sites, she took them to Addis. Here she works as a daily labourer, washing clothes and preparing red pepper for people.

The Men

As with the female respondents, reasons for the men to move to the city are complex. As Table 4.4 demonstrates, their dislocation and displacement arise through a combination of factors, including poor family background, family separation and conflict, and other personal difficulties. As discussed below, other issues playing a part were small land holdings, a 'pull factor' where some participants were told by others in the countryside that life in Addis was better and one could find work there and, in a small number of cases, conscription and ill health also played a part. While many thus came to the capital to seek a better life, all of them now live in poverty.

Lack of adequate land holdings

Five participants—Befekadu, Bizuayew, Getachew, Melaku and Shewangezaw—stated that they came from poor family backgrounds, and although Mesganew's parents were not poor, he said that he ended up poor since he was cheated out of his inheritance. For all these men, who had been farmers, insufficient land was a key factor leading to poverty.

Accordingly, Melaku argued that there is 'a land problem' in Ethiopia. While the population is increasing, the amount of land available, particularly to the poor, is limited and, by custom, poor farmers have to continuously subdivide their land among family members. Melaku said that eventually the farmers can no longer make a living on these small landholdings; as plot sizes diminish with time, increasingly, the land is overused and overgrazed, and there is a lack of fertilizer. As a result, the land cannot yield sufficient harvests to feed the families.

Causes of Poverty

TABLE 4.4: Men's reasons for and context of migration

PLACE OF ORIGIN	BACKGROUND AND CONTRIBUTING FACTORS OF MIGRATION	LIFE IN ADDIS ABABA
• Debre Berhan ~ 130 km north of Addis Ababa (Befekadu, Bizuayew) • Debre Markos ~ 230 km northeast of Addis Ababa (Mesganew) • Gagin Western Ethiopia (Mekuria) • Getsha ~ 500 km north of Addis Ababa (Melaku) • Kaffa, southwest Ethiopia (Tesfaye) • Mekele ~ 800 km north of Addis Ababa (Bekele) • Salatbet ~ 70 km south of Addis Ababa (Getachew) • Wello ~ 300 km north of Addis Ababa (Kebede) • Wollega ~ 500 km west of Addis Ababa (Shewangezaw)	• parents poor farmers with small land holdings • no formal education • family conflict • conscription into army • separation/ divorce • losing one or both parents • illness of self or parent • promise of better life and work opportunities • family reunion	• manual labourer • carrying bags for people

Thus, lack of adequate land is one reason why more and more people come to Addis, only to end up begging on the streets. Melaku told his story:

> I was born in Getsha in Northern Ethiopia about 500 km from Addis Ababa. I have one sister and three brothers. My father died when I was still very young but my mother is still alive. When I grew up I worked as a shepherd and later on as a farmer on my mother's land. But she was very poor and only had a few cattle. Her small plot of land could not support the family and we had difficulties surviving.

Similar accounts come from Bizuayew and Befekadu, both of whom originally came from Debre Berhan, about 130 km Northeast of Addis Ababa. Bizuayew stated:

I have two brothers and one sister. Mother is still alive but father died when I was only seven years old. When I was young, I had some schooling and later became a farmer. But our land was not big enough and we only had a few cattle. [Eventually] we could no longer make a living and I decided to visit one of my uncles in Addis Ababa.

According to Befekadu:

My parents were very poor and lived on a small plot of land. I am the ninth child of my mother, who gave birth every year. I worked as a farmer on my parents' land until it became too difficult to survive on the small plot of land. I planned to work in Addis Ababa and send some money back home to support my family.

As their circumstances in the countryside became increasingly precarious, the decision to migrate to Addis Ababa was also influenced by others suggestions that life in the capital is much better. Although this is often not the case, warning messages are unlikely to reach the country regions, since few of the displaced ever return home to tell their stories. Many men, like Befekadu, are ashamed to go back to their former communities, since they are poor and have not achieved anything. In this way, migration becomes part of a cycle that exacerbates poverty for people who have left difficult circumstances in the countryside.

Pull factor: promises of a better life

Befekadu, Mekuria, Melaku, Tesfaye and Kebede all stated that they heard that life would be better in the capital than in the countryside. According to Befekadu: 'I decided to go to Addis Ababa "to escape the poverty" two years ago. I heard from many people that it would be easy to find work in Addis— and that the life would be much better there.'

Participants, including Bizuayew, Befekadu, Melaku and Kebede, were ultimately disappointed, so now have second thoughts about having come to Addis Ababa.

For example, Bizuayew now thinks that his migration from the countryside was a mistake and that migration might have exacerbated rather than alleviated his poverty; since living in the city he has lost the support of his family and the community networks he had in the countryside.

Causes of Poverty

Similarly, although Befekadu left 'to escape poverty', his expectations were not met in Addis where:

> There are no jobs and life ended-up being even harder than in the countryside. I would like to go back to my family but feel ashamed to go home. People in my village expect me to do well and bring something back to support my family. [This is why] I have not been in touch with them and they don't have any idea of my whereabouts. This is the reason why I am isolated from my friends and family there.

For Melaku and Kebede the promise of a better life in the capital was also not fulfilled and life is hard:

> When I was 23 I decided to leave home. I had heard from people that one can make a good life in Addis Ababa. I was told that there were many jobs and people could earn a good living. But after I arrived everything was different and I found it hard to find any work and make a living (Melaku).

While Kebede's parents had sufficient land and his background was not as poor as most of the other participants, he was still enticed by the capital's reputation:

> Many people in the countryside said that it was easy to get work in Addis Ababa and earn a good income there. So I decided to go. But when I arrived life was very hard and very different from what I had heard from people back home. I tried to make a living by carrying bags for people and sometimes work as a manual labourer (Kebede).

Conscription

The conscription into the army affected only Bekele, Shewangezaw and Getachew, but all three ended up in Addis Ababa as a result. Bekele stated that he did not live in poverty in the countryside before he was conscripted. However, all that changed after he had to join the army and leave his family:

> I originally came from Mekele in Northern Ethiopia, about 800 km from Addis Ababa. I grew up there [and] worked as a farmer for 14 years. I was married with two children. In my native village my parents owned land, farm equipment and animals such as cows, sheep and donkeys. I was happy

in my village where everyone had everything they needed. But one day, I was conscripted into the army to serve in the Eritrean war. This changed my life and I had no choice but to leave family and friends.

Conscription meant that Bekele was dislocated, thus losing everything, so that his life changed forever. After he arrived in Addis, he never managed to return home, and his life of deprivation now seems permanent:

After three years, when the war was finished, I was taken to Addis Ababa and was told that my parents had died. ... [Because] my village was so far away and I did not have enough money for the bus fare, I never made it back home. I [now] have lived in Addis Ababa for 15 years, working as a manual labourer.

Getachew and Shewangezaw, on the other hand, were already living in poverty. Both lost their parents when young and neither objected to being conscripted, seeing the army as a chance to better their situation. Getachew, who originally had come from the countryside, had already experienced the situation in Addis and was hoping that the army would make a positive difference in his life.

Similarly, Shewangezaw did not mind joining the army, as he too had few options and opportunities:

I was born in Wollega in Western Ethiopia about 500 km from Addis and worked as a farmer with my parents and also joined the Boy Scouts in 6th grade. But my father and mother died when I was young. So I discontinued my education and did not mind joining the army, as a young man, when I was conscripted. I was sent to Harar to fight for the next ten years ... [and then] taken further North and spent another 14 years as a soldier.

Although Shewangezaw received some assistance after his long service, he states that there was no ongoing pension and that he had to find work:

After the regime change in the 1980s I was taken to Addis Ababa and handed over my gun. The new government then gave soldiers oil and 50 birr per month and also accommodated them in a rehabilitation centre for two years. But after that there was no pension of any kind and I started working at construction sites around Addis Ababa as a daily labourer.

Just as Bekele's life chances had diminished through the forced dislocation and eventual migration to the city, so had Getachew's and Shewangezaw's hopes for an improvement in their plight through military service not been realised. After their military service all three men eventually joined the ranks of the poor in Addis.

Ill health

Two participants, Mesganew and Tesfaye, stated that one reason they came to Addis was to get free health care and treatment. Mesganew said:

> ... I found a job in a spice factory located in Wollega. There I worked for eight months until I contracted malaria. [Although] I had 800 birr saved up I had to spend 150 birr each time to see the doctor for treatment. Because this treatment became too expensive I could no longer afford to see the doctor and left for Addis Ababa. There I received treatment through the Missionaries of Charity clinic and was admitted to a hospital for one month. When I was better I went to Merkato to start carrying people's bags and now work as a daily labourer.

Tesfaye, who worked on a coffee farm in the countryside, also contracted malaria so had to leave that job:

> [From there] I went to Jimma, about 330 km from Addis Ababa, to work on a flour mill I operated for about two years. I then developed some hearing loss and also memory problems. I heard from people that I could get free health care in Addis through the Missionaries of Charity and decided to go to the city about four years ago. After arriving in Addis I started begging around the churches and later began to make a living by making and selling woollen hats, something I still do today.

PERSONAL ISSUES AND CHOICES

The information provided by the Poor in this section on personal issues is much less extensive than in the previous sections on causes of poverty. Nevertheless, participants still made some comments here. For instance, having migrated to Addis Ababa, participants identified a small number of personal/individual issues that they saw as affecting their own and other peoples' lives. For example, about half of the women saw ill health as a personal cause of poverty, as poor health prevented them from working or limited their already precarious employment options. Some women respondents also began to have doubts about some of their own decisions, as well as questioning the behaviour of the poor themselves. The men were less forthcoming than the women in talking about their situations; instead, they focused more on individual causes of poverty and responsibilities of the poor.

The Women

For Zinash, Aster, Samira and Yelfu, ill health is a major cause of poverty, as being unwell prevents three of them from working and makes it difficult for the fourth to find work. At least two of the women suffer from HIV/AIDS, which they contracted through relationships with men. Yelfu had chicken pox as a child, resulting in the loss of sight in her left eye.

While originally Zinash had reasonable health, she struggled to survive with various casual jobs after she was abandoned by the merchant. However, life then became even worse for her:

> I fell very ill about six months ago and went to the Missionaries of Charity clinic just before I was dying. The doctor there diagnosed TB and also discovered that I was suffering from AIDS. Because of these diseases, I have lost the hearing in my left ear.

Zinash, like Aster and Samira, said that she can no longer work because of her illness and now has to rely on others: 'I used to bake *injera* for people to make my living but can no longer do that now. Now I find it difficult to work. If there is health there is a job. If there is sickness one must seek the help of others.'

Zinash's condition makes her life complicated. She pointed out that because she does not have much money to buy good food, she lacks nutrition to fight her illness. She also said that there is a stigma attached to AIDS and people are reluctant to employ anyone with the disease. According to Zinash, some landlords even refuse to lease places to someone with the condition: 'I cannot tell anyone about my disease, especially not the people I am renting the space from. If they knew about my condition they would evict us from the house we live in.'

Aster, who stated that she is also HIV positive, agreed with Zinash that there is a big stigma attached to this condition. Thus, her illness has become her 'main concern and cause of her poverty'. She confirmed Zinash's view that their illness precludes them from finding work, and further suggested that AIDS sufferers may be vulnerable to exploitation by organisations set up to assist them:

> There are organisations [which] deliberately employ people with AIDS and then exploit and cheat them out of their pay. … I too was employed for three months [in such an organisation] and never got paid. … They knew people in our situation are powerless [and] there was nothing I could do to get my money (Aster).

Although Samira is ill and convinced that her symptoms are those of AIDS, she has not had this confirmed by seeing a doctor. She stated that she is afraid of Western medicine and does not approve of it, as she trusts only traditional healing, which is spiritually based and differs in its methods. Thus, according to Samira, when a child gets sick there are only two things one can do. Either one rubs the child with natural oils or administers a special bitter drink which the child has to swallow. Samira was therefore adamant: 'I only believe in traditional healing. Everyone knows that traditional healing is the best.' Since her 'traditional healer' is sure that Samira suffers from what is called *almaz balechira*,[6] she is convinced that it can only be cured through traditional methods: 'This disease can make you blind and you are not to eat eggs and drink milk.'

Given that Samira refuses to see a doctor, she is unlikely to find out what is actually wrong and no real cure can be found. This is also a choice she is making. As the next section demonstrates, life situations are also affected by one's choices.

Life choices and individual responsibility

Some of the women also reflected on their life choices and how these decisions influenced their lives. For example, Almaz, Fantu, Yelfu, and Fatuma regretted some of their decisions and actions; similarly, Genet and Aster felt that the poor themselves are responsible for their own plight, partly through making poor life choices.

Several other women were more explicit in attributing their poverty to their own actions. For example, Almaz said that she sometimes blames herself for her plight and wonders if she should have stayed in the countryside: 'May be I should have stayed home and tried to get a plot of land there. I should also stay on better terms with my family, with my brother and other relatives.'

After many years of poverty, Fantu too now reported having second thoughts, and wonders if running away from her husband was a mistake. So instead of blaming her poverty and situations on society, she thought that 'society is not to blame for poverty but people themselves. I blame myself for leaving my husband. … But I don't even remember my husband's face now.'

Yelfu and Fatuma also said that they find it difficult to live in Addis Ababa and are reconsidering their choice to come here. Both now feel responsible for their situation and regret some of their decisions. Thus, Yelfu said:

> I now regret the decision of leaving my husband. I was too young to understand the consequences of my action[s]. I think that if I had stayed at home in the countryside, I now would have many children and live well on the land.

Fatuma also reflected the view that society as a whole is not responsible for poverty, and thought that the community normally tries to help poor people. For example, she said that when she lived in a richer neighbourhood, everyone tried to help her by giving her work. So she said that now she blames herself:

> I feel somewhat responsible for my own poverty. I [now] think that maybe it was a mistake to leave the countryside, where all my relatives and support [systems] are. … My poverty might not be as severe at home as in Addis (Fatuma).

Genet believed that, in many cases, the cause of poverty lies with the person rather than with society, as, in her view, people do not want to see others to be poor. She therefore blames some of the poor: 'Some people are poor because they are ill and lack support, but some individuals are healthy and themselves to blame because they are lazy and don't want to work.'

Aster agreed that some poor are lazy and do not want to work: '[Poverty relates to] the laziness of some people who don't want to work. There is also absence of courage and a lack of belief that they can do something or even anything.'

Causes of Poverty

The Men

Although most men looked dejected and depressed when interviewed, they did not volunteer much personal information or their feelings about their situation. Thus, while only a small number of them reflected on themselves, most others commented on the individual responsibility and behaviour of the poor.

For example, while Befekadu, Bizuayew, Melaku and Kebede said that they are disappointed that their expectations about the life in Addis Ababa have not been fulfilled (as discussed in the Displacement and Migration to Addis Ababa section), they did not reflect on their decisions. An exception is Befekadu, who reported that he regrets his decision to come to Addis:

> I would like to go back to my family but I am ashamed to go home. People in my village would expect me to do well [and that] I bring something back to support my family. That is why I have not been in touch with them and they do not have any idea of my whereabouts. [But here] I am isolated from my friends and family.

Although Tesfaye agreed with Befekadu that poverty has to do with 'being isolated, alone, and having no support from family and friends', he added that poverty is the result of 'being old, sick, mentally ill or disabled'. He argued that since sick people cannot work, they lack the necessary income for a normal life.

However, like Getachew, Kebede, Shewangezaw and Mekuria, Tesfaye said he did not feel sympathy for the 'normal poor' and those who are not ill; he placed much of the blame for poverty with poor people themselves:

> The majority of the poor are lazy and morally weak. … There are many opportunities to find work in Addis. [Although] the poor might lack the connections and influence to find work, they do not want to work—even if someone offers them a job. They prefer to be idle (Tesfaye).

Tesfaye also commented on the problem of begging in Addis Ababa:

> Most of the poor people in Addis come from the countryside and had land of their own; but they did not like to continue working on it. Instead, they preferred to come to Addis and walk around begging so as to have an easier life.

While Tesfaye lost his land by having difficulties paying the land tax in the countryside, as discussed earlier, he still thought that some farmers:

> … were so lazy that they did not even manage to pay the land tax required by the government, and therefore lost their land. … Many farmers who gave up their land and came to Addis do not realise how important it is to have land because one can use it during one's entire life time.

The argument that the poor themselves are responsible for their poverty was shared by Getachew and Kebede: '… some of the poor are lazy people who do not want to work, even if there were enough jobs. These people are responsible for their own poverty' (Getachew).

Kebede described the poor as having characteristics and making life choices that include:

- being lazy and not wanting to work
- having bad habits
- drinking too much alcohol
- smoking
- using drugs.

By contrast, while Shewangezaw and Mekuria agreed that people 'should not chew *chat*[7] nor drink alcohol' to make their poverty worse, they did not believe individuals are responsible for their poverty.

In summary, on the whole, poor participants lacked knowledge about structural causes of poverty, instead attributing the causes of poverty to negative social attitudes, lack of community support, the rising cost of living, poor family background and family matters such as marriage and family conflict. The Poor identified significant causes of poverty as migration, displacement, and personal issues such as ill health and past decisions.

4.2 THE PROVIDERS

Box 4.10 shows the five classes of poverty causes identified by the Providers. Each of these five causes is discussed in turn below.

Box 4.10 Causes of poverty identified by the Providers

- structural factors
- societal issues
- governance
- policy weaknesses
- individual issues

STRUCTURAL FACTORS

> Poverty and power is an opposite pair where power is the root cause of poverty. Power [totally] misunderstands the essence of authority and the fact that we are here to serve God. This is why a great man is 'small' and a servant (Provider 7).

Providers 7, 6, 2, 3 and 4 all argued that structural factors cause the crisis of poverty in Ethiopia and elsewhere.

For Providers 7, 6 and 2 in particular, these causes specifically relate to inequality, power and the unequal distribution of resources. Provider 7 strongly believed that poverty is not a matter of chance, but is instead a '... part of the darkness of the mind of wealthy people and represents a scandal'.

In this way of thinking, the causes of the 'scandal of poverty' in the world relate to:

- the great level of injustice in the world
- the fact that some people enrich themselves to the detriment of others
- dictatorships that force people to comply with systems which are good for the powerful but not for the people
- wrongful decisions and choices made by the powerful
- the lack of clarity about what development is and what giving aid and helping people actually means
- the fact that 'development' is often misguided because it is not really addressing people's actual needs
- the fact that development, as it is currently practised, gives with one hand but takes away with the other. This process often involves some people taking from others something that does not belong to them (Provider 7).

Providers 6 and 2 agreed that there is little justice in the world as a whole. Provider 2 pointed to the absence of economic equality, an absence that explains why:

> Poor people work hard but earn very little, compared to those few rich people who get very wealthy with relatively little effort. This kind of inequality is manifested throughout the community and affects every sector and the way society operates as a whole.

However, inequality is not simply an economic issue for Provider 2, who used the concept more broadly; like Provider 7, Provider 2 saw inequality in terms of the abuse of power by the privileged. He argued that inequality can also occur through the manipulation of notions like 'ethnicity and culture', where one ethnic group might receive preferential treatment over another one, or be treated less favourably. 'For example, if a *kebele* official is part of the "Oromo" ethnic group, a person who is "Amhara" might be treated less favourably than another Oromo' (Provider 2).

However, like Provider 7, Providers 2, 6, and 5 also criticised the current model of development and the processes involved in it. As Provider 6 put it: '… poor nations are the dumping ground for cheap Chinese goods, for example. Poor countries also make themselves dependent on wealthy nations, worship foreign goods and fail to develop their own economies.'

Provider 6 explained further that this kind of 'development process' prevents a poor country from developing the technological skills necessary to develop its own resources and to deal with its economic and other challenges. To make matters worse, internal structures in developing nations are often such that they maintain unequal distributions of wealth and available resources. This means that only some parts and sectors of the country are developed, so that mainly the wealthy benefit and the poor continuously miss out.

Provider 4, on the other hand, thought that one of the key issues of development is the lack of opportunity of the poor to be fully functional members of society. For example, the disadvantaged lack participation in the labour market, and poor people, who migrate from rural areas to towns and cities, lack the services they need. Following on from this, Provider 5 argued that greater government input is therefore required in the following areas: 1) the development of the country as a whole, 2) the development of appropriate technology, and 3) the production of goods and services. In addition, Provider 5 felt that 'the government is also developing the wrong kinds of large infrastructure projects, mainly in the cities, instead of addressing the needs of 85% of the population that live in the countryside and depend on agriculture'.

Societal Issues

A number of participants thought that some of the attitudes and cultural values in Ethiopian society contribute directly and indirectly to the poverty in the country. Providers illustrated this idea both in general terms and by looking at specific examples of societal attitudes towards women, institutional/organisational values, and moral/spiritual dimensions.

A good example of how general values influence society was provided by Provider 6, who suggested that:

- there is unwillingness in richer parts of society to give up some of their benefits and to make some sacrifices to help the poor
- there is a lack of dedication by some professional groups and institutions to assist the poor in society. Instead, they work for the betterment of their own situations, rather than fulfil their proper function as a change agent in the community for the common good
- there are too many religious holidays as taught by the churches, days when people are not allowed to work
- there are traditional values and cultural settings which stop people from developing themselves and the country
- there is wastage of time and precious resources by people and the nation as whole.

For most Providers, such as 1, 3, 6, 7 and 4, women are particularly disadvantaged in society. They argued that women continue to have fewer opportunities in the community than men, and that their disadvantaged position is also demonstrated in the way they are treated and viewed by society. Thus, Provider 1 suggested that the societal values system contributes to the ill-treatment of women, as this system condones and legitimises it. For example:

Against the Odds

> The traditional gender division of labour is still at work in some communities, where women are supposed to focus on domestic work, rather than working outside of the home. Here, a woman in a household depends entirely on her husband to give her money on Sunday, to run the household (Provider 1).

In similar fashion, Provider 4 thought that 'gender imbalances in society, where the position of women is less equal, have negative effects on everyone in the community, including children'.

Provider 1 argued that if a woman steps outside what is considered to be her place, there will be communal pressure for her to conform to the 'traditional ways'. Some of these 'traditional ways' and cultural values in society relate to what he considers 'poor thinking' and:

> ... backward attitudes of some of the community leaders, linked to the past traditions. They lack the appropriate knowledge about many issues, limiting the access of community members to many of the opportunities in society (Provider 1).

For Provider 3, culture is important too, but she saw the role of culture from a different perspective. As she explained, she grew up in a patriarchal society with a 'dictatorial government', and in this system people were socialised to honour and obey their father, who makes the major decisions, which his family does not question. For Provider 3, this cultural norm also applies to society as a whole; the government represents the father figure, and expects its people to obey without questioning its decisions and actions. Using 'father' and 'government' interchangeably, Provider 3 said that 'in this culture, I would never ask my father to give me anything and would hope he would provide me with what I need'.

In her analogy, Provider 3 argued that this is the reason why people normally do not request either their rights or the provision of services they are entitled to from the government. In turn, the government does not expect to be asked by society for anything. It only gives something when it wants to and decides who gets what. In this kind of 'family scenario' there are children who invariably are the favoured ones, who have high expectations, and then they are those who can expect much less from the father. The favoured children are also those who are much more likely to ask for things. Consequently:

Causes of Poverty

> ... this system still operates on many levels of society where the wealthier classes anticipate higher rewards than the lower ranks of society. In this way, poor people have very low expectations in relation to their actual government entitlements such as services. While this kind of thinking is changing in society, attitudinal change of poor people, in particular, is slow (Provider 3).

For Provider 3, this cultural system explains why in Ethiopia there is a lack of 'civil society' that would provide a means for people and organisations to come together and address social problems collectively.

Provider 1 agreed and suggested that cultural attitudes indeed shape the lack of institutional and strategic responses to assist the poor. As one instance, he pointed to 'the crisis of population growth', arguing that the reason why family planning is only in its infancy relates to traditional and strongly held community and religious attitudes which still do not favour contraception or other welfare interventions in society. He also pointed out that children are traditionally seen as 'a sign of wealth' by some sections of the population, although poor people cannot afford adequate care for many children. While Provider 1 conceded that it would be much better for the poor to have fewer children, he acknowledged that without proper organisational assistance '... there are some good reasons why the poor have too many children. For example, having more children increases the likelihood that some children actually survive in a poor family' (Provider 1).

Provider 1 further argued that because of traditional values:

> ... people are still asked by churches to give alms on Sundays and during the many religious festivals, draining peoples' resources. Some households don't respect other people and are rude, blaming the poor without knowing anything about them or their situation.

For Provider 3, this situation is made worse through the lack of private and other appropriate media outlets, which can: 1) initiate free public debate and 2) generate ideas for societal reflection without fear of reprisals. Given this, she stated, it is unlikely that any meaningful 'cultural and attitudinal change' can take place in the immediate future, since:

> ... the media feels constrained and therefore tends to serve the interest of the government, rather than feeling free to offer independent analysis. As a result, issues of poverty and policies in relation to such problems are not really properly discussed and analysed (Provider 3).

According to Provider 3, while it is highly desirable that society and its institutions should be free to express opinions and make contributions to the public debates, there are no guidelines about what is 'allowed' and what is not. This lack of clarity makes people insecure and stifles their activities.

While Provider 6 and 7 also thought that some of the cultural values in society have negative implications, they saw the social causes of poverty very much in moral and spiritual terms. For Provider 6, poverty in this context is the result of:

- sinfulness and selfishness of people
- lack of respect for others
- lack of dignity and recognition of people themselves and of their neighbours
- not being able to relate to others
- lack of working attitudes by some of the poor.

For Provider 6, on the other hand, people do not:

- understand God and what it means to be human
- love God and other people
- understand the importance of giving and receiving as human beings
- understand spiritual consciousness in the world, a path people have chosen willingly.

GOVERNANCE

> Politicians are not really interested in solutions and spend most of their time in unproductive meetings, instead of actually tackling the problems of society (Provider 5).

Almost all Providers argued that causes of poverty directly relate to issues of what they see as 'poor governance' and the related inefficient management of resources in the country. For a number of interviewees poor governance is also associated with inadequate public policy that fails to address the key social policy issues in the country.

To explain what is meant by poor governance, Provider 3 defined it thus: '… poor governance applies where systems and structures to govern the country have been developed, which are inadequate or working poorly.'

Providers used various examples to demonstrate how poor governance creates problems in society. Providers 5 and 7 questioned the entire workings and motivation of the political system, Provider 4 pointed to market processes and the economy as a whole and Provider 1 saw poor governance in the context of local government; in addition, Providers 1, 2, 3 and 6 referred to the rural sector and policy formation in a number of areas.

Analysing market processes, Provider 4 felt strongly that:

> … it is irresponsible and inadequate political governance which allows the free market system and its owners to fix prices, so that those who don't earn enough can't buy the necessities of life and their ability to meet vital basic needs will increasingly be weakened. … Politicians have also been involved in the privatisation of public companies/assets, with auctions insured and financed by government banks.

Provider 1 also felt that 'some local bureaucracy' tends to be unaccountable. He used local council as an example here:

> For instance, when someone needs something from a local council office, officials might expect some [payment] to do things. Without money one has to wait a long time in a queue and the poor are often harassed, blamed and not helped. This is how the overall public policy towards the poor can be viewed, where officials often reinforce and perpetuate the marginalisation of the poor.

For Providers 1, 2 and 3, similar processes can be found in agriculture, on which the majority of people in Ethiopia depend. They suggested that because there are a few major landholders who control large tracts of land, many poor people are denied access to land and livelihoods.

For Provider 2, lack of appropriate mechanisms to ensure good governance allows land in the countryside to be controlled and distributed unfairly by government officials. As poor farmers have no voice and power, they are marginalised on small plots of land where they cannot make an adequate living. As Provider 2 explained:

> … those who have power and money have access to local officials and can get close to influence them. They have access to cheap credits and, because of their close relationship to government, they can get land cheaply which they then sell on [the lease] for a much higher price. Thus, the land is not fairly distributed among the population, leading to enormous economic injustices.

And:

> Poor and smaller farmers have little voice and power to influence government officials; [instead] they have to survive on very small plots of land to make a living. When they can no longer survive on their small plots, many of these poor farmers come to Addis Ababa to beg for their livelihood.

POLICY WEAKNESSES[9]

For most participants, governance also relates to the way public policy is made. They were, thus, critical of some of current policies in relation to poverty and other social issues. In the first instance, participants saw problems in terms of the broad policy setting adopted by policy makers. In addition, Providers gave a few specific examples of policy gaps, in areas such as population growth, land/agriculture, basic needs and the development of services. Providers 6, 1, 5, 3 and 2 thought that the general policy setting currently in place needed adjusting.

According to Provider 6, government policy has to be seen in an historical context. He explained that during its history, Ethiopia has gone through many different systems of government, ranging from monarchy to communism to the current free market approach. Further, policy makers always try something new; therefore, there is no coherent policy framework that can be implemented in order to develop the country. Thus, Provider 6 compared

Causes of Poverty

Ethiopia with: '... a patient who goes to see too many doctors [and who] will never be cured, especially if there is never any proper follow-up.'

Provider 5 agreed, pointing out the legacy of the different political systems, and using the environment as an example:

> Society still lives with the legacy of the last socialist regime which made many wrong decisions. Thus, society is not really aware of the enormous environmental degradation facing the country and the fact that the land has been depleted. People still continue to cut trees today damaging the land.

Providers 3 and 2 commented more broadly on policy formation. Provider 3 stated that some existing public policies have not been properly implemented and, therefore, are not working. This problem then is complicated by the lack of public participation and consultation in the development of new policies by the wider community, and 'without any input by society into anti-poverty policy, the real needs of the poor can, therefore, not be addressed' (Provider 3). In addition, Provider 3 pointed out that government policies are '... rarely studied, reviewed, monitored and evaluated, after they have been developed; so it is difficult to see how and if they actually work and what needs to be changed in the future'.

Provider 3 also argued that this situation means that the real problems of society are not always apparent, resulting in a continuation of short-term thinking on the part of politicians and officials, and:

> Before election time, there will be policy promises mainly addressed to the already well off who are educated, have opportunities, knowledge and information. These people have power and influence and are close to policy makers giving them information, resources and benefits that the poor do not have access to (Provider 3)

For Provider 1, policy weaknesses include:

- relevant guidelines and policy implementation that benefit the rich more than the poor
- the economy being a reflection of government policy, leading to some people not paying their fair share of tax
- policies that do not address the provision of basic needs.

To further demonstrate gaps in public policy, a number of specific issues were articulated by individual Providers. Four of these views are discussed below.

1. Land Policy and Population Growth

Provider 3 drew attention to the dire situation many small farmers face in the countryside, where they often cannot sustain themselves. As families grow, their already small plots of land are continually sub-divided between the various family members. Eventually, some people are forced to migrate to the ever-growing urban areas where they often end up living in the streets. However, there is no coherent government policy to address either the problem in the rural areas (via a land policy, for example) or the plight of the poor once they have arrived in the cities.

Provider 2 argued that the issue of lack of land for the poor is even more pressing when population growth in Ethiopia is considered:

> Despite the fact that the population has grown from 25 million about 20 years ago to now 70 million people,[10] government has no policy to control the population growth, which largely consists of poor farmers living on small plots of land they share with their children (Provider 2).

2. Ethnic and Cultural Issues

Provider 2 suggested that division and competition between Ethiopia's many ethnic groups is often the result of a deliberate government policy promoting 'cultural differences' and diversity. This divisiveness then leads to further problems: 'The end result of the implementation of this policy is nepotism and corruption where everyone is trying to get resources and influence instead of working fairly for the good of the country' (Provider 2).

3. Meeting Basic Needs

For Provider 5, the current focus on addressing issues such as HIV/AIDS is misdirected, as he believes that politicians should concentrate on addressing the wider needs of the population instead. For example, there are no policies to address the sharp price increases of important food items such as *teff*, which at the time of interview costs 600 birr for 100 kg.

4. Service Gaps

A number of service gaps were identified by Providers 3, 1 and 4. According to Provider 3:

- while some organisations, such as the *iddirs*, have the capacity to contribute to and address social problems, many other organisations do not get enough financial, technical and other support from the community or the government
- there is a lack of family planning, which means people in Ethiopia have too many children they cannot feed and look after
- there is no adequate legal system to protect the women/girls who have been abused by men.

For Provider 1, service gaps are:

- land and general amenities like water are very expensive and not affordable for the poor
- health care is free in theory, but people need to be a resident in an area, and have an ID and supporting letter from the local council to access free health care. A lot of people do not have these things and are not in a position to obtain health care as a result.

For Provider 4, service gaps are:

- absence of social, educational and other support systems
- inadequate health services, especially for people with disabilities, as existing services are set-up for 'normal' (and better off) members of society.

INDIVIDUAL ISSUES

While almost all Providers identified structural/societal factors as the major causes of poverty, they also acknowledged that, at least to some extent, individuals influence their own situations. Interviewees focused here largely on traditions and cultural values, some of which they thought affect individual behaviour, something they already had referred to in the Societal Issues section of this chapter. Provider 1 summed it up thus: 'There is also a culture of expecting others to help, although someone might be quite lazy and unproductive themselves. This often relates to traditions and upbringing.'

Like Provider 1, Providers 2, 4, 5 and 6 also believed that decisions made by individuals play a role in poverty. Provider 1 made a clear link between societal values, the way they are propagated in the community and the behaviour of the individual poor. He therefore felt that:

> Many poor farmers have been influenced by churches around the country not to work on many days in the year on their land, thus not maximising the potential of their land. Because of cultural values and practices, many people are set in their ways and unwilling to learn new ways of doing things. This keeps their development back (Provider 1).

Providers 1 and 5 argued that some traditional thinking keeps the poor backward. For Provider 1 this means that the poor:

- still use traditional medicine, risking their health and that of their children, especially when they suddenly switch or mix the traditional methods with Western medicine
- are so deprived that they are often dependent on others, lacking the initiative and ability to find alternative options in life for themselves. This dependence sometimes also includes the lack of foresight, where someone might leave their job without having other work to go to and then rely on their family to support them.

Provider 5 agreed, and argued that because of 'outmoded traditions', many poor individuals in the rural areas are incapable of 'using all their windows of opportunities'. This means that:

> ... they often don't use their local resources efficiently enough. They continue growing maize all the time, instead of something else which might have greater benefits. Because of their cultural traditions poor farmers do not like to change and diversify their products but live in the traditional way like their fathers. They keep having too many children they find difficult to feed and look after instead of having less (Provider 5).

Causes of Poverty

For Providers 2, 6 and 4, some of the poor simply have 'the wrong attitude' and 'don't want to work' (Provider 4). As Provider 2 suggested:

> Some people consider begging in the city easier than working the land and thus take the easy way out, hoping to get something for free from society and officials. This can create dependency rather than making the poor self-reliant.

4.3 THE ADVOCATES

All the participating Advocates described the causes of poverty as complex and difficult to come to terms with. For example:

> Causes of poverty are immense and complex. But poverty is not a new phenomenon and existed in previous times, including the period of colonialism (Advocate 2).

> There are natural and man-made causes of poverty. The natural causes include natural disasters, disability and lack of mental capacity. The man-made causes include [the fact that] some people exploit others. Thus, we find the rich and the poor inequity in the distribution of resources, materials, services and money (Advocate 3).

Despite the complexity of causes of poverty, the data provided by the Advocates yielded four key areas through which poverty is discussed, as shown in Box 4.11. Each category is discussed below.

Box 4.11 Causes of poverty identified by the Advocates

- structural factors
- societal issues
- governance
- individual issues

STRUCTURAL FACTORS

All Advocates argued that poverty has structural causes, with some Advocates linking international with local spheres. International arrangements of the trading system and processes of globalisation were largely seen as having negative effects on poor nations and ultimately limiting their economic and social development.

International Level

For most Advocates, structures affecting lives in Ethiopia have to be seen in the global context, and they argued that the international economic system operates as part of the process of 'globalisation', in which rich nations dominate and exploit the poor. According to Advocate 2, while the process of exploitation takes place at the international level, it also affects the national level:

> One example of this is the unfair World Trade Organisation trading system which does not allow poor countries to subsidise their farmers whereas rich nations do. The processes of inequality and exploitation seen on the international stage can also be identified on the national level, where the rich accumulate enormous wealth and don't share it with others (Advocate 2).

Advocates 4, 5 and 3 agreed. Advocate 4, for instance, argued that although people are 'equal in theory', there is an increasing division between rich and poor nations, as well as between people within countries. According to Advocate 4, this polarisation is fuelled on the international level by unstable external markets where powerful countries, dominated by the US, manipulate trade for their own benefits and expect poorer nations 'to obey' their rules:

> If poor countries don't do as they are told, they will face all sorts of pressures including trade embargos. There is actually no 'free trade' and 'fair exchange of goods', and poor nations depend on the goodwill of the more powerful. [This is why] a country like Ethiopia does not receive adequate prices for its goods, such as coffee, which in turn reduces local employment and other opportunities. (Advocate 4).

For Advocates 5, 6, 7, 4 and 1, these global factors mean that the international community does not share its wealth with poorer nations like Ethiopia. For this reason: 'Western countries often do not assist governments in developing nations to reform their internal structures, but are much more interested in taking their resources, such as oil' (Advocate 5).

Consequently, Advocates 1, 4 and 6 thought that many trade restrictions have been developed by rich nations to prevent developing countries exporting to other markets. Advocate 6 even suggested that globalisation is designed by wealthy nations to ensure poor countries remain poor:

> Processes and mechanisms of globalisation actively prevent nations from developing their economies. They deprive poor nations of investment and trade opportunities which they need to develop further. Part of the globalisation model is also warfare, where a poor country might get pushed into buying unnecessary weapons or even entering a war. Wasting precious resources thus (and often dividing its population), these resources are then missing to develop the nation instead (Advocate 6).

Advocate 7 suggested that international processes deliberately generate huge foreign debts in order to entrap developing nations into a cycle of debt and poverty. She argued that the consequences of debt for a country and its people are particularly devastating, as such debt causes extreme poverty and hardship, and servicing debt negatively affects the whole population: 'As the entire nation is trying to service this debt, it lacks the required budget for health care, education and infrastructure and can, therefore, not meet the needs of its people' (Advocate 7).

Advocates 4, 5 and 1 also stated that the global economic system has had major negative impacts on the environment. They argued that while Western-style development precipitated problems such as environmental degradation and droughts globally, it devastated large tracks of land, especially in Africa, land on which farmers depend on for their survival. According to Advocate 4, farmers, therefore, suffer in two ways: 'Not only do farmers get insufficient prices for their goods, they may also struggle to produce a good harvest due to environmental factors, finding it sometimes difficult to make a living on the land.'[11]

National/Local Level

Advocates 4, 5, 1 and 3 maintained that what happens internationally is also reflected on the national and local level. First, they argued that the pain is inflicted on a country by unfair global trade is not shared equally, and the poor suffer the most. Second, even such wealth as is generated is not equally shared.

Advocate 1, for example, pointed out that: 'One of the causes of poverty is the unequal distribution of the resources in the country. [For this] the powerful are responsible, denying the poor their basic entitlements and rights.'

Advocate 3 did not focus on international factors, but believed instead that problems arise because the local economy is not facilitated or managed properly. He argued that resources are appropriated by a few people, benefitting the rich who keep increasing their wealth. At the same time, poverty itself and the gap between the rich and poor is constantly increasing, and:

> One of the major trends in society is that the whole community is being impoverished. An economic oppression emerges as the main controlling mechanism of the distribution of wealth, where the rich directly benefit from the poverty of others (Advocate 3).

Most Advocates, such as 6, 1, 3, 4, and 5, therefore thought that problems of inequality and poverty relate to issues of 'poor governance', which involves political structures and decision-making processes that are not conducive to the development of the country and its public institutions.

SOCIETAL ISSUES

> In the Ethiopian context, there are many social and other factors to be considered where poverty could be viewed 'as a weapon of mass destruction' (Advocate 5).

To highlight social factors which influence the incidence of poverty, Advocates provided a number of disparate views. For example, Advocate 5 stated that poverty relates to:

- greed in society where individual members of the community do not share with each other, and the poor no longer have the opportunity to make a living
- a person may not have enough land to till in the countryside, so decides to come to Addis Ababa and beg
- lack of personal and community resources.

Advocate 7 pointed to a lack of support mechanisms in society for poor people; these deficits apply in areas which include government assistance, the community and even friends. He argued that lack of support can precipitate poverty, especially during difficult times or catastrophic events such as floods. In these cases:

> Families may not cope on their own as people's resources are quickly depleted. In such circumstances, it will be difficult for individuals to recover by themselves without assistance, increasing the likelihood of extreme poverty (Advocate 7).

Advocate 1, on the other hand, saw the rapid population growth as a huge problem, since the needs of too many people cannot be balanced with the available resources. To illustrate the resource shortage in the countryside, she stated that:

> In many of the country regions, plots of land are forever subdivided between family members when children are born and raised. Thus landholdings are often no longer sufficient to sustain families in the rural areas and many farmers therefore migrate to the city, looking for better lives (Advocate 1).

For Advocate 5, lack of resources and the inability to make a living also have the potential to trigger a vicious cycle of social unrest, civil war and poverty:

> Extreme poverty can disrupt social cohesion and create tensions between people. This can lead to civil war and diminish the capacity of the population and the whole country to be productive. War therefore brings social and economic instability as experienced frequently by the whole of the Horn of Africa, including Somalia (Advocate 5).

Social unrest was also on the mind of Advocates 3 and 4. Advocate 3 argued that if social unrest occurs:

- it is either based on ideology or ethnic tensions. Social unrest and war invariably waste a lot of resources, energy and the talent of many people
- the whole country becomes unproductive and its development is stifled

- instead of investing money and resources in people, there will be increasing investment in government.

For Advocate 4 too, poverty may arise in the community if there is conflict between people; indeed, in the worst-case scenario, tensions might be so high that people start killing each other. The causes of such conflicts can differ from community to community. According to Advocate 4, conflict could ensue 'by some people claiming to be from one group in the community and manipulate others in another group'. But conflict could also be instigated:

> … by some individuals providing challenging ideas to society that inflame a situation, resulting in disputes. Thus, people will stop supporting each other and once cooperation between people stops, economic and other development will suffer (Advocate 4).

To demonstrate what he called 'obstacles to local development' Advocate 4 used an example from last year in Gambela,[12] where:

> Christians and Muslims lived in harmony until some 'bad individuals' created trouble and the Muslims started fighting Christians. After fighting began people got killed and houses and churches were burned down. As a result, 400 people lost their homes in the community and still need assistance to rebuild their lives. Families affected by this continue to struggle, have little to eat and their children cannot go to school.

Societal Attitudes Towards the Poor

For Advocates 2, 7 and 1, cultural issues also need to be considered, especially the way people have been socialised to accept poverty. Advocate 2 thought that: 'Society, including the government, the churches, NGOs and the rich, think it is normal to be rich and to be poor. They give 1 birr to the poor to absolve themselves and think that this is all the poor deserve.'

Advocate 2, therefore, argued that the community takes it for granted that:

- the local, 'traditional ways of doing things' are correct
- poor people do not have access to education
- the rich do not share with the poor.

Advocate 3 and 7 agreed, suggesting that the whole of civil society accepts poverty as a given and keeps reinforcing that view. For Advocate 3, this view does not only include organisations such as the churches and NGOs, but also the political system:

> Churches, in particular, perpetuate the ideology that poverty is normal and sanctify the poor by suggesting that only the poor can go to heaven. The same applies to the culture of the political system which accepts the absence of education for a large part of the community. But by allowing access to education to only a few people, the system also maintains and reproduces itself and the dominance of a minority over the majority of the community (Advocate 3).

According to Advocate 7, stereotypical attitudes towards the poor in society also lead to discriminatory practices in institutions. She used the example of banks and other lenders, which tend to be reluctant to lend money to poor people because they are often characterised as 'deviant and untrustworthy' by the community. For Advocate 7, poverty can thus be exacerbated by the unwillingness of institutions and organisations to assist the poor:

> Despite the fact that the poor might actually have the skills to set up businesses, for instance, banks are unlikely to provide credit facilities to them. Since poor people cannot meet the necessary lending requirements, such as providing collaterals or guarantors, they cannot get access to capital in order to improve themselves and their situation (Advocate 7).

In addition, Advocate 7 argued that there are also gender and political biases against women, so that many lenders hold 'old patriarchal' views and do not want to lend money to women. She pointed out that this is a significant issue, since it is women who often hold families together, being the ones who budget and act responsibly. For Advocate 7, negative societal attitudes towards the poor in the banking sector can also lead to spiralling debt crises for entire families. Since the poor are locked out of the normal lending mechanisms, they might have to go to expensive money lenders who charge very high interest where:

> ... it is very difficult for the poor to pay back the money that was lent to them. Sometimes this forces poor farmers to sell their land, cattle and other

possessions, impoverishing them even further. The burden of debt affects every member of a family, condemning numerous people to a life in poverty. This actually resembles the debt crisis of the nation (Advocate 7).

GOVERNANCE

Following the structural and societal analyses, the Advocates provided a definitional framework for poor governance and how it relates to poverty. The governance–poverty relationship is conceptualised broadly below, before its application is illustrated with concrete examples.

Advocate 6 defined poor governance in the following and typical way:

> Poor governance means that there is lack of basic democracy and transparency, where regimes are not accountable, serving their own clients rather than society. The system is also characterised by corruption, and public property is misused and squandered.

And:

> Decisions are made by politicians without consulting the public and the poor have no voice in the decision making process at all. Thus poor peoples' houses are demolished to make way for roads, without actually asking them, a process that further increases the number of the very poor and the homeless.

Advocate 3 agreed that poor governance means that, ultimately, a government is not interested in the views of its own people, and:

> ... if someone shows interest in contributing to the public debate, then this will automatically be interpreted as 'political' and seen as undermining the politically accepted process/status of the government. This hinders the full participation of the community and increases the political control and passivity of the population.

For Advocates 4, 3 and 5, the lack of good governance also affects the distribution of wealth and resources in the country. Accordingly, while everyone has 'a birth right to be equal with others, in some poor countries there is no democracy where people find themselves in superior and inferior positions' (Advocate 4).

For Advocate 3, many politicians are trying to 'gain and improve themselves through the political process, rather than working for the poor and the greater good of society'. He suggested that in the worst-case scenario, this political ambition can lead to the oppression of the population and end in political instability. Therefore, people need to learn lessons from the past:

> For example, revolutionary governments in the past brought in new ideologies in the name of equity. While some of this ideology was based on socialist ideals of equality, in practice, the implementation of these ideas resulted in poor governance and negative situations where the economic development of the country suffered and many people became poor (Advocate 3).

Similarly, Advocate 4 thought that 'poor governance and administration' means that leaders of a country might not act in the best interest of their people, since they may:

- be dishonest and take bribes
- engage in drinking and illegal activities
- fail to look after their own people/population
- prevent political freedom/democracy and ensure that they cannot be removed from their position.

For Advocate 4, all of this then increases the likelihood of poverty:

> … if the incidence of poverty in society becomes disproportionate, conflict between people will increase, making it harder to make the necessary changes for the better. Thus, lack of freedom, security and safety are all part of poverty.

Advocate 1 agreed; in her opinion 'poor governance' means that:

- a lot of resources are wasted by strengthening the power base and survival of politicians and the wealthy, rather than serving the country
- there is still insufficient trust by Ethiopians living overseas, who could potentially make a big contribution to the country's development.

Taking the argument further, Advocate 3 suggested that poor governance undermines the trust between civil society and the government, so that many people withdraw from active participation in society. In his view, this affects particularly: 1) the young who question their support for the political system and the work of the government, and 2) members of the intelligentsia who are leaving the country. He argued that the latter is of great significance because: '… there has been a big "brain drainage" and exodus of skilled people who should actually assist in the development of the nation' (Advocate 3).

However, Advocate 3 admitted that there are two competing processes. He explained that the loss of learned and educated people is actually due to the greater freedom allowed by current government policy:

> Whereas, in the past, other governments have tried to control the intellectuals and prevent them from leaving the country, current policy allows them to leave. The result of all this is that much productivity in the country is lost on all levels, especially in the economic sphere (Advocate 3).

Policy Weaknesses

> There is a basic lack of vision for society by government and policy makers in order to implement proper societal policies to develop the whole nation (Advocate 6).

The majority of Advocates argued that current public policies do not address the needs of the poor, as a sample of responses demonstrates in Box 4.12. For some interviewees, the policies implemented also favour the rich and powerful over the poor.

For Advocate 6, government offices also lack the capacity to provide sufficient services to the public because:

- there is a lack of proper planning towards development and little 'is really evolving for the poor'
- there are no proper standards and norms applied in public policy, because policy makers only think in terms of 'programmes' and want to fit the poor into a scheme.

Box 4.12 Lack of pro-poor policies

ADVOCATE 3

'There is a poverty of thinking and planning at work … and a political bias, in that politicians make decisions for the rich rather than for the poor.'

ADVOCATE 6

'There is a lack of pro-poor policies, particularly for the 85% of the rural poor instead of the current pro-rich policies.'

ADVOCATE 5

'Current policies don't [create] the opportunities for the poor to improve themselves in society, nor do they facilitate employment options.'

ADVOCATE 1

'There is a lack of planning without clear priorities/consideration given to the needs of poor people and families in the community.'

Concrete policy failures in a number of areas are illustrated by Advocates 2, 4 and 5:

- Public infrastructure building projects. These fail to address the needs of the public and the poor in particular, who lack access to basic services such as sanitation, clean drinking water, housing and other public utilities. Instead, resources are devoted to subsidise the rich and middle class, by building a ring-road, for instance.
- Resources in the rural areas. Whereas middle-class households in urban areas are connected to the water and sewerage system, a typical rural person has no access to water and needs to walk for hours. The longer the walk to get the water, the lower the rate of production and the likelihood of economic consumption, and the higher the health cost to the people involved.
- Security in slum areas. The poor are excluded from safety and security, and are highly exposed to crime and diseases such as HIV/AIDS.

Individual Issues

> Lack of knowledge, formal education, skills training and self-respect, at the personal level, increases the likelihood of poor people to scramble for resources (Advocate 6)

While most of the comments made by the Advocates did not relate to the poor as individuals, they acknowledged that individuals play a part in their situation. Thus, Advocates 1, 3, 4, 5 and 7 briefly referred to some of the poor's behaviour, attitudes and characteristics that might contribute to their plight.

For Advocate 4, poverty can relate to the behaviour of individuals. For example, some poor people do not want to work despite 'the fact' that 'God says everyone has to work to earn his daily meal' (Advocate 4).

Poverty can also be the outcome of 'a misunderstanding' between a married couple. If a family breaks down, this might then initiate a cycle of family poverty, where:

> The husband might start drinking and behave badly after arguing with his wife. The man then may lose his job and his family will find itself in poverty. The man might also be lazy, have multiple partners and be unwilling to work. He might spend his money on drink and gambling and neglect his plot of land by not ploughing it (Advocate 4).

While Advocates 5 and 3 conceded that poverty can relate to 'ill health and the inability to work due to sickness' (Advocate 5) and 'the spate of HIV/ AIDS infections and other illnesses which undermine the productive forces in society' (Advocate 3), they also pointed to personal shortcomings of the poor. Advocate 5 defined these as:

- lack of initiative to do something
- lack of inventiveness
- laziness and dependence on others for help
- fatalistic thinking, for example, that 'God created me so He should feed me'
- lack of education.

For Advocate 3, on the other hand, poverty can relate to the mentality of the poor, who '… have created their own world and become very submissive. They have resigned themselves to their situation and no longer desire a better world. They have totally given up' (Advocate 3).

Advocates 7 and 1 also thought that some poor people contribute to their situation. According to Advocate 7:

> Some confuse their life circumstances in that they misallocate their funds/resources and spend it on alcohol, smoking and gambling. They waste existing opportunities and the education of their children in exchange for their own recreation, leisure and friendships, and then blame the life they lead on either God or fate. Other poor people are just happy with what they have and don't think much about their future. They may hold 'traditional beliefs' which are backward, holding them back in their development and progress.

Advocate 1 argued that many poor farmers, for instance, are losing the incentive to be self- reliant and hard working, but also explains that emerging negative attitudes to work have been influenced by the enormous environmental degradation in the country. Due to drought and other environmental issues, insufficient harvests in many parts in the countryside reduce the likelihood that farmers will be willing or able to plant and prepare the land for the following year. Thus, 'as more and more people become dependent on handouts and aid each year, their culture of self-reliance and hard work also changes' (Advocate 1).

Summary

Just as with the definitions of poverty in the previous chapter, respondents articulated the causes of poverty in a multifaceted/multidimensional way. While the Poor reflected on their personal experiences rather than on wider societal factors, Providers and Advocates drew on their knowledge of structural and other broader causes of poverty.

Interviews with the Poor suggest that their identification of causes of poverty largely depends on individuals' experiences; that is, on their life histories, daily struggles to survive and interactions with other people, which are embedded in social structures and practices. This complexity of connections means that, for the Poor, the causes of poverty are enmeshed, dynamic and cyclical. Compared to the other two groups, the Poor demonstrated little awareness of structural causes of poverty, although they had some notions of inequality, especially in relation to the rising divide between the rich and poor. Most poor participants felt unsupported by the community. The vulnerable position of women was confirmed in this chapter, and poor women clearly had even fewer choices and opportunities than their male counterparts. Growing up in a patriarchal society, and usually carrying the added burden of child-rearing, the women's lives are more precarious and often less under their own control, than those of the men. Poverty cycles also appeared to be intergenerational, involving combinations of poor family background, family breakdown/conflict and insufficient land to survive on in the countryside. In addition, there was a lack of education and opportunities, such as employment, displacement and migration to Addis Abba, plus personal issues, such as ill health, loneliness and social isolation. While some of the women questioned their own life choices, the men were less self-questioning of themselves. To some extent, both female and male participants also looked at the behaviour and responsibility of poor people themselves in relation to causing or contributing to their poverty situation.

The Providers demonstrated a good working knowledge of poverty issues and causes, although they lacked the personal experience of poverty. Thus, although their ideas reflect their knowledge of and empathy with those experiencing the difficult reality of poverty, they expressed these ideas in wider and more abstract terms than the Poor. For this group, the crisis of poverty in Ethiopia is caused by structural factors such as social inequality, unequal distributions of wealth and the lack of opportunity for poor nations arising out of an unfair global Western-style development model. Providers also commented on cultural issues such as societal attitudes towards women, institutional/organisational values and moral/spiritual dimensions in Ethiopian society as direct and indirect causes of poverty. Almost all Providers argued that causes of poverty directly relate to poor 'governance', which leads to inefficiency and to inadequate public policy that fails to address key social policy issues to meet citizens' basic needs. Providers also identified inadequate land policy and service gaps in areas such as education and health care. While mostly commenting on structural/societal factors of poverty, Providers acknowledged that individuals also influence their lives and situation. Respondents here

Causes of Poverty

focused largely on traditions and cultural values, some of which they think negatively affect individual behaviours of the poor.

The Advocates also painted a complex picture of poverty causes, identifying structures, society, governance, public policy and individual factors. Advocates' analysis of structural issues such as economic globalisation was more comprehensive than that given by the Providers; Advocates here viewed current international trade as unfair and exploitative, affecting poor nations negatively and limiting their economic and social development. Advocates also suggested that global inequalities are perpetuated in various ways on the national level, and argued that both individuals and institutions too readily accept poverty as a given, and that various negative societal attitudes work against the poor. While Advocates also described how lack of good governance and related local systems can hinder the progress of the nation, their analysis of this factor was not as extensive as that of the Providers, perhaps because of differences in their areas of work. Nevertheless, Advocates reflected on how current public policy and inadequate support mechanisms both relate to poverty and fail to address the needs of the poor. Finally, like the Providers, this group also identified some attitudes and behaviours of the poor as causing poverty and preventing the remediation of poverty, as discussed more fully in the next chapters.

Above Private mansion, Sarbet Area. K. Serr

Bottom New building construction on Haile Selassie Rd. K. Serr

Above Yakatit (February) 12 Memorial, Sidist Kilo. K. Serr

Bottom Addis Ababa University, Sidist Kilo. K. Serr

Above Street scene, Bole Area.   K. Serr
Bottom Dwelling, Piazza area.   K. Serr

Above Street scene, Kazanchis.
K. Serr

Left A back lane, Kazanchis.
K. Serr

Above Hong Kong Island, China. K. Serr

Bottom Homeless men, Addis Ababa, Ethiopia. A.M. Friala

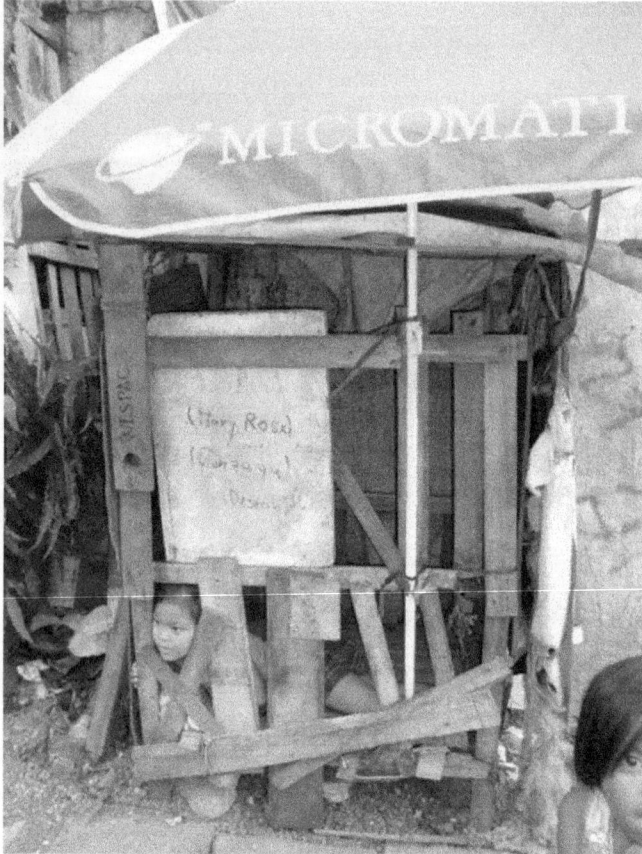

Left Street children, Cebu, Philipines. A.M. Friala

Above Atlantis Resort Hotel, Bahamas. Villa suite with ten bedrooms, four bathrooms, butler, and kitchen staff costs $24, 000 per night. This is about the equivalent of 50 years of a typical salary for a waitress in Addis Ababa. Picture and description from hotel website

Bottom *Favelas*, Salvador, Brazil. K. Serr

Above Rubbish recyclers, Cebu, Phillippines. A.M Friala   K. Serr

Above Female manual labourer on building site, Addis Ababa. K. Serr

Bottom Drying chilli, Addis Ababa. K. Serr

Above Street sellers, Sidist Kilo. K. Serr

Bottom Homeless woman, Addis Ababa. A.M. Friala

Above Woman with a disability, begging. Addis Ababa. K. Serr

Bottom Night shelter for men, Addis Ababa. A.M. Friala

Above Charcoal stove for cooking, Addis Ababa. A.M. Friala

Bottom Former leprosy sufferer, begging. K. Serr

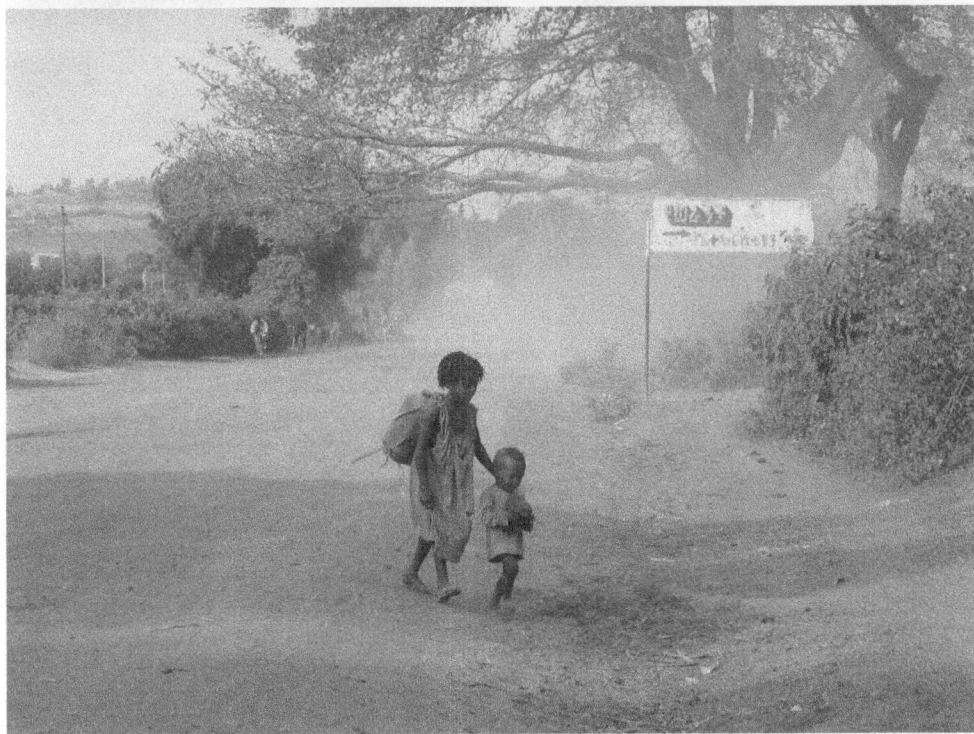

Above Rural village, Northern Ethiopia. K. Serr
Bottom Child carrying water, Southern Ethiopia. K. Serr

Community toilet block and clothes washing drums. A.M. Friala

Locked communal toilets, Addis Ababa. A.M. Friala

Homeless man outside church compound, Addis Ababa.
A.M. Friala

Above Femal labourers on building site, Addis Ababa. K. Serr

Bottom Female wood carrier, Entoto Mountain, Addis Ababa. K. Serr

Above New villa construction, Sarbet, Addis Ababa. K. Serr

Bottom Makeshift shelter, near Sheraton Hotel, Addis Ababa. A.M. Friala

Above Pastoralists, Northern Ethiopia. K. Serr

Bottom Makeshift shelters of homeless people, Addis Ababa. K. Serr

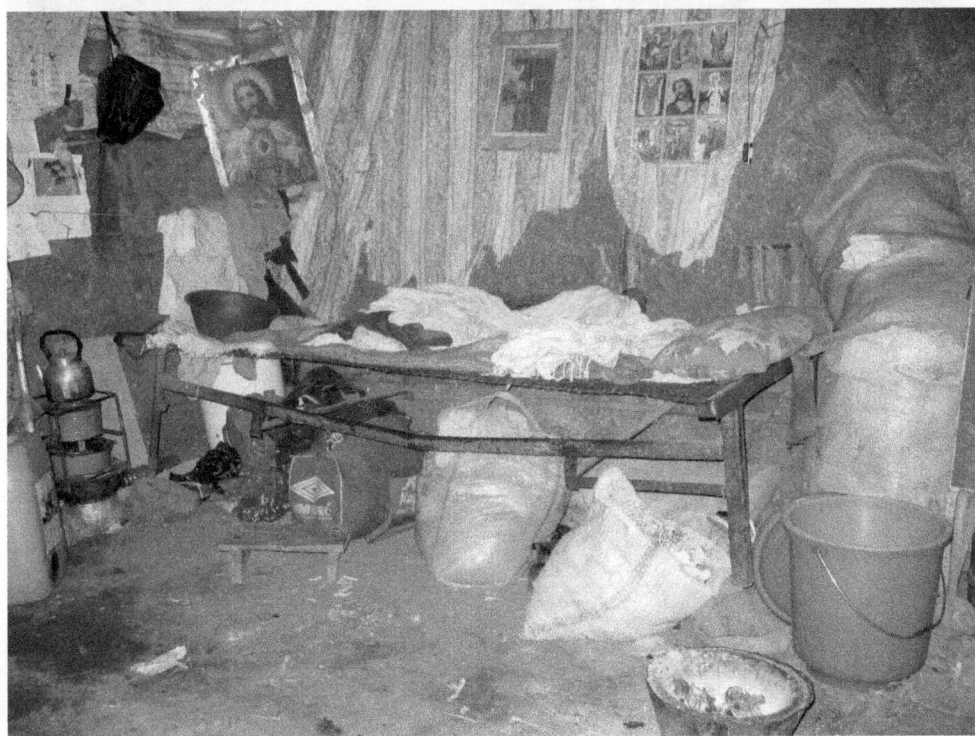

Above Gate of Bole Medhanealem Church, Bole. K. Serr

Bottom Interior of a poor family's dwelling, Addis Ababa. A.M. Friala

Recipients of food handouts, Addis Ababa. A. Tilahun

Village mosque, Southern Ethiopia.
E. Lyn

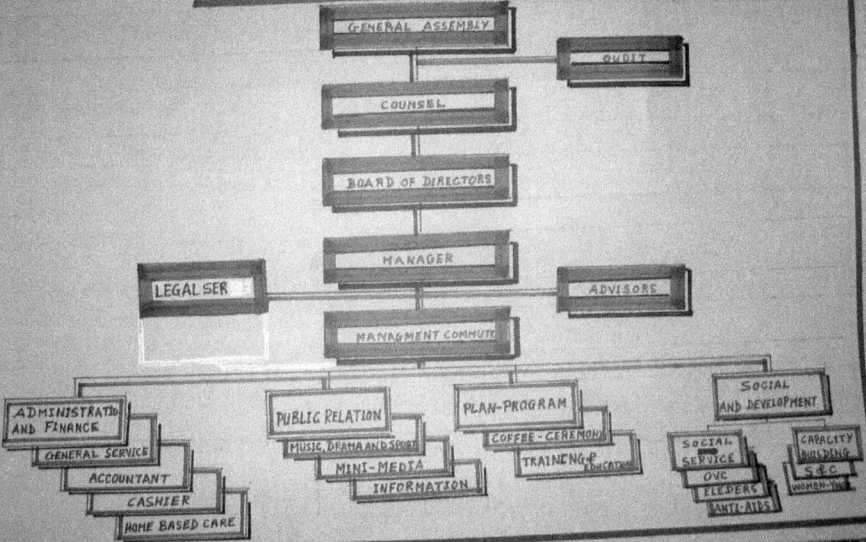

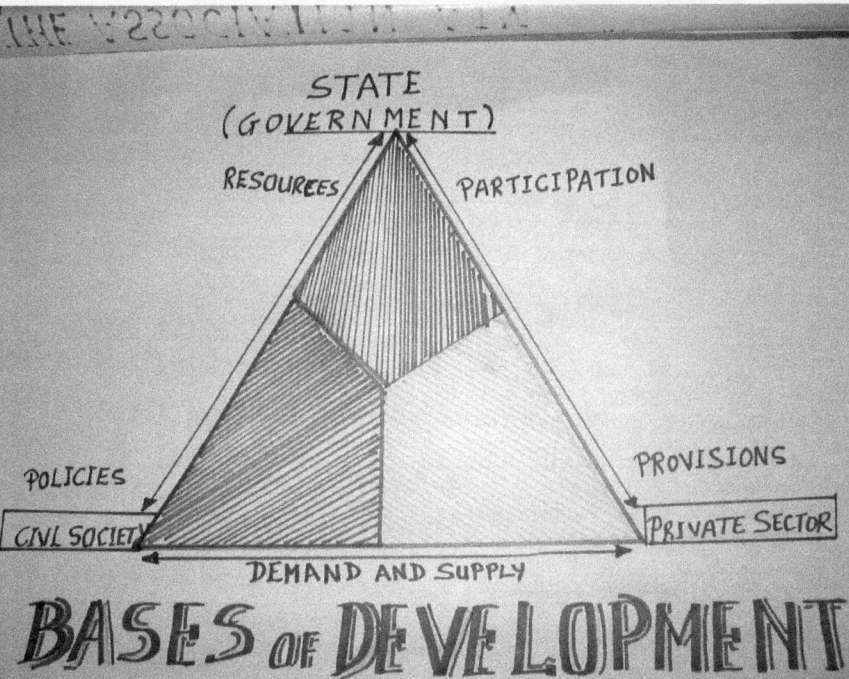

Above Organisational chart of local Iddir. K. Serr
Bottom Developmental paradigm of local Iddir. K. Serr

THE ASSOCIATION'S AREA OF FOCUS

- POVERTY REDUCTION (capacity builing)
- AIDS PREVENTION AND CARE OF PATIENTS
- ASSISTANCE TO ELDERLY AND ORPHANS
- ESTABLISH WOOD AND METAL WORKSHOPS
- ESTABLISH 1-6 KINDERGARTENS
- ESTABLISH CREDIT AND SAVING ASSOCIATIONS
- ESTABLISH SERVICE COOPERATIVE
- CONSTRUCT A CLINC.
- ESTABLISH I.G. NOT BASED ON PROFIT MAKING
- ADVOCACY AGAINST HARMFUL CUSTOMARY PRACTICES
- DEVELOPMENT WORK IN COORINATION WITH LOCAL KEBELS AND SUB-CITY.

THE ASSOCIATION AIM

- To under take social work by organizing the member's knowledge, labour, money and participating in development activities carried out by administration.

- To assist eledery people with support AIDS orphans and other orphans.

- To help to improve the lives of youths from poor families by opening small-scale income - generating project.

- To estabish a community centr where the elederly can meet to find means where by their knowledge and experience can be passed on to the next generation.

- To implement the association's objectives in collabration with govermental and non-governmental organizations, agencies and individuals.

Above Focus areas of local Iddir. K. Serr

Bottom Overall aims of activities of local Iddir, Addis Ababa. K. Serr

Chapter Five

BARRIERS PREVENTING FULLER PARTICIPATION OF THE POOR

None of the research participants provided much data in answer to the question about barriers to fuller participation by the Poor. Informants in each group felt that they had already answered most of the 'barriers' questions when discussing the 'causes of poverty'. It became clear that, in many ways, barriers overlap with causes, further demonstrating the cyclical nature of the poverty experience. Many participants also believed that the lack of opportunities in society experienced by those who are less fortunate in the community act as significant barrier to the poor in their attempts to have better lives. Lack of opportunities especially applies in societies with strongly hierarchical social structures and scarce resources; in such societies an often unassailable advantage is held by those with wealth and power. Given the paucity of data generated for this part of the study, it was not possible to develop a robust categorisation of themes for discussion. Nevertheless, participants provided some new ideas, while reiterating some themes mentioned previously.

5.1 THE POOR

Seven women contributed material for this chapter, while Belaynesh, Genet and Kedega felt that they had nothing more to add. Nine men supplied additional information, Getachew being the one exception. Although having little material for analysis made it difficult to develop meaningful categories, the data for both women and men were loosely organised around societal/community and personal issues, with some gender similarities and differences emerging, mostly in the Personal Issues section.

SOCIETAL AND COMMUNAL ISSUES

Much of what was covered here is associated with the lack of life chances and opportunities such as education, work/low income and not being able to join community organisations.

The Women

Most of the material here came from Fantu, Yelfu and Almaz. Fantu felt strongly that having no opportunities in life prevented people from achieving anything in society. In her own case, education was one of those missing opportunities: 'I have no education and find it difficult to get work. [For example,] sometimes organisations look for cleaners, but even for those jobs they want people to have some basic education.'

Fantu also stressed that people 'like herself' have fewer than average chances to get employment, since they do not have family and relatives with influence and connections in the community. Without those networks, said Fantu, the need to be educated is even greater.

Both Yelfu and Almaz said that an important barrier in their life is not being able to join an *iddir* community association. They felt this is an important obstacle, since *iddirs* support their members by providing various services. Being a member of such an organisation also makes people part of the community. Thus, Yelfu stated that while she would like to become a member, she does not have enough money. She also explained that when people have made no contributions for many years, it is difficult for them to join an *iddir* and that she has now given up hope of doing so:

Even if I could spare some money, I would first have to repay the owner of the house where I live, for all her support over many years. It would not be fair for me to join the association and pay them instead of giving her something back (Yelfu).

Like Yelfu, Almaz said that she does not expect ever to be able to afford the membership fee of an *iddir*, so feels excluded from this important aspect of participation in society.

The Men

Without money I simply cannot live properly and also have no influence and power in society (Bizuayew).

For a number of men, such as Bekele, Kebede, Shewangezaw, Bizuayew and Mesganew, lack of money and income constituted a significant barrier to their fuller participation in society. However, they placed different emphases on the impact of inadequate money on their lives.

Bekele focused on the quality of life he cannot have. Lack of income for him is a result of being unemployed, as 'without a job and adequate income I cannot live a decent life'. Kebede, on the other, hand emphasised that as a result of insufficient income, 'housing is a big problem for me. I have to sleep with total strangers—in such horrible conditions.' Kebede also suggested that his situation is made even harder, since he has no family or other connections to support him, financially or otherwise.

Melaku focused on a different problem arising from lack of money, as he wants to establish a business or buy land but cannot get the necessary start-off capital and financial assistance to realise his ideas. Thus, he called this problem a '50,000 birr financial barrier', the sum he thought he would need.

By contrast, the ambitions of Befekadu, Tesfaye and Shewangezaw are much more modest. They do not have enough money to join an *iddir*, and Tesfaye stated that membership of a community association is simply too expensive, costing 'about 20 birr per month'. In addition: '… if the association has been going for some time, a new member needs to contribute back payment to make up the time they have not been a member. Thus, many people cannot afford membership' (Tesfaye).

157

Like the women, these men saw membership of an *iddir* as very important because of the support and services it provided to its members. As Befekadu explained:

> *Iddirs* help with the burial of its members and assist their families during the entire process. But if someone in the community is not a member and dies, they do not receive a proper burial with a religious ceremony. Then their families, friends and neighbours cannot attend and they will be buried by the municipality instead, without a priest and ritual.

While most men's barriers related to insufficient income, Mesganew, Mekuria and Befekadu also mentioned the lack of societal opportunities. For Mesganew, for instance, this lack includes his difficulties in getting an ID from the *kebele* and, most importantly, the lack of training and work opportunities: 'I only want a job, even if they don't pay me and just give me food. But I want to have some training to better myself.'

Also, Befekadu and Mekuria thought that their opportunities in life have been very limited. For both men this meant growing up without formal education. As Befekadu said: 'I have no education or knowledge [and] can't be like other people because I am poor. I can't participate in the community and don't even know how, because my world view is very limited.'

Personal Issues

Both women and men believe that barriers to their fuller participation are the feelings of isolation from the community and their shame for the lives they lead. These barriers of isolation and shame are exacerbated for the women due to their illnesses.

The Women

Most women, such as Yelfu, Almaz, Fatuma and Fantu, stated that they miss being part of the community and expressed feelings of loneliness and isolation as a result of being excluded in their community.

Almaz felt herself to be especially affected. Living on the streets with her two children, she pointed to her great need for social interaction and support. Not having such support has, therefore, social and psychological implications for her: 'I am cut off from people and feel very lonely and isolated. … I miss human contact and feel I will die without it.' Thus, Almaz said that she is losing hope, as she knows that she has no way of joining and being part of the community: 'My life is outside in the streets. … I am not like other people who have a home.'

Similarly, Fatuma said she was ashamed of her life because she lacks the company of friends and relatives, and being poor makes her feel stigmatised and isolated: 'I am never invited by other people and am labelled poor and am ashamed [of it]. I don't even have anything to make coffee.'[1]

Getting on in years, Fantu is also alone. She reported feeling that she does not belong anywhere in Addis; instead, she longs to go back to Gondar one day to show her children where she originally comes from. But she also said that she has given up hope of ever getting there: 'I don't have the means to take them there. It is two days to travel by bus and a full day's walk into the countryside.'

Illness

Aster, Zinash, Samira and Almaz identified their illness as a significant barrier to their participation in society. For most of them, illness means living with HIV/AIDS, feeling stigmatised and cut off from people in the community. Their feelings about and reactions to their illness are varied. Aster, for example, has difficulty finding employment and, without any income, has to rely on begging to support herself.

Zinash said that she deliberately keeps to herself so that nobody will find out about her illness. She pointed out that people are afraid of AIDS and often avoid people with the disease. Therefore, she said: 'Nobody knows about my illness but my children because of the stigma so I suffer in silence. The children are very supportive and promised to look after themselves.'

Thus, being isolated, both women lack supportive social relationships and cannot participate in their community in any meaningful way.

Similarly, AIDS is a barrier for Samira: '… because of my sickness I cannot work and people around me discriminate against me. AIDS has a stigma attached to it.'

While the other women complained about the effects of AIDS, Almaz told of 'a broken arm' and her distrust of Western medicine, making her life on the streets even harder. Although she has been told that she can get free health care at the Missionaries of Charity, she refuses to see a doctor: 'I am afraid of Western medicine and only believe in the traditional way of healing that comes from bathing in the *tsebel*?' (Almaz).

The Men

Like the women, men like Befekadu, Melaku, Mekuria, and Bekele feel isolated and ashamed of their situation. Being poor, without friends and family, they have lost self-confidence and find it difficult to relate to others.

Melaku, for example, stated: 'I have difficulty interacting with other people because I lost my confidence. I feel ashamed of my poverty, lack of money and dirty clothes.'

These men talked of missing their families and their places of origin, and lamented the fact that they have left their homes. Bekele explained his situation: 'I miss village life and the holidays there. ... In Addis I am alone, have no family and friends and have no one to share the festivities with.'

Bekele thus felt bitter about the past. He said that he still remembered how he was not poor when conscripted into the army and parted from his family forever. As he never managed to get back to his village after he was released, he can only wonder what his life would have been like if he did not have to leave. Now he is lonely in the city, recalling only the good things about his life in the village:

> People were happy [in our village] and they loved and helped each other. Everything people needed was available and no one was without food. If someone was in need, neighbours would help and share what they have, for example, a goat. Life is different in Addis Ababa where there are rich and poor people, but the rich do not share with the poor (Bekele).

Despite providing little data for this chapter, the Poor still made some contributions. Their comments covered some societal barriers, such as lack of opportunities, education, income and personal barriers, such as lack of belonging, shame, isolation and illness.

5.2   THE PROVIDERS

> Given the long history of problems in the country, things are complex and there are many barriers in society. [This is why] there are no easy and simple solutions and positive change will, therefore, take time and cannot come quickly (Provider 3).

Like the Poor, most Providers presented little additional material for this chapter, and Providers 2 and 5 had no further comments to make about barriers to fuller participation of the poor in society. Likewise, the lack of responses from this group prevented categorisation of the material. While Participants tended to reiterate some of their earlier views on causes of poverty, a few new ideas were developed, and these insights have been organised around a brief discussion on three issues: injustice/inequality, governance and societal barriers.

For Providers 7, 1 and 6, the main barriers to the poor participating more fully in society are: 1) the great injustices between countries and people, 2) the unequal distribution of wealth and resources, and 3) lack of good governance. Providers 1 and 6 saw current circumstances 'as a crisis' which, to them, indicates that government policy around the world favours the wealthy over the poor and needy in society. Provider 1 suggested that this situation is exacerbated in developing countries:

> Many studies undertaken by intellectuals/academics are not widely available and used by the public. There are few processes of evaluation and scrutiny of public policy to see whether it actually works or is successful in what it sets out to do.

For Provider 6, changing the conditions of poverty will be a major challenge; overlapping with earlier discussions on the causes of poverty, he classified barriers as:

- lack of good governance
- lack of visions to develop the country
- too much bureaucracy
- absence of democratic processes
- lack of real opportunities in society to develop oneself
- difficulty in implementing new ideas in the current socio-political climate.

Provider 4, on the other hand, identified the practice of begging as a key barrier, an obstacle which prevents the whole community from 'moving on and progressing forward'. He believed that begging relates to an outmoded 'cultural tradition and way of thinking', and he explained that the tradition of begging has its historical roots in the church,[3] where:

> ... young seminarians called *yek'olo temari* used to beg for their living in the course of their education, a process which could take up to ten years before students could become priests. Begging then was seen as a way of life, even for sons of dignitaries living in famous monasteries such as in Bahar Dar and Gondar. This tradition lives on and has also influenced other groups in society today, to make begging acceptable and part of the current Ethiopian culture (Provider 4).

Provider 4 thus thought that churches needed to change the way they operate and become part of changing peoples' attitudes towards begging.

Provider 1 agreed and drew attention to the culture of almsgiving, where many people give money to the churches to help the poor. In his opinion, the way almsgiving is currently organised does not ensure that the money actually reaches the poor, since 'there is currently no transparency about how much money is actually given to churches and what happens with the money'.

A more extensive commentary on barriers was given by Provider 3, who started by looking at the culture of society, where 'it is unusual' for people to speak out:

> Despite the fact [that] people expect most things from the government, they normally do not actually ask for them. This is made worse since there is a current trend where government is trying to reduce its responsibilities to its citizens further. However, while people are not ready to speak out for their rights, it needs to be seen if the public will accept increasing lack of services, poverty and other social problems in the long run (Provider 3).

In addition, Provider 3 identified other obstacles holding back the country and its people:

- economic problems, such as lack of income, unemployment, low wages/salaries and lack of opportunities to set up small businesses
- current technology, which is backward and needs to be improved
- lack of full democracy, so that people are afraid and unable to 'experience freedom of expression in terms of speaking and writing'
- lack of knowledge about rights and obligations by citizens who are unsure what the government policies exactly are

Against the Odds

- lack of adequate public facilities, such as housing, health care services and education
- inadequate resources in the education/training sector lead to skills shortages, especially for the young who constitute the majority of the jobless
- the existence of a culture which generates too much bureaucracy in the workplace and where people are too inefficient with their time in the office. This inefficiency includes not reviewing work plans, inadequate learning skills and not preparing work tasks properly. These negative work practices can be found at all levels in society and hold back the development of the community.

Compared with the direct accounts of the experiences of the Poor, comments made by the Providers are more abstract, as they focus on systemic and structural barriers rather than on barriers experienced at the personal level. For this group, barriers relate to issues of injustice/inequality, inadequacies in government and policy and the way social/cultural traditions hold back the development of individuals and the country. As with the barriers identified by the Poor, those identified by the Providers are cyclic and intermeshed.

5.3 THE ADVOCATES

> There are many big buildings going up everywhere—but we don't know where they come from and how they will benefit the poor (Advocate 6).

Of the three groups interviewed, the Advocates provided the least information for this chapter, and Advocates 1, 3 and 4 made no comments. As with the Providers above, insufficient data made classification and categorisation impracticable. Therefore, the following discussion reflects disparate themes, presented below from the more abstract responses to the more concrete.

For Advocate 2, lack of education is a significant barrier because uneducated people lack the ability to participate constructively in society. For this reason, 'education could be benchmarked against poverty and be seen as an important indicator of the problem'.

Advocate 6 thought that there are 'basic problems' in the way government and policy makers 'communicate' with the community. Being critical of policy makers, Advocate 6 argued that the policy makers do not share their plans and visions with the public, so it is not clear how they want to develop the country. For example:

> If we provide development for the rich we also need to inform the public—in an organised way, why this is so and how it will create jobs and solve all the other problems, so that people can be part of this vision (Advocate 6).

For Advocate 5, cultural and religious obstacles need to be taken into consideration. He stated that there are too many religious feast days in a year, a situation supported by churches. This means that on many days per year farmers and workers are not allowed to work or are discouraged from working 'regardless of the fact that some of the work actually needs to be carried out'. Some denominations also consider poverty as a curse rather than a social problem that needs to be addressed. As a result of this kind of teaching, the poor often have a very fatalistic view about life and their own poverty. Advocate 5 argued that changing attitudes is fraught with difficulties and dilemmas:

> The teaching of the churches has placated the poor into accepting their plight. They largely refrain from expecting from others what they themselves do not have. Thus, a double bind will emerge if churches should change their teachings. By suggesting to the poor that they should no longer accept and tolerate poverty as 'normal', long-held attitudes and behaviour patterns of the poor may become much more demanding and even result in increased crime rates.

While the comments of Advocates 6 and 5 dealt with abstract barriers, Advocate 7 identified more concrete barriers in the community, which include:

- lack of financial resources and other endowments
- lack of social and political networks to assist the poor
- lack of knowledge and skills, so poor people cannot articulate their needs

- traditional beliefs and fear of the unknown, which hold people back from progressing
- physical disabilities of people.

Summary

Although the responses of the three groups in this chapter were very limited compared to their contributions to other areas, participants still provided some useful insights into the barriers to fuller participation of the poor in Ethiopian society. As in the previous two chapters, the main differences between the Poor and the two professional groups lay in the insight into poverty gained by the unique experience of the poor. Thus, the Poor provided direct and practical examples of poverty barriers that affect them, while the responses of professional groups were more abstract and removed from the direct poverty experience.

For the Poor, the data provided by women and men show similarities and differences. In the Societal and Communal Issues section, the women focused more on lack of education, the men on lack of income. Lack of opportunity for education and the inability to be part of community organisations were mentioned by both groups. Although both women and men suffered from isolation and lack of meaningful social interaction, the women were much more focused on the barriers caused by their illnesses, especially HIV/AIDS. Comments made by the Poor strongly confirm the cyclic nature of poverty, in which each factor can be a cause, effect or barrier. For example, a common component of the cycle described by the Poor involves a series of sequential and interlocking issues: inadequate education leads to deficits of employment, income, living standards, health, housing and opportunity, which, in turn, again leads to inadequate education for the next generation.

For the Providers, barriers involved issues of injustice, governance and societal obstacles. Here, the Providers reflected on inequalities in the distribution of resources and issues of poor governance; cultural barriers were also thought to keep the community from progressing and removing barriers to the fuller participation of the poor. Apart from one more detailed commentary, there was limited discussion of the role of government and of the churches' historical links to begging.

The Advocates provided the least material for this chapter. While the findings hinted at issues of injustice and poor governance, again discussion was restricted by lack of detail. Nevertheless, the Advocates detailed both some concrete barriers and a limited number of structural, societal and individual barriers. In addition, an important issue emerged concerning the role of the church and its influence on the thinking of the poor and society in general.

Chapter Six

SOLUTIONS TO POVERTY

This chapter looks at how the three groups—the Poor, the Providers and the Advocates—formulated poverty solutions and suggested different ways to alleviate the problem. As in previous chapters, their responses showed that the Poor mainly rely on their experiences of deprivation and poverty, while the two professional groups draw on their experiences of working in the field and from poverty-relevant concepts they have developed.

6.1 THE POOR

> I find it difficult to imagine what the solutions to poverty are (Almaz).

Initially, the Poor found poverty solutions difficult to develop. At this stage of the interviews, they were already exhausted from telling their stories and describing their situations. While living in poverty, they clearly had never thought about how poverty could be addressed, nor did they ever expect to be asked by anyone how to solve it. The women, in particular, had difficulties with this question; having had even fewer chances in life than the men, they were over-burdened by their harsh and unforgiving lives and the responsibilities to their children. While lack of education and relevant professional experience made this task still harder for the Poor, they did develop some good ideas and valuable insights.

As Box 6.1 shows, the responses made by the Poor fell into three categories. In their reflections, the Poor responded sparingly about societal and individual solutions, but commented much more extensively on the role of government, proposing a number of schemes and services they thought should be provided by government. The three categories are discussed below.

Box 6.1 Poverty solutions offered by the Poor

- society
- government
- individuals

Society

Both female and male participants understood society as including many classes of people, organisations and institutions, such as NGOs and churches, but as they felt that government belongs to the state, they chose to comment on it separately. Neither gender provided much detail about societal solutions to poverty.

The Women

Women participants had great difficulties in formulating societal solutions, and their answers here were tentative and lacked detail. Some general thoughts on what society could do to solve poverty were provided by Zinash, Yelfu and Aster, presented below. These general thoughts are followed by a small number of comments about the work of the churches.

Commenting at the general level, Zinash thought that:

- the wealthy in society should lend money to the poor, without any interest payment, until they can pay it back
- the churches should preach to society to stop poverty

- NGOs should support the government in its efforts
- the able-bodied poor should work hard and get themselves out of poverty.

For Yelfu, solving poverty requires co-operation at all levels, so that:

- society as a whole should work together
- people among themselves should help each other
- every member of the community should use their labour and serve the community.

Aster, on the other hand, commented on the roles of both churches and NGOs, saying that:

> I expect society to create a more supportive environment for the poor and help them. I want the churches to continue to provide material aid such as food and clothing. NGOs too should provide the poor with their basic necessities according to the organisation's capacity.

While Aster said that she wants churches to continue their current work, Almaz, Kedega and Belaynesh expected much more assistance from them. Almaz thought that while churches give food during holidays, food should be provided every day instead, and she also expressed her unhappiness with the financial aid given by the churches:

> Instead of giving the needy sometimes 5–10 cents during the festivities, churches should give much more money to those who find it difficult to survive. The churches should do many things for the poor, but they don't do it (Almaz).

For Kedega too religious organisations are not doing nearly enough for people like herself and her two children: 'The churches are not doing anything for us [so] the solution is with God. He gives me hope and I expect Him to give me good health.'

While Belaynesh said that she hopes that the churches continue to help the poor, she agreed with Kedega that they have to do a lot more since, at the moment, 'it is only God who can really improve the lives of the poor'.

The Men

Like the women, the men had difficulties with the notion of how society could contribute to poverty solutions, and the four brief comments in this section came from Befekadu, Getachew, Mekuria and Melaku. Befekadu said:

> I want everyone in society to support the poor more. Society should be much more understanding and make [greater] efforts to offer work to people whenever possible. For example, someone could employ me as a security guard.

Getachew, Mekuria and Melaku all thought that people in the community should share what they have with each other, especially with the poor. For Getachew, this should be done voluntarily as 'it would be the right thing to do' and '… is morally right because the Bible says so. If this was done then there would be no longer a problem [in society].'

Similarly, Mekuria and Melaku felt that giving and taking between people is important; however, they focused more on those who can actually afford it. As Mekuria said: '… the rich in society should play a greater role and share their wealth with the poor so that they have enough to live on.'

While Bekele thought that support for the poor, such as food, clothing, housing and job opportunities, should be provided by NGOs, most of the other men thought that the provision of welfare services is mainly the role of government.

GOVERNMENT

The governmental level drew most responses, and all the Poor clearly thought that the government had the main responsibility for the population and therefore should play the key role in poverty alleviation. Despite their initial hesitation, the Poor developed detailed recommendations for service provisions, including various ideas on income support benefits.

The Women

> I believe that the government is not playing its part or we would not see so many *lemagns*[1] on the streets (Samira).

Box 6.2 Almaz's comments on the role of government in solving poverty

THE GOVERNMENT SHOULD:

- invest in the country
- create job opportunities by establishing factories and industries
- provide credit to the poor without interest
- provide free housing to the poor but no food if they get the housing
- provide food only to those who have no jobs, but provide no money
- protect the elderly and disabled and provide them with all they need depending on their needs
- provide free health care for everybody.

All women thought that government must be involved in assisting the poor and developing poverty solutions, and they commented on a number of areas which they identified as needing improvement. One example of the changes proposed by the women is shown in Box 6.2, where Almaz outlined her suggestions about the role of government.

Almaz's comments exemplify responses made by the other women, who all proposed extensive assistance to the poor in the form of employment opportunities, income and financial support, education, housing, health care and in a small number of other areas, each outlined more fully below.

Employment

All women except Genet felt that more job opportunities should be created for poor people. However, only a small number of women suggested how this could be done, and their main suggestions were:

- establishing more industries in rural areas (Zinash)
- greater investment in the whole nation in order to establish more factories (Aster)
- assisting the poor with business opportunities by making office space or land available, especially to young unemployed people (Yelfu).

Income and financial support

All the women believed that some kind of income or financial support should be provided to the poor, but differed in their views on what this support should consist of and how it should be distributed. For example, some women argued for a national income-support benefit scheme, while others wanted to see some financial assistance to the poor only in certain circumstances. Details of ideas about income-support schemes and financial assistance are given below.

Income support

Various opinions about both recipients and amounts for income-support schemes were offered by the women. For example, Almaz and Fatuma wanted income support given to all the poor, including the unemployed; Aster and Belaynesh sought to restrict benefits to the elderly and people with disabilities; Samira wanted only an old-age pension to be paid to everybody.

In terms of payments, Fatuma thought that 200–300 birr per month would be sufficient to meet peoples' needs. Almaz, on the other hand, said 'the allowance should be about 500 birr per month so that the poor can really survive'. She also wanted to support the disabled and elderly to a greater extent than the unemployed, by paying them a higher allowance than the 'able-bodied poor'. As she was not quite sure about how much money they should receive, she stated that, in any case, 'the poverty situation of the poor should be studied before providing financial assistance.'

Like Almaz, those who wanted to support only the elderly and people with disabilities were equally divided and not sure how much income should be paid. While Aster agreed with Almaz that the benefits required depend on peoples' needs, Belaynesh said she would pay this group an allowance of 500–1,000 birr per month.

Financial assistance

While Yelfu, Samira, Zinash and Genet did not necessarily support a general income-support scheme for the poor, they did propose financial assistance consisting of various loans schemes including:

- general loans, to be paid back, assisting people who experience hardships (Yelfu)
- small grants for people to set up businesses (Fatuma)
- start-up capital for the able-bodied poor in the order of 30,000 birr, so that they can establish small businesses. This money would need to be invested wisely (Belaynesh)
- start-up capital for people to build houses or to set up small business, such as a kiosk to sell tea and other groceries (Zinash)
- credit facilities for the 'healthy poor, something like a common fund so that people can borrow at no interest to assist them. However, this fund should not be accessible to the ill because they cannot give back the money' (Samira)
- a credit scheme where poor people can get credit without paying interest. This could then help Genet who would like to buy a kiosk to support herself (Genet).

Education

While the majority of women requested more educational opportunities, they provided very little detail about how this could be achieved. A small number of women suggested that this could be done by:

- providing free education for all people, because without education 'one cannot do anything' (Yelfu)
- providing free education, especially for adults. Fantu stated that she would still like to go to school, despite her age, in order to improve herself and have better chances of getting a job (Fantu)
- linking educational opportunities with 'on the job training' (Samira).

Housing

> [Having] a house is very important, because it makes people independent of others. One can cook or take food back home. One can feel safe and able to invite friends and neighbours to socialise with. One can be more confident and feel better about oneself (Yelfu).

All women agreed that housing is a key area that needs to be addressed. While they acknowledged that there are possibilities of assistance through local *kebele*s, they argued that local housing options are highly insufficient, and that the application process is much too difficult, so that most people miss out on being assisted. The women therefore suggested a national housing scheme for the poor, which would assist in making houses and shelters available. These facilities should be either subsidised or free.

While Fantu, Fatuma, Genet and Samira argued for subsidised housing, a minority of women thought that housing should be free for the poor. Opting for a subsidy, Fantu said: 'Houses should be provided to the poor, with only nominal rents to pay. If housing is thus available, other monies can be spent on other important necessities like water, electricity and food.'

For Aster and Almaz, on the other hand, the poor 'are already too poor' to pay for housing, which should be paid for by the government scheme. However, there are conditions:

- Someone should not get free housing as well as free food (Aster).
- Free housing should only go to those poor who have nothing to eat and nowhere to live (Almaz).

Health care

Aster, Fatuma, Fantu and Belaynesh wanted free health care for everybody in society, not just for the poor. While they stated that existing services are inadequate, they provided little detail about how the system could be improved. The only two comments came from Fantu and Belaynesh.

Fantu argued that the current process of obtaining health care at the local *kebele* needs to be made easier:

> Once a person has demonstrated that they are poor, their file should then be proof enough of the person's poverty for the future. The next time they are sick, they should automatically receive the health services without having to go through the same process again.

Belaynesh agreed with Fantu; she also wondered whether the local NGO network can play a role in providing health care for the poor.

Other suggestions

A small number of additional suggestions came from Fatuma, Fantu and Genet. Fatuma would like to see assistance for people to go back to the countryside and their farms, a policy that could include assistance in the form of land, money and farm equipment.

Others proposed food subsidies for the poor, including:

- free wheat for poor people, as it is now too expensive (Fatuma)
- subsidised general food items (Genet)
- subsidised wheat, *teff*, cereals, oil, onions, pepper and other necessities for the poor (Fantu).

The Men

> The government should play a bigger role in the solutions of poverty, by creating more welfare services to support the poor (Bizuayew).

Like the women, the men saw the government sector as having the major role in tackling the issues of poverty. Their responses produced an interesting array of ideas and useful suggestions, identifying many of the gaps in the services they believe are necessary to meet the needs of the poor. An example of the range of poverty solutions suggested by the men comes from Shewangezaw, as shown in Box 6.3.

Although he made recommendations about housing, healthcare and access to ID, most of Shewangezaw's comments focused on income support for the poor. He, therefore, started his list of solutions with a call for equal opportunities in education, training and remuneration. Although not all participants' responses were as detailed as those of Shewangezaw overall the men's suggestions for poverty alleviation were perceptive and constructive. The men's ideas, discussed below, relate to the following areas: education and training, employment, income and financial support, housing, health care, support for people from the rural sector and other types of support. While comments on these categories vary, the men did pay close attention to employment and income-support issues.

Box 6.3 Shewangezaw's poverty solutions

The role of government should be to:

- provide formal free education and training for everyone
- ensure peoples' wages are adequate to live on
- ensure wages are in accordance with levels of training
- provide income benefits for all poor people in need
- provide income benefits for unemployed young people until they get a job
- provide pensions for the ill, elderly and disabled until they die; these benefits could be passed onto their surviving children after death
- provide pensions to all soldiers. Shewangezaw argued that other public servants also receive pensions, so it is not fair for some soldiers to have no income in old age. He therefore suggested the sum of 360 birr per month, an amount that would be enough for him to live on
- provide public shelters for the poor. Shewangezaw cited an example of a public shelter in Nazreth, where they house and feed poor people, and give work to some of them. Shelters should provide single rooms to each person to ensure privacy. Rooms do not have to be big, but the size should also be suitable if a family member needs to stay there. Rooms should be equipped with clean mattresses, blankets, water containers and cooking equipment/ utensils. Shelters should also have access to clean public toilets and showers
- provide a way of organising the poor into associations so that they can support themselves. Such associations could be modelled on the *iddir* system, but set-up specifically for the poor
- provide free health care services for all, as the current system is not adequate
- provide better access and a process to obtain ID, as poor people have great difficulties getting them.

Education/training

Education received little prominence in the men's comments, the only four responses coming from Mekuria, Befekadu, Tesfaye and Bizuayew. While Mekuria and Tesfaye proposed 'free education for all members of society', Befekadu and Bizuayew recommended better job-training opportunities for young people and educational courses for adults. As Befekadu pointed out: 'I would like assistance for people to go to school or training, particularly those who cannot read and write. This would help people to find work after school so that they can support themselves.'

Employment

> Once you have a good job you will have money ... and [then] you can have 'everything' (Bekele).

For all men, employment was important in the 'fight against poverty' and was seen as one of the main solutions to the problem. Thus, participants wanted to see the creation of job opportunities for all poor people, and especially for the young (Getachew, Bizuayew, Mesganew, Mekuria and Melaku), the middle-aged and the elderly (Kebede), and for those without education and qualifications (Getachew). For Kebede and Befekadu, for example, this means that we must: '... treat all people equally by creating job opportunities [in society] for people over the age of 40, like jobs as security guards or in farming' (Kebede).

All men felt that the government should play a more active role assisting the poor with employment. When asked how this could be done, almost all participants advocated job-creation schemes in the countryside, for people to work on the land. The only additional suggestion came from Melaku, who proposed a combination of schemes to create jobs in factories, organisations in both the government and non-government sector, and the countryside. Work created in the countryside would thus give '... many people the opportunity to find work. [These could be in] environmental and related projects, land clearing activities, the creation of farmland projects to farm the land' (Melaku).

In order for people to get the right job, Befekadu and Tesfaye suggested that:

> ... an official listens to someone like me, assesses my capacity and then links me to the right job ... because I really want to work and be independent (Befekadu).

> For those who are able to work, assistance should be provided in finding job opportunities by using educated and knowledgeable government officials to link the unemployed with the available work (Tesfaye).

Mesganew, Melaku, Bizuayew, Getachew and Kebede were all in favour of sending young unemployed people to work on land development projects. Mesganew, for example, felt that such a government scheme should '... pay

6 birr for women and 8 birr for men, per day, and should be organised on a voluntary basis'.

Mesganew said that young people could volunteer for the working schemes in the countryside, while others like Melaku believed there should be no choice: 'While this work should be offered to those interested in the first instance, others should also be forced to accept it even if they don't like it.'

Other similar examples about how to create work opportunities (on an involuntary basis) related to farming projects suggest:

- projects organised as cooperatives to benefit all members, particularly for the young, who should have to work without choice (Bizuayew)
- projects modelled on previous government initiatives 'where unemployment was lower and people worked on coffee, oil seed and other farms' (Getachew)
- projects for the 18–40 year olds, where people would be able to volunteer at first but could also be conscripted into it like in the army (Kebede).

A final suggestion about employment came from Shewangezaw, who wanted assistance given to former soldiers to find work 'after their service ends, to make them more independent'.

Income support and pension schemes

> … there should be some income support for all [the] poor and money given to unemployed young people until they get a job (Shewangezaw).

All men except Bekele proposed income support and pension schemes in various forms, to provide income benefits for all the poor and the unemployed, and pensions for people with disabilities and the elderly. The suggestions made varied between general payments to everyone in need to a more targeted approach for different groups.

Income support
Over half of the participants—Melaku, Mekuria, Getachew, Mesganew and Shewangezaw—wanted a temporary cash support scheme that would provide

income to all poor people, including the unemployed. The only exception was Tesfaye, who thought that 'anyone who earns more than 50 birr per month is not in poverty. No money should be provided to the young and those who are able to work.'

While there was agreement on the necessity of providing income support for those in need, there was disagreement about how this should be done, for how long and the amount to be provided, as illustrated in Table 6.1.

TABLE 6.1 Male participants' suggestions for income support payments

PARTICIPANT	SUGGESTIONS FOR INCOME SUPPORT	AMOUNT
Getachew	• provide income for all the poor and unemployed until they get a job • support should be based on what people might need in order to cover their basic necessities, although the minimum amount payable for a person should not be less than 1,000 birr • this 'estimated sum is based on the cost for housing (300 birr), food (400 birr), clothing and other expenses (300 birr)'	1,000 birr per month
Melaku	• provide income to the poor, plus financial assistance and support to families so that they can stay together and support each other	300 birr per month
Mekuria	• pay income support for every poor person 'for one year only, so that they can create business and other opportunities for themselves' • no benefits after one year	500 birr per month
Mesganew	• provide income directly to the poor, instead of 'being channelled to other people before it reaches the poor'	10,000 birr per year (i.e. 833 per month)

Pensions

For those who are no longer able to work, due to old age and ill health, there should be a life pension. This income can [then] also be used to assist their families (Tesfaye).

Almost all men argued for the introduction of a pension scheme to support the elderly, permanently ill and people with disabilities. A small number of participants, such as Shewangezaw, Getachew and Tesfaye, also wanted to see pensions allocated to former soldiers 'since public servants receive pensions, it is not fair for some soldiers to have no income in old age' (Shewangezaw).

As for income support, opinions on pensions varied. For example, Getachew said that there should be:

> ... pensions for the elderly, the sick, disabled and mentally ill. These groups should get the same amount of 1,000 birr each month. But people with a disability should not receive any more money or support than the able and other poor, because this group is already better supported by the community as people feel sorry for them. They can also earn extra money by continuing to beg in the streets. ... But the mentally ill are the poorest of the poor, as they cannot work. They should receive special treatment and be taken to *tsebel*, for example, and be provided with all other necessary services to take care of them.

Table 6.2 further illustrates the differing ideas on pension payments, advocated by the men.

Housing

While the majority of the male participants thought that housing was important, they gave few details on this issue. Some argued for free public housing to assist the poor, while others thought that it should only be subsidised. Thus, they lacked consensus, and the range of their solutions was wide, as shown by the following suggestions:

- public housing for a nominal cost (Mekuria)
- subsidised private or public housing for the poor, so that they can rent at a nominal rate (Kebede)
- affordable houses through the local *kebele*s (Getachew)
- subsidised housing for the elderly, the disabled and those who cannot or do not want to be farmers or business people (Bizuayew)
- free dormitory-style shelter accommodation (Melaku)
- free shelters, 'where some of the needy can be housed, clothed and fed— all in one place' (Tesfaye).

TABLE 6.2 Male participants' suggestions for pension payments

PARTICIPANT	SUGGESTIONS FOR PENSION PAYMENTS	AMOUNT
Bizuayew	• provide a one-off grant for the elderly and the disabled. This money should be used to meet their initial housing and other essential needs • the allocation of this money should be supervised and controlled	40,000 birr
	• provide pensions to people who can no longer work • as people with a disability already receive more support from the community than other groups, pension entitlements should be assessed according to their need	100–150 birr per month, depending on situation
Kebede	• provide pensions for people over the age of 50 and their families, so that no one has to beg	500 birr per month
	• provide pensions for people with a disability • these should be less 'as they already have a lot of support from the community'	up to 400 birr
Mesganew	• provide support for people with a disability, the sick, the blind and elderly • there should be a system which assesses peoples' needs • cash amounts should be based on the assessment • pensions should be more than income support for the unemployed, as they cannot work	N/A
Shewangezaw	• provide pensions for the permanently ill, elderly and disabled until they die, which could be passed onto their surviving children after death • provide pensions to all former soldiers	360 birr per month

Rural/land issues

> If I had money I would do anything to get my land back. I would hire a lawyer or even bribe someone to get it back (Mesganew).

Almost all respondents—Kebede, Bizuayew, Befekadu, Getachew, Mekuria and Mesganew—wanted targeted support for people to be able to go back to the countryside. Getachew felt that such a move would help to relieve 'the unsustainable population growth in Addis Ababa', where:

> … most of these people are farmers who can no longer make a living on their land. Those who are already in Addis should therefore be encouraged and supported to go back to work on their land again. They should be assisted financially and also with fertilizer.

Mesganew, Befekadu and Mekuria agreed, proposing resettlement assistance to those who want to go back home, as Kebede said:

> Assistance could take the form of giving land to the uneducated and those who want to farm it, a travel allowance to get back to the rural area, financial assistance to start farming or establish a business, so that people can become self-reliant.

Bizuayew thought that a one-off financial grant in the order of 80,000 birr could be provided to those who want to be farmers or business people:

> This would allow them to set themselves up and buy land, animals, etc. or start a business such as a taxi, a [delivery] truck or a shop. But once someone received this grant, they would no longer qualify for any other kind of assistance. [The] allocation of monies should be supervised and controlled by the government.

Getachew also wanted to see work carried out in the rural sector itself; he further suggested stopping migration to the cities, by assisting and developing cooperatives in the countryside:

> The system of cooperatives should be rebuild so that rural farming communities can support each other. Cooperatives are successful in sharing resources between people because they can sell their produce better and also help the poor (Getachew).

Other types of support

A small number of additional types of support were proposed:

- free wheat to the poor so they can at least bake bread (Bizuayew)
- food for the elderly and the people with disabilities (Bizuayew, Tesfaye)
- free health care for everyone (Mekuria, Getachew)
- assistance and a better process for people to get an ID through local councils, since it is very difficult to find work, get into training, etc. without identification (Befekadu, Getachew, Bizuayew, Kebede).

INDIVIDUALS

Very few responses were made under this section by the Poor. On the whole, participants were unsure what individuals could do to redress poverty and how realistic it was to expect individuals to play a part. The women, in particular, seemed already overwhelmed with their poverty experiences and saw very few options for change in their lives, least of all, ways to alleviate poverty. While the women thus made even fewer comments than the men, both groups responded with descriptions of a kind of work ethic they felt should be maintained by society and by themselves.

The Women

> I want to improve my life but my efforts are in vain, so I hope that God will help me one day (Genet).

While more than half of the participants thought that the poor need to be part of the poverty solution, they did not know how this could be done. This difficulty explains their limited response.

Nevertheless, as shown in Box 6.4, three women suggested that the poor need to work hard and take more responsibility for themselves, and Aster even thought that some of the poor ask for too much assistance, saying that all too often '… they appear in front of the government and the NGOs to tell them their stories and problems'.

SAMIRA:

'... everyone who is healthy should work and those who are sick should go begging on the streets. This also includes the elderly and the disabled.'

FATUMA:

'... once people are educated, they are responsible to find work themselves and everyone should work hard and try their best.'

ALMAZ:

'... I think that poor people should work hard and get a job, where they can at least earn about 500 birr per month. Then they can rent a house. It would also be good to start a small business and not having to work for other people. My business idea is selling *injera* or vegetables, such as potatoes, and spices.'

The Men

Like the women, the majority of the men's comments related to hard work and individual responsibility, and only a few participants acknowledged the limits of individual actions. While some suggested that the poor should work hard and get educated to improve their job opportunities, they were not mindful of their earlier comments in Chapter Three about how difficult it is to get jobs and an education when one is poor.

Mekuria, Mesganew, Tesfaye and Getachew demonstrated what they expect of individuals. Mekuria said that the poor should: '... work hard and be free of vices and bad habits such as drinking alcohol, smoking and using drugs. The individual should also use their money wisely and not waste it on unnecessary things.'

Mesganew too did not support idleness and pointed out:

> One has to do any kind of work and work hard. Job opportunities should be based on capabilities. ... But even 'unable' people could be employed as ticket collectors, for example. ... We [simply] can't say that someone can't do anything; even if a man is without legs, he can still work with someone else who has legs.

Tesfaye and Getachew also advocated a strong work ethic, and Tesfaye proposed that people should:

- try and improve themselves through education and hard work to save money that lasts throughout a life time
- perhaps start a small business or buy land and be farmers, buy cattle, sheep and other livestock.

According to Getachew, the poor need to maximise their employment options: '… everyone should ensure to get their ID from the *kebele* so they get assistance with finding employment.'

While Tesfaye and Getachew supported the work ethic, they also recognised the importance of families and friends in providing support and assistance during times of difficulty. As Tesfaye pointed out:

> Families are very important in life. They give people support when they are sick and in trouble. Children are also assets and can look after their parents when they are old and can no longer work. Boys, for example, can work on the farms and girls do the housework. Children can also be educated to bring in money and help their parents with their earnings in old age.

While Getachew agreed, he also saw individuals and families as part of a more holistic approach to addressing poverty:

> People need stable families to support them. Without families poor people, in particular, have a difficult and hard life. Families [and] individuals [together with] government and society as a whole should [all] be part of the solution to poverty.

Getachew and Bekele also knew the limitations of individual actions, and were quite philosophical about their situation, a stance that seems to help them survive. Thus, Getachew thought: 'People should try their best and not lose hope. … Tomorrow, there is another day.' And Bekele said: 'I trust in God since no one else can help me and I have no other options in life. I am too proud to beg.'

The Poor, as a group, had initial difficulty in responding to the challenging task of formulating poverty solutions. Being absorbed in their lives of extreme hardship, their comments on how society and the individual could address poverty were brief, while they made more extensive suggestions on the role of government. Nevertheless, while they had never been asked such difficult questions, and despite their lack of education and professional experience in this area, the Poor responded positively to the challenge and made many contributions in this chapter.

6.2   THE PROVIDERS

Of the three groups, the Providers made the most extensive comments in this chapter, showing their knowledge and skill in developing ideas and policies. As shown in Box 6.5, their responses fell into five categories of solutions to poverty.

Box 6.5 Poverty solutions offered by the Providers

- society
- government
- churches
- non-government organisations (NGOs)
- individuals

Society

> To deal with the problems of Ethiopia requires the dedication and focus of the entire nation (Provider 6).

While more than half of the Providers felt that everyone in society should be part of the poverty solution, a small number felt that the wealthy need to make a significant contribution in the community. For some Providers, there also needs to be cultural and attitudinal change in order to tackle issues of poverty.

Providers 7, 3, 6, 5, and 2 strongly agreed that solving social problems, such as poverty, requires the cooperation of all sections in society. According to Provider 5, therefore:

> ... all citizens need to get involved in the community and see what can be
> done to deal with social problems. They should work with government, do
> what can be done—and not always expect help from outside.

Similarly, Provider 2 thought that without such cooperation the necessary transformation could not take place. In agreement, Provider 6 advocated for a national poverty strategy where:

> All stakeholders in society, including the churches, NGOs, the people,
> the professionals and the government, have also responsibilities to work
> for the common good. Everyone, therefore, has to focus on the problem
> and develop [and be part of] a national strategy. The government should
> facilitate this by getting all the relevant stakeholders together.

While there was agreement about the necessity of a joint community effort, Providers 5, 3 and 7 still thought that the major responsibility to help the poor rests on the shoulders of those 'who can afford to share what they have' (Provider 7). Thus, Provider 3 expected 'the elders and professionals such as medical staff' to give some their time to the community and not be selfish. They should also 'share their knowledge and not be corrupt'. Provider 5, on the hand, had wealthy individuals and organisations in mind:

> The wealthy should not wait until the poor are so desperate that they will
> challenge the rich to provide them with what they need. Instead of only grabbing
> as much money as they can, the wealthy and institutions in society like the
> banks, should assist the poor and contribute to the development of the nation.

Provider 7 agreed, saying that the rich and powerful should:

- discover their own dignity [by assisting the poor]
- start serving/contributing to humanity and the poor
- start sharing what they have with others
- change existing unfair structures, step by step. This can be done by raising peoples' consciousness and an awareness of the world around them.

For Provider 7, the current inaction of those who could help the poor relates very much to the absence of moral principles and standards, where there is '... a lack of awareness of the real value and importance of people in terms of what a person is, what his/her needs are and that each person relates to another'.

As Box 6.6 makes clear, Provider 7's outline of moral principles gives each person value, worth and responsibilities towards others. Thus, while she argued that everyone has a role to play in the community, she reiterated that the rich and powerful have an obligation to assist the poor, since they are in a position to do so.

Box 6.6 Provider 7's moral principles

Each person:

- has intrinsic value and worth
- is an important part of humanity
- relates to and depends on others
- has needs and aspirations which depend on society
- has responsibilities to other people and the community as a whole.

Provider 7 thus felt strongly that people need to become more self-aware and conscious about themselves, because 'if someone is really conscious as a person then they won't allow anyone to be in poverty', and '... this also would help to develop closer and more meaningful relationships between people in the community'.

For Providers 2, 1, and 3, the necessary attitudinal change can only come about by addressing some of the cultural values in the community. These Providers thus suggested that people have to move away from those traditions which 'hold them back from developing better ways and thinking' (Provider 2). Accordingly, people need to be more open-minded and their actions should be based on 'rational thinking rather than on emotions, culture and religion' (Provider 3). In terms of poverty, Provider 2 and 3 suggested that:

> Societal attitudes towards work and poverty need to be changed. Poverty has to be discussed openly and the population must no longer tolerate and accepted it. ... Society needs to embrace popular participation so that all people can make their contribution to the community (Provider 2).

> It should also be recognised that poverty is not acceptable and 'God given' (Provider 3).

However, for Providers 3 and 1 attitudinal change also needs to include issues of gender, disabilities, health, and development: '… people need to be open to new ways of thinking, explore their global and regional surroundings and learn to use the existing opportunities' (Provider 3).

Finally, Provider 1 suggested that 'doing away with harmful traditional values' would assist the progress of the nation. This change could be achieved by:

- managing local resources better
- increasing labour discipline, which should be taught in school and by the churches
- collectively collecting money for the poor
- developing partnerships with local *iddirs* which have good systems in place to identify poor peoples' needs and develop good programmes to meet them
- engaging NGOs for the long-term solutions of poverty (Provider 1).

GOVERNMENT

All Providers believed that government was the most important institutional structure in society, so should play the largest role in the fight against poverty. Comments made here fall largely into three categories: Governance, Policy Development and Implementation, and Provision of Services.

Governance

Most Providers argued that good governance is important in dealing with social issues such as poverty. While their views varied, participants agreed that the main role of government was to serve the community and meet the needs of the people. In this context, their comments on governance were meant to be constructive and were made to suggest improvements in the system.

Thus, Providers 2, 5, 3 and 7 emphasised different aspects of good governance. For Provider 3, for example, government can be most effective if it builds trust between itself and the population. In his view, this can be done by allowing people to participate in all levels of society, especially in relation to the social, economic, political issues. For this reason: 'The government should also fulfil all the promises it makes in the media and continue to reform the way civil services are provided to the population' (Provider 3).

Box 6.7 Provider 3's views on good governance

GOVERNMENT SHOULD:

- provide legal protection to the population and educate the police force to comply with the law and not to harass people
- deal with corruption and enshrine its control into legislation
- provide a clear budget to each government department based on community need
- monitor how well government services are actually provided by different departments
- provide relevant information to society about what is happening on the global, regional and local levels and how events affect the Ethiopian community
- organise different forums where it can listen to the community and help people to come up with their own solutions
- provide free media outlets where people can learn about society, their rights and responsibilities.

Box 6.7 shows how Provider 3 mapped out other aspects that he considered important in governance. Apart from recommending appropriate legal protection for the population, improvements on corruption and services, Provider 3 also suggested good governance should inform and educate the population so it can assist government. Thus, he felt that 'if people know what kinds of problems they face, they are much more likely to be able to help government to solve them' (Provider 3).

While Provider 5 wanted officials to reconsider 'the centralised system of government which makes it difficult to serve the population at the different local and regional levels', Provider 7 had a much more direct message to politicians. For the government to function properly, she felt that politicians should:

- learn to pray and ask themselves what is expected of them
- listen to their people and get to know them
- address the needs of the population
- become 'real human beings' and serve the common good of their people
- unite people and society as a whole (Provider 7).

Two other views on governance came from Providers 4 and 6. Provider 4 was concerned about the power and influence of economic forces and the practices adopted by 'big business'. According to Provider 4, these vested interests have the potential to corrupt public policy and undermine the efforts to meet the needs of the population. For this reason he suggested:

> ... [we need] more government regulation of the market system and take active steps against the embezzlement of public funds through unfair dealings with private companies, especially in the area of buying and selling. We also need to prevent big business from joining the executive, since this can lead to corruption (Provider 4).

Provider 4 further argued that to safeguard good governance, the government needs to:

- fight corruption in society
- be democratic, allow pluralistic governance and welcome political opposition parties to play a role in the community
- allow separation of power at all government levels
- allow a strong and independent judiciary that is free from the influence of the head of the executive, institutionally, legally and financially
- improve the decision-making process of government to give the poor some input.

Provider 6, on the other hand, felt that government should:

- provide government which is less bureaucratic and more efficient
- empower public servants to make decisions in one office, rather than at many different locations
- keep peace and order in the community.

Policy Development and Implementation

Comments made by the Providers included general ideas on policy development, as well as on specific economic and business, employment and rural policies.

General policy development

In the first instance, Providers 2, 5, 6 and 1 stated that government policy should target the needs of the population. To be in a position to do so, officials need to remain independent of vested interest groups, including the private sector.

In this context, Providers 1 and 2 argued that policy makers should be mindful of the influence of the wealthy and powerful, and 'be supportive of the poor rather than favouring the rich'. According to Provider 2, this also means that the government should recognise:

> … the importance of the private sector as a significant stakeholder in society, which should not only make profits for itself, but also be a force to contribute positively to the well-being of the country. The private sector should therefore be convinced to take its social responsibilities seriously and make societal contributions.

In similar fashion, Provider 3 and 7 felt that there should be a deliberate approach to encourage 'big business' and 'wealthy individuals in society to make a greater contribution to the community and the poor' (Provider 3). Provider 7 thought that such a policy could be underpinned by media campaigns, using TV and other outlets, 'to raise awareness of the plight of the poor and society's responsibility for them'.

Provider 5, on the other hand, looked for a much greater willingness on the part of officials to engage the community in policy formation, 'so that people can develop their own solutions'. He also suggested '… a clear general policy to deal with the food shortages and rising prices of important food items'.

Provider 6, too, wanted to see greater community involvement where 'government will first define the general policy direction and then convince the population to follow and help to implement it'. Provider 6 also proposed a new policy framework for the work of NGOs, as he is very concerned about the current practices of some of the larger organisations which mainly focus 'on the continuation of their existence as organisations':

> Many funding proposals of these NGOs, often from overseas, seek to attract money in order to survive as an organisation, rather than actually addressing the social problems of the local community (Provider 6).

Provider 1 agreed, and called for better processes and guidelines to evaluate the work of the NGOs in terms of whether they benefit society and the poor.

While Provider 2 concurred, he also thought that good public policy has to be based on sound research that studies social problems and ultimately '... lead[s] to the development of better social services for the needy, and should not just address the short-term but aim to benefit society in the long-term'.

Specific policy issues
In addition to their general comments on public policy, some Providers elaborated on a small number of specific areas such as:

Economic and business issues

For Providers 2, 3, 4 and 1 economic policy is important 'in order to develop the country as a whole' (Provider 2). They largely agreed on a national strategic approach to assist the various stakeholders in society, while still being mindful of the special needs of the poor.

Thus, while supporting economic development and related infrastructure projects, Provider 4 wanted to remind policy makers about the plight of the poor when undertaking projects, such as building roads. He stated:

> For instance, houses of the poor have been demolished in the past to make way for roads without any consultation with the poor. Nor were there any arrangements/provisions made for resettling the people actually affected by this development. Poor people, therefore, have nowhere to go and receive no support to continue their lives. Adequate processes need to be put in place to consult with poor households and also to provide the necessary support for the resettlement of people (Provider 4).

Other responses made by this group stated that poverty solutions should:

- provide assistance to the private sector, which includes various projects to aid the economy and improve national infrastructure; relevant projects should also target specific areas of need, such as housing and benefits for the poor (Provider 3)

- develop economic policies which make the poor a 'real stakeholder' and beneficiary in the economic system (Provider 1)
- develop processes by which tax policies can be evaluated in terms of their effects on businesses in different sectors (Provider 1)
- assist poor people with tax concessions to enable them to set up small business, to help with the start-up phase (Provider 1).

Employment

Providers 2, 6 and 4 thought that government policy should address the problem of employment. For Provider 6, for example, 'this was one of the first priorities because when people have adequate income everything else will follow'.

Other comments included the need to:

- develop industries, in areas such as construction to create employment opportunities for the poor (Provider 2)
- create work and employment opportunities for everyone in the community (Provider 6)
- encourage individuals and groups to establish small business to generate employment options (Provider 4).

Rural issues

Providers 2 and 5 wanted to see specific policy addressing the needs of the rural sector. An overall comment about landownership of the country comes from Provider 2 who thought that:

> Land should be owned by society and not the government as it is a key factor in the country's economic development. Whereas land can currently only be leased, private landownership would allow for the land to be bought and sold and distributed fairly, especially to the population in the countryside.

Provider 2 also argued that the rural population, in particular, is very vulnerable to food shortages, as exports drive up prices for local people: '… basic items such as *teff* are currently too expensive and controlled by influential people close to officials, who can manipulate the system to increase their profits' (Provider 2).

He, therefore, suggested a policy which 'encourages that food grown locally should first be used and consumed locally, where it is very scarce', instead of exporting it.

Providers 2 and 5 also felt strongly that government should play an active part in population control. Other responses from Provider 5 included the need to develop policy on:

- protecting the overall environment and the land
- developing infrastructure in the countryside, where the majority of the population live
- developing irrigation schemes in the countryside
- assisting farmers to increase production
- providing seed money to farmers.

Provision of Services

> The cycle of poverty needs to be broken by providing basic necessities, education, information and opportunities. There also needs to be attitudinal and cultural change in society [to make this possible] (Provider 3).

While most Providers wanted to see the development of welfare services to meet the needs of the poor, one exception was Provider 4, who argued that:

> Welfare systems like those practised in Western countries are not the answer, as they produce psychological dependencies where people lose their ability to fully function in society. Therefore, it is essential to be fully employed.

Provider 4 also thought that the government should not support the 'laziness' of those who do not want to work, and instead should take active measures against them. Nevertheless, even Provider 4 was for promoting affordable welfare services 'with easy physical access for people and the creation of better living conditions for the poor by subsidising housing'.

While Provider 4 thus argued against extensive assistance for the poor, the majority of Providers supported it, commenting in small numbers on income support, food assistance, education, and housing and health care.

Income support

Providers 2 and 4 recommended the introduction of an income support system to '... support those in need, such the elderly and people with disabilities' (Provider 2). Provider 2 thus wanted to see the introduction of an old-age pension scheme, especially for those '... who have worked all their lives, [with] a pension which should be indexed against price rises'. Although supportive of financial benefits for the elderly, Provider 2 was not in favour of supporting 'the young as they should find work to support themselves'.

Provider 4 agreed with the introduction of these benefit schemes to be funded by the government. However, he also suggested that the required government funding could be supplemented through a joint effort between local councils and churches via:

> ... a process whereby churches collect donations for the poor from the community, not based on the principals of handouts but based on a more targeted approach of providing direct financial assistance to the poor (Provider 4).

Food and other subsidies

Providers 2 and 4 also commented on the provision of food and other assistance as solutions to poverty. For example, Provider 4 wanted to '... control food markets so that basic food stuffs and other necessities are affordable and also of good quality. This needs to be area-specific to address local and regional needs.'

In order to meet the basic needs of the poor, Provider 2 wanted to '... subsidise basic food and other necessities/items so poor people can have enough food and clothing'.

Education

Most Providers wanted to improve access to and quality of education, arguing that government should:

- provide free education (Providers 2, 3 and 4)
- improve the quality of education for children (6)
- make it more possible for all children to go to school. Achieving this educational goal would need the supply of transportation for children in remote rural areas, where children have no access to education because

of the great distances they have to travel. Transportation would also reduce the incidence of abduction of children, who sometimes fall prey to unscrupulous abductors on the way to school (Provider 5).

Housing and health care

Providers 3, 4 and 2 commented on the need of housing for the poor, suggesting that it was necessary to:

- provide basic housing services and options for the poor; Provider 3 points out that 30–40% of young people are forced to stay with parents as they have no other options
- provide cheap and subsidised public housing for the entire population (Provider 4)
- provide housing subsidies to the community so that everyone in society has adequate shelter (Provider 2)
- assist people with affordable housing and other social services to enable them to work (Provider 4).

A small number of Providers (2, 3, 4) felt the need to improve the health care system to better meet the needs of the population, and particularly those of the poor.

CHURCHES

> Those who serve the church, including priests and bishops, should never forget who they are. They must remember the fact that their mission is to serve the poor and that there should not be a divide between the poor and rich in society (Provider 7).

All Providers except Provider 1 commented on the power and influence of the church and its potential to be a positive force in the community. Yet participants thought that the churches could make a greater contribution to society and, in particular, to the alleviation of poverty.

While the mission of the church is seen as very important (see Box 6.8 for instance), Providers 5, 3, 4 and 2 also thought that the teaching of the various churches has a significant role to play in assisting the community.

PROVIDER 5

'The churches should reconnect with their mission to serve the poor, instead of just building more churches and places of worship.'

PROVIDER 6

'Churches need to return to their roots to serve the poor and also be much more active in the development of the country. They have many followers and can mobilise them for that purpose.'

PROVIDER 3

'Churches should serve the poor. Their focus should be on development issues, and the money and resources they have must be used for the development [of the country].'

Providers 5, 3 and 2 agreed that the churches 'need to teach people to work hard, rather than encouraging them to pray to God so that He will provide for them' (Provider 2). They also agreed that the number of religious festivals should be reduced and the 'churches should encourage their followers to work more days in the year and condemn begging' (Provider 3). Similarly, Provider 5 said that priests in rural areas '… need to teach the community to be more productive by reducing the number of religious festivities, where people are asked by the churches to stop working on their land during that period'.

Providers 3 and 4, on the other hand, wanted churches to use 'their considerable influence in society and over their followers' (Provider 3) to teach about:

> … modern education, health care and wrong beliefs (Provider 3).

> … moral duties, to become self-reliant, independent and productive. They should teach people to care for others and discourage begging in the streets and near churches (Provider 4).

Finally, Providers 4 and 2 suggested more practical solutions. For example, Provider 4 thought that:

... Churches should also use the funds they receive through the collection of alms to assist governments by providing services to the poor. [With their funds] they can also help NGOs to develop income-generating projects for the community.

Provider 2, likewise, argued that all churches should use their considerable resources for the community and make a much greater contribution by:

- providing more of the necessary services to the poor, including food, shelter and clean water
- providing appropriate training schemes for job creation, especially in the rural areas
- working together among themselves (all the denominations) and pooling resources with each other.

NON-GOVERNMENT ORGANISATIONS (NGOS)

These organisations should not only focus on the provision of services to the poor but also advocate for them in society. [For example] they should lobby the government to make better social policy for the poor and also implement it (Provider 5).

While Ethiopia has a very extensive network of NGOs working on poverty issues, Providers' comments about the work of these organisations were scarce.[2] For example, while Provider 7 simply thought that NGOs should 'continue with their work and see it as their due', only Providers 5, 2 and 3 made some brief observations.

These three Providers thought that the work of NGOs needed significant improvement to serve the poor better, with Provider 2 arguing that:

... many NGOs currently only use 10% of their budgets for the poor and 90% for themselves and their overheads. This inefficient system and current practice is perpetuated as NGOs not only design development projects themselves but also implement them.

Provider 2 therefore suggested that the government should regulate the work of NGOs, which should:

Solutions to Poverty

- only be allowed to manage projects, but not control their implementation
- concentrate on the fulfilment of the basic needs of the poor before working on other projects
- develop sustainable projects which use appropriate technology and are relevant to local people, to make them more independent rather than dependent.

Similarly, Provider 3 pointed out that 'some NGOs do not really implement what they set out to do originally', and:

> … Another problem is the fact that aid from foreign donors often gets channelled through government, where the money then may or may not be used for relevant community purposes. … While there is a lot of money that goes to international NGOs, some of the donations should also be used to support local NGOs and institutions (Provider 3).

According to Provider 3, NGOs need to target their work much more clearly 'on poverty alleviation and building community capacity'. To improve their work, NGOs, thus, should:

- be more informed by societal need, involve the participation of the wider community and integrate people's local knowledge for the development of the whole country
- develop local people's capacities so that they can play a greater part in their own development
- assist in the required attitudinal and cultural change of the population so that people learn how to speak up about their problems and participate more fully in society
- incorporate a human rights framework into their projects
- work on the causes of poverty, rather than focusing on the consequences
- support indigenous agencies in their work with local communities to strengthen civil society.

INDIVIDUALS

> While governments can make laws, it is actually the people in society that have the responsibility to comply and work for the common good. For

example, whereas some people keep things clean, others come along and urinate in public places (Provider 6).

Most of the Providers suggested that individuals in society have a major role in contributing to poverty solutions, by improving themselves and their lives.

As Box 6.9 demonstrates, many participants wanted the poor to make the most of their opportunities, work hard, develop self-respect and self-reliance, and improve their chances in life in whatever way they can.

Box 6.9 Providers' comments on the role of individuals in society

PROVIDER 6

'People should work hard and improve their lives whenever they can. They should develop self-respect, uplift good citizenship and work towards the good of the whole community.'

PROVIDER 1

'Individuals should use their own resources better and more efficiently. They should become more economical, eat less meat and more vegetables. The poor should also work together as a group and investigate their options and opportunities to increase their long-term benefit.'

PROVIDER 4

'Individuals should work hard and be self-reliant. They should be productive as well as contributing to their families and society as a whole.'

PROVIDER 3

'It is individuals that make up families and society as a whole. It is therefore important for them to have self-respect and educate themselves as much as possible.'

PROVIDER 5

'Individuals have to be determined to change and improve themselves.'

Two further examples come from Providers 3 and 5. According to Provider 3, the poor should:

- learn throughout their lives to respect others, use their knowledge to develop themselves, but also their community and country
- do the right thing by their neighbours
- take responsibility for themselves and others
- do their homework and find out about government policies and their constitutional rights. Then they need to fight for the freedom of their country and their rights
- change those traditions which are detrimental to development and keep those which serve the community well.

Provider 5 advocated for improvements in the rural areas. He pointed out that:

> ... people need to start changing some of their traditions and ways of thinking. They need to educate themselves better about new farming practices and also have fewer children. They need to diversify their food production, grow different crops and develop better processes by using newer technology.

To illustrate his point, Provider 5 used one example 'where there were 6000 farmers seeking food assistance, despite the fact that there was water available from a local lake and river [to grow food]'. According to Provider 5, the locals did not utilise this resource for nearly 13 years, until a local NGO initiated a project with the farmers. Since then, the people are much better off by using their local reserves and no longer depend on food handouts. Thus, Provider 5 reiterated that:

> Solutions to poverty do not only involve the actual wealth and availability of the land, people also need to have the knowledge about how to use their available resources well at the local level. Compare the yield of a rich farmer per hectare with that of a poor one. There is a big difference, where the rich farmer gets much more out of his land than the poor.

Provider 3 also wanted the poor to realise that they have entitlements and request them from society, rather than simply trying to survive with their own limited resources: 'It is now time for the poor to request from the government that it provides them the kind of services they need and they are also entitled to' (Provider 3). Provider 3 further suggested that the poor need to work together, organise themselves and tackle their problems collectively.

A minority and alternative view was stated by Provider 7, who did not focus on poor peoples' improvements, but on every individual in society. According to her, all people need to start sharing with each other and realise who they are, because:

> When I really deeply know who I am and who God is, and who the other is, I will live accordingly. That means I will respect my own dignity, give the respect due to God and to the other person. Matters of justice will automatically fall into place, moral life will fall into place and poverty will no longer exist (Provider 7).

Provider 7 also questioned the wisdom and tendency in society to gain material wealth and follow the 'race for riches'. Instead, she advocated for people to moderate their needs and even consider voluntary poverty, in order to have a more fulfilling life:

> Poverty can also be a value in that I can choose to be poor, moderate my needs and, therefore, free myself as a person. This will enable me to have better relationships with others, especially with the poor (Provider 7).

Providers made a major contribution in this chapter by developing extensive and constructive proposals to solve poverty, making insightful comments on societal issues and governance, and proposing a role for government that includes a national welfare system, with detailed service provisions for the poor.

6.3 THE ADVOCATES

As with the Providers, data presented by the Advocates fitted into five categories, under which the discussion has been arranged. As shown in Box 6.10, the responses fell into five categories. Compared to the Providers, however, comments made by the Advocates were less extensive and detailed.

- society
- government
- churches
- non-government organisations (NGOs)
- individuals

SOCIETY

While Advocates 7, 2, 3 and 6 thought that society should do more to solve poverty, their responses in this area were rather brief. Advocates reminded society about its responsibilities, such as promoting a joint community effort.

For Advocate 7 and 2, poverty is a moral issue and should not be tolerated by the community. Thus, Advocate 7 stated that society should 'open itself' and '… face its moral responsibility to make poverty a top priority, where the needs of the poor have to be met. This could be done via an ongoing and sustainable process of philanthropy.'

In the same way, Advocate 2 asked for collective awareness and societal action:

> Poverty is abject and every morning people in the community should feel sickened, especially the rich and powerful. Collectively, people should not accept this situation as normal, and the less the poor themselves accept their own plight the better.

Advocate 3, on the other hand, did not believe poverty is a single issue, and, therefore, it cannot be isolated as such. For him, poverty '… is linked to many other social issues which affect civil society as a whole and, therefore, [it] needs to be seen in the context of systems and governance reform'.

Advocate 6 agreed, proposing a holistic community response that involves:

- reinvigorating cooperatives
- organising community participation
- forming interest groups in order to negotiate with government

- agreeing on a democratic and societal vision of government in order to eradicate poverty
- developing volunteerism to provide leadership to the community in terms of poverty alleviation.

GOVERNMENT

> Whatever government does, it needs to realise its dependence on the population for a positive result. Participation of the community in societal activity creates a partnership between government and society, and the mutual understanding and basis required for a joint effort (Advocate 3).

As with the Providers, the Advocates' comments on the role of government included discussion of: Governance, Public Policy, and Provision of Services, as set out below.

Governance

As most Advocates give the government primary responsibility for developing the nation and ensuring the well-being of its people, they see good governance as essential in tackling social issues such as poverty.

For example, Advocate 3 suggested that whatever government is in power, it has the main responsibility for solving poverty since 'it controls the system and also receives tax revenues'. Accordingly, government should invest the taxes it collects back into the community. The government also has the primary responsibility for the population's health care, education and the provision of all necessary services. For Advocate 3, therefore:

> The power invested in government should be used to alleviate poverty by introducing all the mechanisms/systems required for progress and development in the nation, in order to change the livelihood and conditions of the population. … [Thus] there needs to be a change in the system of governance, which cannot be achieved without the active participation of society on all levels.

To illustrate the meaning of good governance, Advocates 3 and 6 presented a number of requirements. Advocate 3, for example, believed any government should:

Solutions to Poverty

- show that it respects its citizens
- directly consult or listen 'to the heart of its people'
- avoid working for its own political gain and address the needs of the poor
- avoid simply pretending to be democratic and interested in the improvements of the living conditions of the population without following this with action
- avoid creating passivity in the population, as this minimises the potential for development.

In similar fashion, Advocate 6 thought that the government's role is to:

- increase the level of democracy by implementing a process of decentralisation
- inform all 'actors' within society of their rights and responsibilities to ensure and enable local democratic processes
- be more inclusive and transparent
- implement fiscal decentralisation to give more power and financial independence to local areas. This would result in greater economic growth and performance in local areas, such as the growth corridor between Addis Ababa and Nazreth.

Box 6.11 shows other, similar responses by Advocates, including comments on rights, democratic process, and transparent systems and policies.

In many ways, the Advocates saw good governance as linked with the development of sound social and economic policy. Thus, they first made some general comments on public policy, then on specific policy areas. Finally, there was a brief discussion on the delivery of services for the poor.

Public Policy

Advocates 3, 7, 1, and 2 commented quite broadly on the overall policy approach, and on what they saw as the role of the government.

For instance, according to Advocate 1, government needs to develop and oversee a national social and economic policy:

Box 6.11 Advocates' perceptions of good governance

ADVOCATE 4

Government should:
- ensure everyone's rights in the country are protected
- ensure that there are good democratic processes
- ensure the political leaders 'are good' and act in the best interests of the nation.

ADVOCATE 1

Government should:
- bring together all relevant stakeholders, systems and structures to ensure that policies are implemented properly, including by government at different levels
- be accountable through transparent processes of governance and be responsible for the monitoring and evaluating the policies it has developed and implemented.

ADVOCATE 5

Government should:
- maintain peace through law and order
- fight corruption and enhance democratic processes internally. This would also increase accountability and raise the credibility of the government sector.

Government should have the overall responsibility for developing relevant policies via the parliament, and talk to the population as a whole and initiate a dialogue about poverty that involves all people in society, thus making everyone accountable in the end.

For Advocates 3, 1 and 2, for this to be successful, government needs to build consensus between the different stakeholders in society, making sure it '...creates favourable conditions for the participation of the whole community in social, economic and educational activity, and investigates the tools necessary for such participation' (Advocate 3).

Advocate 2 also wanted the government to lead the creation of a national consensus about the need for poverty to be eradicated and the fact that it is not a normal situation. He argued that there should be '... [an awareness] that poverty is not an acceptable thing, requiring the collective will [to action]

Solutions to Poverty

from all institutions and the political system. It needs a kind of "Marshall Plan" where everyone is involved' (Advocate 2).

While Advocate 2 invoked the idea of a 'Marshall Plan', Advocate 3 called it a national strategy. He strongly recommended extensive societal participation and a need to:

> … identify the best ways and methodology to gather the required knowledge and expertise from all the relevant sectors and stakeholders in civil society, such as the churches and NGOs. A close partnership with relevant organisations would then assist the government in prioritising policy to address and minimise the extent of poverty (Advocate 3).

To make a national strategy work, Advocate 7 thought it is important to align government regulations with relevant policy settings, to ensure that they are consistent with each other. Finally, for Advocate 2, a national plan and strategy needs to involve:

- societal awareness of the relevant poverty issues
- the creation of wealth
- the development of services without any delay to address the needs of people
- the benchmarking of institutions and organisations against the aims of national strategy. For example, the work of NGOs is currently too paternalistic and they spend more money on their own arrangements than on the provision of services for the poor.

Specific policy issues

Advocates also addressed a small number of specific policy issues and commented on economic development, employment and education.

Economic development and employment

Advocates 5, 4 and 7 thought that economic policy needs attention.

Advocate 5 took an international focus, feeling keenly that economies of poor nations such as Ethiopia depend very much on international markets and 'the goodwill' of richer countries. For this reason, policy makers should try hard to:

- encourage rich nations to provide 'real development options', instead of the ever increasing mechanisms of dependency, which result in the exploitation of poorer nations
- encourage fair trade between nations, so that coffee-growing nations such as Ethiopia can get a fair price for their goods from rich countries
- negotiate better trade conditions through the World Trade Organisation
- encourage the cancellation of the enormous debt that has been accumulated by poor nations. If this was to occur, governments should increase their budgets in the areas of relevant infrastructure projects, health and education
- encourage wealthy nations to increase their development assistance funds for poor countries.

The others commented on the national/local level, with their suggestions including recommendations that policy makers should:

- discourage the implementation of 'the trickle-down theory', and implement processes of social justice and equality where the entire nation can share in the profits of the economy, instead of only a small minority of society (Advocate 5)
- study the basis on which the national debt is created and paid, and also how this system is connected to the local political system. Since money spent on servicing debt is lost to the nation, a reduction of debt can assist in meeting peoples' currently un-met needs (Advocate 7)
- ensure that there is a favourable internal and external economic environment to build and develop the economy (Advocates 4, 5)
- align different programmes and policies of development projects between different organisations so that they all adhere to a national strategy of poverty (Advocate 7).

While Advocate 5 agreed with a strong role of government in public policy, he was not in favour of it in the area of employment. For him, government should only facilitate the investment opportunities for business, while creation of employment should come from 'the market and external sectors'. Therefore, Advocate 5 stated government policy should:

- change peoples' attitudes and expectations, as they still expect the government to provide employment opportunities
- encourage micro-finance to give the poor the opportunity to set up their own businesses
- encourage the banking sector to lend money to the poor.

Provision of Services

> What we really need is basic welfare provisions such as food, shelter, health care, etc. for all those who are ill, disabled and [for] the elderly who can no longer work (Advocate 4).

While the majority of Advocates wanted to have the needs of the poor met, they did not comment in large numbers or in great detail in this section. The few available responses propose a national welfare system, the provision of financial assistance and a limited number of general welfare services to take care of the poor.

Advocates 5, 4 and 1 argued that in order to meet the needs of the poor, a national welfare system should be developed, as only such a system can deliver all the services needed. Advocate 5 thus called for a nationwide:

> … integrated approach of basic services, mainly for the most vulnerable in society such as the ill, disabled, women and children. Assistance provided would include areas such as financial help, food security/nourishment, housing, clean water/sanitation, primary health care.

Advocates 1 and 4 agreed that services need to be integrated and linked with relevant support, because as Advocate 1 added: '… simply building houses for the poor, or giving them some food, would still exclude them from all the other services they need and, thus, exclude them from participating in society the way they ought to be'.

Financial assistance

Advocates 4 and 5 were for the provision of income support for the most needy. Thus, Advocate 5 proposed:

... developing an income-support system for the nation, either through the government or charitable sector. If income would be provided to people where they are located, it would reduce their need to come to the major cities looking for help. This system should include unemployment benefits and the provision pensions for the elderly and disabled people.

Advocate 5 also suggested establishing a poverty line of 350 birr per month 'under which people would be considered poor and in need of assistance'. In addition, he would encourage the giving of alms, with collections conducted in an organised way. According to Advocate 5, this would ensure that:

> ... the most needy in the community ... can be targeted for assistance. The increased income thus generated could be used in a variety of ways, e.g. providing the poor with a stable lunch, erecting shelters for the homeless, providing travel and other assistance to those who want to return to the countryside.

For Advocate 4, financial assistance provided through an income-support system would be able to help rebuild peoples' lives, especially those from the rural areas where '... money could either be used to farm the land or start a business. If people have land they can farm, grow vegetables and, therefore, have things to eat' (Advocate 4).

General welfare provisions

Suggestions regarding the provision of services for the poor include the following:

1. Accommodation (Advocate 5) should be provided by developing a system of subsidised public housing for the poor, through which the poorer sections of the community can access affordable shelters. However, this housing should not only be located in the poorer parts of town so as not to upset the current mix of populations around the city. Segregation of the poor from wealthier people in society may increase social tensions between these groups if the poor are 'locked out' of richer areas.
2. Free health care for all (Advocates 1, 4, 5, 7). According to Advocate 1, 'the current health care system should be made much less bureaucratic

and more easily accessible to the public. Local government could assist in this process.'

3. Better council services through local *kebeles* (Advocate 1), where offices could be made multi-purpose facilities and offer a variety of services to the public. These services should not only be provided to those people who reside in houses in that specific location (with house numbers) but also to the homeless and poor.

4. Clean water and sanitation to be provided in all city and rural areas (Advocates 1, 4, 5, 7).

5. Free education for all, so that people are prepared for the workforce (Advocate 5, 4, 7). Advocate 4 called for a more targeted approach to improve educational opportunities for the poor in the entire system because 'everyone in society who has no money also lacks access to education and the opportunity to contribute to the community. They also can't help themselves, because if people have access to education they can solve everything.'

6. An information centre to be staffed by social workers and other trained staff (Advocate 5). This centre could resource poor people and provide information about where to get employment. It could also inform about the various schemes of self-help and income-generating projects like the example of a local rubbish collection/recycling scheme run by the poor.

Churches

> Churches need to rediscover their roots and missions and promote their solidarity with the poor to achieve societal change. Churches can make a significant contribution in the fight against poverty because of their multi-faceted composition and nature (Advocate 3).

Most Advocates, except 1 and 2, argued that the churches have a significant role to play when it comes to poverty alleviation. Their responses covered the mission of religious institutions, as well as practical things they can do to help the poor.

Advocates 7, 3, 5 and 6 all felt that the churches need to remind themselves that their key mission and responsibility in society is to work for the poor. This is illustrated by Advocate 7's comments on the mission and also about the need to assist in practical ways: 'Churches should practice what they preach and remember their own doctrines to serve the poor, instead of just paying lip service to it. Churches should also look at creating job opportunities for the poor.'

Likewise, Advocate 3 believed that the churches have the opportunity to develop comprehensive solutions, as they can address both the material and the spiritual needs. For him, the churches could do this in cooperation by:

- becoming a voice for the voiceless and an advocate on behalf of the poor to reduce their hardship
- advocating for a system change to allow participation by all stakeholders in society
- establishing a favourable climate to create partnerships in society with concerned organisations, people and the poor themselves
- using their privileged position to better network with other stakeholders and develop common strategies
- creating initiatives for dedicated change
- providing psychological and social support, training and skills development for the poor
- supporting different kinds of projects to assist the poor while, at the same time, continuing with advocacy.

Similarly, Advocate 5 argued that while churches are powerful and wealthy institutions—with great potential to assist 'in the fight against poverty'—this opportunity to make a more significant difference to the community and the poor is largely unfulfilled. Thus, he first reiterated that:

> Churches should know and remember their own social doctrine on which religious teaching is actually based, including the fact that every person has a right to life, human dignity, human and economic rights, and the right not to be in poverty. In this sense, religious orders should explain to the poor who they are and what to expect from life (Advocate 5).

For Advocate 5 churches, therefore, need to:

- know the plight of the poor and actively advocate on their behalf
- provide services to the poor as much they are able to. As the situation of poverty is wrong and an unacceptable state, it requires to be rectified

Solutions to Poverty

- develop a common approach between the religious denominations and work together towards the reduction of poverty as a sector.

Advocate 5 felt strongly that churches of all denominations need to cooperate for the common good of society. He argued that to achieve this, churches need to trust each other and focus 'on the need to service the poor'. The basis for such cooperation should be:

> ... the knowledge that poverty needs to be a temporary problem and that organisations should work together to make poor people independent of services. The cooperation between institutions may include the development of a common focus and aims, the assessment of problem areas, the identification of service gaps, and the sharing of resources to assist the poor (Advocate 5).

While Advocate 5 wanted cooperation between religious institutions, Advocate 4 disapproved. Instead, he proposed a 'healthy competition' between the different organisations, believing that this will ultimately benefit the poor as each church can offer different services and choices. To substantiate his argument against cooperation, he compared 'the situation between the different churches' with '... parents who have twelve children, where each child has their own ideas. Thus, it would be impossible to get a consensus about poverty reduction policies between the different organisations' (Advocate 4).

Advocate 4 also saw a much more limited and traditional role for the church in poverty alleviation, with its main responsibilities to:

- encourage people to believe in God and live their lives in harmony
- give hope to the poor
- initiate educational activities
- develop some welfare programmes, such as health clinics so that the poor have access to some of these services for free.

Another variation of thinking about the function of religious institutions is provided by Advocate 6. He too argued for a greater societal role of the churches, which should:

- continue to advocate moral frameworks for society towards peace and security
- continue and improve their service delivery activities
- engage in positive social change and transformation towards greater social justice
- engage in social advocacy for the protection of the disadvantaged.

Non-Government Organisations (NGOs)

Just like the Providers, most Advocates made either no comment on the role NGOs should play in poverty solutions or, if they did, they were sparing. Thus, while only Advocates 7, 1 and 6 responded, only Advocate 6 was in favour of the work of these organisations.

Rather than encouraging the NGOs to provide more services, Advocates 7 and 1 wanted to see their work abandoned. Advocate 7, for instance, thought that:

> One of the main problems with their work is the necessity to continuously raise funds, rather than concentrating on the provision of services. Therefore, the government should consider taking over some of the NGOs programmes to make them more sustainable.

However, while their work 'continues unrestricted', Advocate 7 felt that NGOs really need to:

- become more accountable and transparent for auditing purposes, to prevent corruptive practices
- develop and concentrate on a social justice agenda to advocate for the poor
- open up employment options for a variety of people, not just for their own people
- target their work and services much more carefully to meet the needs of the poor more effectively.

Advocate 1 was even less in favour of NGOs, suggesting that their work be totally phased out:

215

> Their presence makes people dependent on their activities, which in turn generates more demand for their work. [It also deflects from] the responsibilities of the government—and, in fact, of the responsibility every citizen has for assisting the underprivileged.

While Advocates 7 and 1 were quite negative about the work of the NGOs, Advocate 6 was more positive. He wanted to see these organisations improving their services and make greater contributions in the community, namely:

- take initiatives to empower communities
- deliver services and transfer knowledge to local communities
- serve the community as a kind of watch-dog to expose 'scandals' of poverty and systems of bad governance
- advocate on behalf of the poor and give a voice to the voiceless
- use their power and influence to promote new thinking and campaign for social issues
- develop relevant pilot projects to demonstrate good governance, e.g. in land management and systems development in partnership with government
- transfer their projects to the government after they were successfully set-up
- work together as a sector in a coordinated way to ensure better outcomes for the poor
- work towards better connections between the NGO sector and the government.

INDIVIDUALS

> Individuals should have a vision for themselves and develop dreams, ambitions for their families and immediate communities (Advocate 7).

As in the previous section, only three Advocates responded; again, their comments on how the poor can help themselves and improve their own lives provided little detail.

For Advocates 5, 1, 7 and 6, the poor need to start believing in themselves, have dreams and visions. The poor should also realise that '… poverty is not acceptable and think about what could be done to address the problem. They could organise themselves and get information about what is being done and by whom' (Advocate 5).

All three Advocates agreed that the poor should start working together. For Advocate 7, the poor should develop small joint business enterprises, since 'potential gains from working together could be significant, where the proceeds of profits from such projects could be distributed fairly among the members of the local community'.

Advocates 1 and 6, in particular, wanted the poor to play a much more active part in the community by 'standing up and be[ing] counted'. Thus, Advocate 1 argued that while the government should take responsibility for the welfare of its citizens, the poor need to organise themselves and make their voices heard. She expected that if poor people actively requested assistance from local government, it would be more likely that there would be a positive response to their needs. Advocate 6 agreed, and developed an entire plan of action for the poor, who should:

- take more responsibility and explore every opportunity to escape poverty
- be committed to collective action, for example, by taking an active interest in their local surroundings and cleaning the streets, supporting local regulations and dealing with sewage problems. Such action would help to change peoples' attitudes that the poor are dangerous and delinquent
- organise themselves and the beggars and request that their rights to houses and basic services should be met by the authorities
- choose delegates and make representations to local government about their plight, including lack of housing, rather than being chased away as individuals by the police. This would ensure that their concerns are heard and that their rights as citizens to services could be met by councils
- make sure that begging is not becoming a lifestyle, and the poor do not simply go from one NGO service to another, being passive recipients of handouts
- inform themselves of wider developments in their country
- have visions of a better life and demand their rightful place in society.

Summary

Participants' comments provided interesting insights and ideas on poverty solutions. The Poor initially found it difficult to formulate poverty solutions, as they lacked relevant experience and had never been consulted about such matters. Nevertheless, they responded well to this challenge by providing useful suggestions and ideas on how to tackle poverty. While the Poor mainly talked from personal experience, Providers and Advocates provided wider perspectives, because of their education and professional experience. All three groups requested more support from the general community and relevant institutions/organisations, but saw the government as having the main responsibility for poverty alleviation.

Interviews with the Poor showed that they are absorbed in situations of extreme hardship, so that their foremost request is for direct relief from society, government, NGOs and churches. Thus, the Poor's solutions included: income and financial support, employment/job creation, greater access to education, housing, health care, greater levels of *kebele* support and particular assistance for the rural sector. There were very few responses about how the Poor themselves could address poverty; the women, in particular, seemed overwhelmed by their deprivation and saw few ways in which they could be part of the poverty solution. While the women made fewer comments than the men, all the Poor gave a few suggestions about the kind of work ethic they felt should to be maintained by society and also by themselves.

The Providers, although one step removed from the poverty experience, demonstrated a robust understanding of the issues and articulated the most extensive poverty solutions of all the groups. Based on their knowledge and experience, Providers suggested anti-poverty policies across many areas: society, government, NGOs, churches and individuals. Solutions thus suggested by this group were complex and multilayered. While they called on the wealthy to share some of their wealth and resources with the poor, they also argued for a national poverty strategy and for society to tackle poverty together. Providers felt that the government should play a key role in addressing the needs of the population by providing strong leadership in society and good governance through an appropriate legal, administrative, moral and institutional/organisational framework. Providers also thought that some cultural and attitudinal change in the community was needed, and that public policy can address poverty through economic and business regulation, tax policy, employment creation and rural assistance. More specifically, most Providers argued for the development of national welfare services, including income support and pension schemes, food subsidies for the poor and greater access to educational opportunities, housing and health care. All Providers felt that churches should use their influence and resources to address poverty, and that this could be done by a return to their mission to serve the poor. While most Providers worked for NGOs, their comments on this sector were scant; they suggested that NGOs have an important contribution to make, but could use their resources more effectively. Finally, the Providers want the poor to make the most of their opportunities, work hard, develop self-respect and self-reliance and improve their chances in life.

Interviews with the Advocates showed that they are the furthest removed from the poverty situation. While their ideas on poverty solutions covered the same areas as discussed by the Providers (society, government, NGO, church and individual), their comments were far less extensive than those made by the Providers. Advocates too thought that the government has the primary responsibility for developing the nation and meeting the needs of its people. Commenting on governance, policy development and service delivery systems, Advocates called for a consultative democratic process characterised by accountability, rights, freedoms and justice. Such a process would bring together all stakeholders, enable the government to lead the nation and build a national consensus about how best to fight poverty. Public policies should then address economic development and aim to get fairer trade agreements in the international system and a better deal for the nation; study the reasons for and reduce the national debt; create a more equal distribution of wealth and resources locally; and create more employment, micro-finance and other local development options for the population.

While Advocates were in favour of developing and extending welfare provisions for the poor, many did not comment, and their responses were less comprehensive as those of the Providers. The few recommendations here included the provision of financial assistance for the poor and the rural sector, and the development of welfare services such as subsidised accommodation; better provision of health, council and support services; and improvements in sanitation and access to education. Nevertheless, of all groups, the Advocates demonstrated the best knowledge of international causes of poverty and how they affect poor nations. Advocates also thought that churches and NGOs should make a significant contribution in poverty alleviation. Like the Providers, this group felt that the churches should act according to their mission to serve the poor and provide a moral framework for society to work together. Similarly to the Providers, very few Advocates commented on the role of NGOs. A few Advocates also commented on the role of the poor, suggesting that the poor needed to work together, demand services, develop visions for themselves, realise their potential and be careful that begging is not becoming part of an entrenched lifestyle.

Chapter Seven

CONCLUSION

The global economic crisis, the most severe since the Great Depression, is rapidly turning into a human and development crisis. No region is immune. The poor countries are especially vulnerable, as they have the least cushion to withstand events. The crisis, coming on the heels of the food and fuel crises, poses serious threats to their hard-won gains in boosting economic growth and reducing poverty. It is pushing millions back into poverty and putting at risk the very survival of many. The prospect [of failing] to reach the Millennium Development Goals (MDGs) by 2015, are already a cause for serious concern (The World Bank 2009, Backpage).

While the repercussions of the latest financial crisis are still being felt around the world, it is too early to say how Africa and the rest of the developing world will be affected. What is clear, however, is that this current crisis is part of a periodic and systemic failure of an economic model based on neo-liberal principles, a model in need of urgent reform and:

... a fundamental reorientation in economic thinking based on an overall philosophy of capitalism, where capital serves the well-being of the society at large (the majority of which lives on incomes from labour) rather than the other way around (UNCTAD 2010, p. 46).

As we have seen in this book, this system gives unfair advantage to rich nations, producing unprecedented inequalities in wealth and poverty, between and within nations. In the context of economic globalisation, Ethiopia is one of the poorest countries in the world, and despite its best efforts and real achievements in social and economic development over the last few decades, poverty is still a major problem this nation has to grapple with.

As the faces of the deprived are often hidden and hard to understand, this small study of poverty in Addis Ababa gives a voice to some of the victims of poverty. Significantly, the findings and recommendations presented below do not rely on the expertise of so-called poverty experts; instead, the analysis of the material is based on information given by the 'real experts' of poverty, the poor themselves. In addition, the study compares the voices of the poor with those of a small group of professionals providing services to the deprived (the Providers) and researchers/policy makers working in this area (the Advocates). Based on the interviews conducted with these three groups, the following sections present the findings of the study in relation to the research questions and recommendations about how to alleviate poverty.

FINDINGS

Respondents in all three groups identified many areas of deprivation experienced by the poor, underlining the need for concepts of poverty that embrace great complexity and going far beyond lack of income and resources, to encompass deprivations across the totality of the human condition. These deprivations include income poverty, unemployment/underemployment, substandard accommodation, lack of food, social isolation, and emotional/psychological problems. Respondents also showed that poverty relates to societal and structural arrangements; lack of education, opportunity and participation; inequality and injustices; and the way people behave and feel about themselves and others in the community. These responses paint a diverse and complex picture of poverty, demonstrating that poverty is multidimensional.

A summary of the findings of this study is presented below, in order of the four questions asked of respondents. For each question, the responses of the Poor appear first, then the responses of the Providers and finally of the Advocates.

Findings Relating to Definitions of Poverty

The Poor

The Poor are the real experts on the poverty experience, and the interviews highlight the importance and value of listening to their voices. The data this group provided show both that their experience of poverty is multidimensional and that usually they are deprived of even the basic needs. Poverty for them represents many combinations of interacting needs, such as lack of money, food, appropriate housing and sanitation, and the presence of a range of negative emotional/psychological states and poor health. Data analysis also made clear that the women tend to be more vulnerable and deprived than the men. Contributing to this gender difference is the fact that all the women interviewed were single parents, raising children under difficult circumstances, while none of the men was responsible for children. In addition, it was shown that homeless women are particularly insecure and often at risk of being raped. Thus, the lives of female participants are clearly different from those of their male counterparts, although there are also similarities.

The Providers

While interviews with the Providers showed them to be one step removed from the direct experience of poverty, they did have a good grasp of what it means to be poor. This group confirmed the multidimensional nature of poverty, including the lack of fulfilment of basic needs and further effects of lack of money and resources. The Providers also identified urban/rural variations in patterns of deprivation; these differences included the lack of opportunities and rights, and cultural and spiritual issues.

The Advocates

The Advocates' understandings of poverty were the furthest from actual poverty experience and the most highly conceptualised. Although this group paid scant attention to the effects of income poverty, perhaps assuming them, they reiterated the multifaceted nature of the problem. Some Advocates looked at the international and local contexts of development, identifying some of the more abstract issues behind poverty. Others acknowledged that the basic needs of the poor were not met, although their accounts of those needs were not as detailed as the accounts of the other two groups. The Advocates also made important observations about the poor's lack of participation in society, and presented interesting views on how societal and cultural attitudes towards the poor can differ.

Findings Relating to Causes of Poverty

The Poor

Interviews with the Poor suggested that the way they identified the causes of poverty depended largely on their experiences; that is, on their life histories, daily struggles to survive and interactions with other people, all of which are embedded in social structures and practices. This complexity of connections means that, to them, the causes of poverty are enmeshed, cyclical and dynamic. Because their daily struggle to survive requires their total energy, this group demonstrated little awareness of structural causes of poverty, although they had some notions of inequality, especially in relation to the expanding gap between the rich and the poor. While most participants felt unsupported by the community, the vulnerability of women was especially evident, their choices and opportunities being even more restricted than those of their male counterparts. For example, growing up in a patriarchal society and usually carrying the burden of child-rearing, the women tended to feel more precarious and to have even less control over their lives than did the men. Information given by the Poor also showed that poverty tends to follow intergenerational cycles, involving combinations of poor family background, family breakdown through death or conflict and insufficient land to survive on in the countryside. In addition, the Poor experienced a lack of education, few opportunities for employment, displacement and migration to Addis Abba, plus personal issues such as ill health, loneliness and social isolation. While some of the women questioned their own life choices, the men did so much less frequently.

The Providers

Providers saw the crisis of poverty in Ethiopia as caused at the national level by structural factors such as social inequality and unequal distributions of wealth, and at the international level by an unfair global Western-style development model, which they saw as producing a lack of opportunity for poor nations.

Providers also commented on how cultural phenomena in Ethiopia, such as attitudes towards women, institutional and organisational values, and moral/spiritual qualities act as direct and indirect causes of poverty. Almost all Providers argued that causes of poverty relate to poor 'governance', which leads both to systemic inefficiency and to inadequate public policy across many areas, including land policy, education and health care. This chain of causation means that key social policy issues are neither addressed nor implemented, so that citizens' basic needs are not met. While the Providers commented most frequently on structural/societal causes of poverty, they also thought that individuals influence their own lives and situations, largely because of traditional cultural values, and that these in turn contribute to individuals' poverty.

The Advocates

The Advocates painted a complex picture of poverty causes, identifying social and economic structures, governance, public policy and individual factors. Advocates' analysis of structural issues such as economic globalisation was more comprehensive than that provided by the Providers, and Advocates viewed current international trade as unfair and exploitative, affecting poor nations negatively and limiting their economic and social development. Advocates also suggested that global inequalities are perpetuated in various ways on the national level, and argued that both individuals and institutions too readily accept poverty as a given, and that negative societal attitudes work against the poor. While the Advocates also described how the lack of good governance and related local systems can hinder the progress of the nation, their analysis of this factor was not as extensive as that of the Providers, perhaps because of differences in their areas of work. The Advocates thought that current public policy and inadequate support mechanisms are causes of poverty, but also argued that some of the attitudes and behaviours of the poor themselves are part of the problem.

FINDINGS RELATING TO BARRIERS

The Poor

The Poor strongly confirmed the cyclic nature of poverty, in which each factor can be cause, effect or barrier. Thus, the common presentation of the cycle describes a series of sequential and interlocking issues: for example, inadequate education leads to deficits of employment, income, living standards, health, housing and opportunity, and these factors can in turn lead again to inadequate education for the next generation.

The Providers

For the Providers, barriers were injustice, poor governance and societal inequities, including inequalities in the distribution of resources. They also thought that cultural barriers arose from the roles of the church, and that these barriers worked against the fuller participation of the poor and kept the community from progressing.

The Advocates

While the Advocates hinted at issues of injustice and poor governance, their discussion of barriers lacked detail. Nevertheless, they identified a limited number of structural, societal and individual barriers. They also commented on the role of the church and its influence on the thinking of the poor and of the wider society.

FINDINGS RELATING TO POVERTY SOLUTIONS

The Poor

Necessarily absorbed in the demands of extreme hardship, the Poor offered solutions to poverty that were rooted in requests from society, government, NGOs and churches for direct relief. The Poor's solutions thus included income and financial support benefits, employment/job creation, greater access to education, housing, health care, greater levels of *kebele* support and assistance for the rural sector. While they made extensive comments on the government sector, they gave very few responses about how the Poor themselves could address poverty. The women, in particular, seemed overwhelmed with their lives of deprivation and saw few opportunities to be part of the poverty solution.

The Providers

Although not personally experiencing poverty, the Providers had a good working and conceptual understanding about the issues, and used their knowledge and skills to develop the most extensive poverty solutions of all groups. Their solutions encompassed actions by society, government, NGOs, churches and the individual efforts of the poor, and they stressed that action was needed at multiple levels. For example, while they called on the wealthy to share resources with the poor, they also argued for a national poverty strategy, and for all sectors of society to tackle poverty together. Providers felt that some cultural and attitudinal change in the community was needed if such a goal were to be achieved. Like the Poor, this group also saw government playing the key role in any poverty solution, by providing strong moral leadership and good governance through appropriate legal, administrative and institutional/organisation. Providers argued that good public policy should first and foremost address the needs of the people through various strategies including economic and business policy, tax reform, employment creation and assistance for the rural sector and environment. Most Providers argued for the development of national welfare services, including income support and pension schemes, food subsidies for the poor, greater access to educational opportunities, housing and health care. All Providers felt that churches have a major contribution to make in addressing poverty, and that this could be achieved by the churches rediscovering their mission to serve the poor, and by using their influence and resources. While most Providers worked for NGOs, their comments on this sector were scarce; comments suggested that NGOs have an important role to play but could use their resources more effectively to meet peoples' needs. Finally, this group believed that the poor should make the most of their opportunities, work hard, develop self-respect and self-reliance, and improve their chances in life in whatever way they can.

The Advocates

Advocates' comments on solutions again showed that they are the furthest removed from the poverty experience, but the most knowledgeable about the broader social, political and economic concepts. Thus, of all the participants, they demonstrated the most knowledge of international causes of and solutions to poverty. While their ideas addressed areas similar to those raised by the Providers, their comments were far less extensive than those made by the Providers. Like the other two groups, the Advocates thought that the government has the primary responsibility for developing the nation and meeting the needs of its people. Commenting on governance, policy development and service delivery systems as ways of tackling poverty, the Advocates called for a consultative democratic process which entails accountability, rights, freedoms and justice in order to bring together all members of society. Such action, they argued, will enable the government to lead the nation and build a national consensus about how best to fight poverty. Public policies should then address economic development, aiming to get fairer international trade agreements and a better deal for the nation. Advocates further advised studying the reasons for the national debt and ways of reducing it, as steps to achieving a more equal distribution of wealth and resources locally. They also suggested creating more employment, micro-finance and other local development options for the population. While the Advocates were in favour of developing and extending welfare provisions for the poor, their comments were not as frequent or as comprehensive as those of the Providers. The few recommendations here included the provision of financial assistance for the poor and the rural sector, the development of welfare services such as subsidised accommodation, better provision of health, council and support services, and improvements in sanitation and access to education. Advocates also thought that churches and NGOs should make a significant contribution to poverty alleviation. Like the Providers, this group felt that the churches should act according to their mission to serve the poor and provide a moral framework for society to work together. Very few Advocates commented on what the poor themselves could do to alleviate poverty.

RECOMMENDATIONS

> ... all citizens need to get involved in the community and see what can be done to deal with social problems. They should work with government, do what can be done—and not always expect help from outside (Provider 5).

Based on the responses of the Poor, the Providers and the Advocates, a number of recommendations concerning the alleviation of poverty were developed. These recommendations are grouped into five areas: society, government, churches, NGOs, and individuals, discussed in that order below.

SOCIETY

- Poverty must be seen as a moral/ethical issue and should not be tolerated.
- National cooperation and consensus between all institutions, government and citizens should be further developed to create a better society and to tackle poverty. To this end:
  - societal awareness of poverty issues needs to be increased and promoted
  - community participation and civil society development need to be encouraged
  - democratic principles and visions of society need to be promoted and sustained
  - every member of society needs to work and contribute to the common good, people should help and support each other, and volunteerism in the community needs to be developed.
- Inequality and unequal distribution of wealth and resources need to be kept in check so that everyone in the community has the opportunity to participate to the best of their ability. Those who can afford it should share some of their wealth and resources with people in need. 'Big business' and wealthy individuals should be encouraged to make a greater contribution to society.
- Positive cultural and attitudinal changes should be promoted in the community to assist social and economic development; gender equality needs to be institutionally reinforced.

GOVERNMENT

All respondents felt that the government had the most important role to play in meeting the needs of the population, and had the ultimate responsibility for poverty reduction. Recommendations made here are organised under three areas: governance, general policy issues and specific policy issues.

Governance

- Continue to provide strong leadership in developing and overseeing national social and economic policy.

- Play the key role in bringing together all societal stakeholders, coordinating relevant systems and structures, and ensuring that policies are implemented properly at different levels of government.
- Continue improving good governance by combating corruption and developing accountable and transparent processes of government and civil services through:
  - promoting the separation of power at all levels of government, and encouraging a strong and independent judiciary
  - enhancing pluralistic/democratic processes through popular participation, e.g. the development of civil society, supporting free media, welcoming political opposition parties to play a role in the community, ensuring peoples' rights are protected and informing all 'actors' within society of their rights and responsibilities
  - monitoring and evaluating policies which have been developed and implemented
  - ensuring that policy makers are independent of special interests groups and act in the best interests of the nation.
- Improve the government's decision-making by:
  - giving communities (and the poor) greater input into the process, and directly consulting with and listening to the 'heart of the people'
  - making government services less bureaucratic and more transparent and efficient
  - decentralising and improving civil service systems to serve the population at local and regional levels, and empowering public servants to make decisions in one office rather than in many different locations.

General policy issues

- Focus national development on the well-being of the population to ensure that peoples' needs are met.
- Promote the implementation of social justice and equality.
- Re-evaluate and monitor the implementation of neo-liberal economic policies.
- Ensure 'benchmarking' of institutions and organisations against the aims of the national strategy, and monitor, regulate and evaluate their work to ensure agreed service agreements and expected outcomes are met.

- Implement fiscal decentralisation to give more power and financial independence to local areas.

Specific policy issues

Recommendations on specific issues cover the following four areas: economy, employment, rural issues and welfare/social protection provisions.

Economy

International level

- Encourage rich nations to provide 'real development options', instead of implementing mechanisms of dependency and exploitation of poorer nations. In this context:
  - discourage the negative polices of economic globalisation and neo-liberalism, and encourage fair trade between nations so that coffee-growing societies such as Ethiopia can get a fair price for their goods from rich countries
  - negotiate better trade conditions through the World Trade Organisation, including the cancellation of debt accumulated by poor nations so that governments could use more money to improve infrastructure, health and education, and the increase in development assistance funds for poor countries.

National level

- Discourage the implementation of the negative processes of globalisation, including the use of 'the trickle-down theory', structures of inequality and the unequal distribution of wealth and resources, so that the entire nation can share in the profits of the economy.
- Study how national debt is created and paid for, and try to reduce debt liabilities, so that additional monies can be used to develop the nation and provide necessary services to the population.
- Ensure a favourable internal and external economic environment to build and develop the economy and make the poor a 'real stakeholder' and beneficiary in the economic system.

- Align different programmes and policies of development projects between various organisations so that they all adhere to a national strategy of poverty and meet peoples' needs. Part of such a strategy would encourage individuals and groups to establish small businesses and the banking sector to lend money to the poor.

Employment

- Encourage greater investment and economic development in local/rural industries by assisting the private sector (e.g. with tax concessions) to create employment projects that would aid the economy, improve the national infrastructure and address specific areas of need, such as housing for the poor.
- Develop public sector schemes in urban and rural areas to create jobs in factories and various organisations in the government and non-government sectors.
- Develop and support income-generating projects such as small businesses and cooperatives, particularly for the young and poor people (e.g. through tax concessions and/or micro-finance to enable the set-up and start-up phases).
- Investigate and support ways the poor themselves can organise into associations so that they can support themselves. Such associations could be modelled on the *iddir* system, but set up specifically for the poor.
- Set minimum standards to ensure that peoples' wages are adequate to live on and are in accordance with level of training.
- Develop information/job finding services where trained staff can assess peoples' capacities, provide information and link job seekers with employment.

Rural issues

- Develop strategies to support rural communities, reduce migration to the cities and help people living in cities to relocate back to the countryside (e.g. with cash incentives and travel allowances). Assist the rural sector by:

- developing infrastructure and support systems in the countryside, where the majority of the population live
- promoting and developing cooperative farming where people can share their resources to get better results in sales and profit margins
- assisting farmers to increase production through the development of irrigation schemes, the provision of seed money and advice about how to protect the environment.

Welfare/social protection provisions

In order to meet the needs of the poor, all participants agree on the need to develop a national welfare system and to increase assistance in the following areas: income support and financial assistance, food and other basic necessities, accommodation, education, health, and council and other services.

Income support and financial assistance

Income support
- Introduce a national income support system to support the unemployed until they have employment and those who are temporarily sick. These benefits should be in accordance with the established poverty line.
- Expand and develop a universal pension scheme to support the elderly and people with a permanent disability, and provide pensions to all current and former soldiers.

Financial assistance
- Provide one-off (non-repayable) emergency grants to cover housing and other essentials for people most in need, including the elderly and the disabled.
- Develop a credit scheme where poor people can get credit without paying interest when experiencing hardships.
- Provide small grants/start-up capital for poor people to set up small businesses, such shops and grocery stores.

Food and other basic necessities

- Subsidise basic necessities such as clothing and household goods.
- Subsidise food stuffs such as wheat, *teff*, cereals, oil, onions and pepper.
- Control food markets so that basic food stuffs and other necessities are affordable and of good quality. This control needs to be area-specific to address local and regional needs.

Accommodation

- Improve and expand the current system of public housing and basic services, and provide cheap/subsidised housing for everyone who needs it, and:
  - identify and develop affordable housing stock through the local *kebeles*
  - integrate public housing into mainstream society to create a mix of populations and prevent segregation and social tensions between different socio-economic groups.
- Develop a system of free/subsidised emergency housing options, including dormitory-style shelters, to meet the needs of the poor and the homeless, with priority given to those in most in need.
- Develop a system of supported accommodation facilities to cater for the special needs of children and young people, families, women, the elderly and people with disabilities.
- Develop a loan scheme to provide start-up capital for people to build houses.

Education

- Improve access to and quality of free education, especially for the poor, and assist children in remote rural areas by providing free transportation. This measure would have the additional benefit of reducing the incidence of abduction of children on the way to school.
- Provide better educational opportunities and 'on the job training' options for adults who want to improve their life chances and have access to the job market.

Health

- Expand and improve the existing system of health care services to meet the needs of the population better, and:

- make current system less bureaucratic and more easily accessible to the public
- improve maternal health system and related services
- promote and develop family planning centres and offer greater birth control mechanisms.
- Provide/improve clean water and sanitation systems to all city and rural areas.

Council and other services

- Reduce bureaucratic processes in local and regional government offices to improve public access to services.
- Consider developing local *kebele* offices into multi-purpose facilities, to offer a greater variety of services to the public.
- Improve procedures to assist the poor, the homeless and non-registered residents to obtain local services, including greater assistance in obtaining an ID.
- Assist communities in the development of community associations such as *iddirs*, so that they can support each other and the poor.
- Develop information/support centres staffed by social workers and other professionals. Such centres could resource poor/unemployed people by providing various types of assistance and information, and could also inform the public about the various self-help and income-generating projects, such local rubbish collection/recycling, run by the poor.

CHURCHES

- Continue to provide spiritual and moral leadership in the community, encourage people to believe in God and live their lives in harmony, peace and security.
- Remember that their roots/mission is to serve the poor and actively assist them.
- Work towards greater social justice and equality by being a voice of the voiceless and advocate on their behalf to reduce their hardships, and:
  - develop a common approach and cooperation between the different religious denominations towards poverty alleviation, and use their influence, knowledge and opportunities to assist in the development

of comprehensive poverty solutions to address human needs, both materially and spiritually
- develop partnerships with other stakeholders, such as NGOs and all levels of government, and be part of agreed anti-poverty strategies
- pool resources and work together as a sector to improve and increase their delivery of free and accessible welfare programmes for the poor, including the provision of financial assistance, food, health care, shelter, sanitation/clean water, psychological and social support
- innovate/create new service delivery programmes to reduce poverty, especially in areas such education, training/ skills development and job-creation schemes
- reduce the number of religious festivals, encouraging followers to work more days in the year
- condemn begging.

NGOS

- Target work and services better, to meet the needs of the poor more effectively.
- Work together as a sector in a coordinated way to ensure better outcomes for the poor. NGOs should also become more accountable and transparent for auditing purpose, to prevent corruptive practices.
- Develop closer partnerships with churches and other stakeholders to support the government in its efforts at poverty alleviation.
- Be more informed by societal need, by involving the wider community, and integrate local people's knowledge in the development of services/ projects for the development of the whole country.
- Promote new thinking on social issues based on human rights/social justice agenda, and assist the government to develop good public/social policy to alleviate poverty.
- Work more on the causes of poverty rather than focusing on the consequences, and:
  - support indigenous agencies in their work with local communities to strengthen development and civil society
  - initiate sustainable projects and services which are relevant to local people, using appropriate technologies. These projects should meet the needs of the communities, make them more independent and develop

peoples' capacities, so that they can play a greater role in their own development

- empower communities by giving a voice to the voiceless in society, increase employment options for local people and transfer knowledge and projects to communities or government after they were successfully set-up
- develop relevant pilot projects to demonstrate good governance and systems development in partnership with government.

INDIVIDUALS

- Realise that poverty is not acceptable, and develop visions and dreams for themselves to have a better life.
- Be more committed to the common good by taking an active interest in their local surroundings, such as cleaning the streets, supporting local regulations and dealing with sewage problems. Such action would help to change peoples' attitudes about the poor being dangerous and delinquent.
- Be careful that begging is not becoming a lifestyle and people are not simply going from one NGO's services to another, being passive recipients of handouts.
- Organise themselves to ensure that their concerns are heard. Thus, they should demand their rightful place in society and request that their rights as citizens to services, e.g. houses, and basic needs be met by the authorities.
- Take more responsibility for themselves and others, and take active steps to lift themselves out of deprivation, and:
  - develop self-respect and self-reliance by improving themselves through education, finding employment and working hard to save for the future
  - start a small business or buy land and be farmers, buy cattle, sheep and other livestock
  - ensure one has an ID in order to gain employment
  - do the right thing by their neighbours and work together as a group to increase their life chances and options in society
  - change those traditions that are detrimental to self-development and keep those that serve the community well.

Concluding/Final Remarks

1. Concepts, causes and solutions of poverty need to be reformulated to reflect the multidimensional, interactive, complex and cyclic reality of the poverty experience. To achieve this, the voices of the poor must be heard and integrated into poverty research and the development of public policy.

2. Public policy should also draw more extensively on the knowledge of service providers, advocates and other related stakeholders.

3. As this study shows, the research participants hold significant goodwill, which constitutes a valuable resource in the fight against poverty. The participants are well disposed and well placed to play a constructive role in the task of addressing poverty, and to cooperate with other stakeholders in society and with all levels of government.

4. The critical leadership role of the government in developing the country and reducing poverty was a common theme throughout the study.

GLOSSARY OF
LOCAL TERMS

TERM	EXPLANATION
almaz balechira	Herpes zoster, also called shingles, is an acute viral infection affecting the skin and nerves, characterized by groups of small blisters appearing along certain nerve segments (Ethiopia 2008).
Amhara	Indigenous ethnic group.
Amharic	The indigenous and official national language of Ethiopia.
birr	The national currency of Ethiopia, which is divided into 100 cents.
bule	A colloquial term for left-over food given to beggars by restaurants.
chat	*Catha edulis* is a green leafy shrub grown 'on warm, humid slopes between 1,500 m to 2,800 m'. *Chat* 'cultivated in Yemen, Kenya and in Ethiopia, has been consumed for centuries in these regions, and is legal in Ethiopia' (Gordon and Carillet 2003, p. 228). People chew the leaves and suck the juice, which has a mild stimulating effect.
Derg	Military socialist government that ruled Ethiopia between 1974 and 1991.
dihinet	One of the terms used to describe poverty.

gabi	A traditional hand-woven blanket-like shawl made from thick cotton. Ethiopians wear the gabi as protection from the cold.
iddir	A membership-based community organisation. These organisations assist families mainly in the burial of their family members, although some also provide various welfare programmes. All members pay a minimal fee on a monthly basis.
injera	The staple food of Ethiopia; it looks like a pancake. Prices vary according to quality. Low quality, cheap injera is usually dark, coarse, sometimes very thick, and is made from millet or sorghum. Good quality injera is pale, regular in thickness, smooth and free from husks and is always made with teff (ibid., p. 83).
kebele	The local and lowest level of government which can issue identity cards and assist with housing and free health care for the poor. Since early 2011, this has been replaced by woreda in Addis Ababa.
lemagn	The term used for a beggar.
listro	Boys earning a living as shoe shiners by cleaning shoes. They normally get paid 1 birr (about 6 US cents at the time of writing) per pair of shoes.
Oromo	Indigenous ethnic group.
Piazza	Original Italian term for a precinct at the centre of Addis Ababa, with a square.
plastic bet	This is a house on a wooden frame covered with plastic sheets, normally rented for about 20 birr per month (at the time of writing). While the plastic gives some protection against the rain and wind, it is very cold at night.
shiro wot	One of the cheapest sauces, vegetarian, usually made from powdered lentils sautéed with onion and other spices.
teff	Eragrostis tef is an indigenous cereal that grows mainly in the highlands and from which the better injera is made.
tsebel	Holy water, usually located near an Orthodox Christian church; refers to a natural spring where people gather and bath. The spring water is also used for baptisms and is believed to assist in healing.
tukul	A hut made from straw, usually 3–4 meters in diameter and 1.50–2 metres high and built directly on the ground/mud.
yekesel midija	A cast iron pan which uses charcoal to cook food.
yek'olo temari	Traditional seminarians begging to pay for their living during the course of their education, before becoming priests.
zebegna	A guard who traditionally is paid very little, sleeps in a tin shack inside the compound of a residence and is supposed to guard the premises 24 hours a day.

METHODOLOGY

This project is part of an international pilot study called *Shattered dreams*. Developed and led by Dr Klaus Serr, Australian Catholic University, the research was conducted between 2005–06 and 2008–09. The project took place in three communities: Melbourne, Australia (in partnership with Catholic Social Services Victoria); Munich, Germany (in partnership with Caritas Germany); and Addis Ababa, Ethiopia (with assistance from Hope Enterprises and from staff at the Ethiopian Catholic University of St Thomas Aquinas). The impetus for this project stemmed from the fact that most studies on poverty are undertaken by 'experts in the field', while people living in poverty are rarely consulted about their experience and understanding of poverty. Research such as this is of critical importance, because unless anti-poverty policies developed by professionals include the expressed needs and experiences of the poor, solutions are unlikely to be effective.

AIM AND OBJECTIVES

The main aim of this study was to gain a greater understanding about poverty by enabling the poor themselves speak about their experiences, and then contrasting these views with those of small groups of professionals working in the poverty area. The purpose of the study was thus not to test or build on established poverty concepts or theories; instead, it set out to increase insight into the conditions of a very deprived group of people by using an explorative and open-ended approach. Therefore, the project's main objectives were:

1. To gain knowledge about a small group of poor peoples' attitudes, perceptions and insights about their situation. To this end, the current stage of the project was carried out in Ethiopia, one of the world's poorest countries.
2. To ascertain the opinion of a few key stakeholders, such as service providers and policy makers, about poverty issues in the same society.
3. To identify and explore inter-group differences in attitudes, perceptions and insights about what it means to be poor, about the causes of poverty and how poverty could be solved.

Research Questions

The same core questions were asked of all participants:

1. How do you define poverty?
2. What are the causes of poverty?
3. What are the barriers which prevent fuller participation of the poor in Ethiopian society?
4. How could poverty be relieved or solved?

Where necessary, subsidiary questions were used to prompt relevant responses; see details in the following section.

Methods

This study followed a qualitative research approach, using in-depth, semi-structured interviews that focused on the four open-ended main themes of poverty definitions, causes, barriers and solutions, as shown above. Despite not having a set of detailed questions and not wanting to test conventional poverty concepts, the researcher's interviews were guided by a general understanding of poverty concepts. For example, while the first question 'What is poverty' aimed to uncover possible new dimensions of poverty, it was also important that issues related to absolute poverty (lack of necessities such as food, shelter, clothing) and basic human needs (lack of necessities and basic services) were covered by probing, if necessary. This approach helped ensure that no significant matters of interest were left out. Questions on poverty causes, barriers and solutions were also organised around different levels. For instance, the question on causes included 'What can the different levels of Society, Government, Churches, Non-Government Organisations, Personal/Individual do about poverty?' In keeping with the explorative nature of the research, recursive questioning was used, that is, there was a 'relationship between the current remark and the next one' (Minichiello *et al.*, 1990, p. 112). Nevertheless, interviewees' attention was always redirected, if necessary, to ensure that their comments related to one of the key questions posed. This technique was often aided by directive and relevant probing via secondary questions relating back to original questions posed (see also Liamputtong 2009).

All interviews in Ethiopia were conducted by Dr Klaus Serr. Each interview took about one hour, during which time only written notes were taken. While there are limitations to handwritten notes, this approach was used to reassure all participants that their information would not be misused and that they could speak in confidence. To ensure accuracy of contents, the interview notes were read to each informant, who was then given the opportunity to correct or add to what he/she had said.

Interviews with the Poor were conducted in Amharic,[1] the official language of Ethiopia, with the help of two qualified and experienced social workers who also had a sound knowledge of social science research. While the researcher was familiar with some of the cultural practices, the interpreters were also able to guide the researcher in cultural matters, to ensure participants were dealt with in personally and culturally appropriate ways. Interviews with the policy makers and welfare providers were conducted in English, as the professionals were drawn from government/non-government organisations and universities, where English is spoken widely.

Convenience sampling was employed, as this allowed the researcher both to access poor participants (including *lemagn*s and homeless people) at one convenient site with assistance from Hope Enterprises, a Non-Government Organisation, and to recruit professionals with relevant expertise, who were willing and available to be part of the research (Hesse-Biber and Leavy, 2005).

Thematic analysis was used where, after extensive reading of the material, major categories/themes were developed. These were organised around the main four question areas, and analysis was assisted by and validated through peer review.

Research Participants

The following participants were interviewed for this study:

1. Twenty poor people (10 women and 10 men). Characteristics of participants were as follows:
   a. Age: the age range for women was 19–55 (with one not certain) and for men, 23–66.
   b. Marital status: of the women 6 were widowed, 2 divorced, 2 separated; of the men 9 were single and 1 married; whereas all women had children, only one man did.
   c. Ethnic/religious backgrounds: of the women 8 classified themselves as Amhara, 1 Gurage, 1 Tigre. Seven women were Christian Orthodox and three Muslim; of the men 9 classified themselves as Amhara and 1 Oromo,[2] all being Christian Orthodox.[3]
   d. Education: of the women 7 had no formal education, 3 at least grade 6 (1 each of 6, 7, 8); of the men 6 had no formal education, 3 had grade 6 and 1 grade 4. Poor participants were volunteers identified by the staff of Hope Enterprises, Addis Ababa (Ethiopia) and interviewed at Hope. Throughout this text, this group is identified as the 'Poor'.
2. Fourteen professional informants from various religious and non-government organisations: seven service providers, and seven academics and policy makers, all interviewed at their offices around Addis Ababa. This group is identified as the 'professionals' and then differentiated according to their professional roles: the term 'Provider' was used for those whose work involves service provision to the poor, while the term 'Advocate' refers to people who work in research/academic or policy-making capacities.

Recruitment

Recruitment of poor participants took place at Hope Enterprises, which gave permission for this research to occur at its facility. The process of recruitment was as follows:

1. The research was announced and explained to the poor by staff at the agency. Expressions of interest were sought from the poor who wanted to participate voluntarily in the project. The selection criteria for participation in the research were that volunteers:

   - Were willing to cooperate and provide the information required
   - Had the cognitive abilities to understand the task required
   - Were not under the influence of alcohol or any other substance which may interfere with the research.

2. Providers and Advocates were approached by letter through Australian Catholic University (ACU) to solicit participation from those interested. This letter included and referred to the ACU Key Informant Information Letter, explaining the project. Of the initial respondents, the 14 final informants were selected on the basis of their expertise and experience in this area.

Ethics

Ethics approval for this project was sought and granted through the Australian Catholic University Human Research Ethics Committee (No.V200607 52). Accordingly, all participants received the requisite information about the research and agreed to be part of it by signing a consent form. For illiterate participants, letters of consent form were filled in by the interpreter after the project and the process has been explained to the volunteer. It was noted on the form that the participant had understood the project and the purpose of the interview task, and agreed to participate. Confidentiality was assured for all participants. All the poor participants chose a fictitious first name at the interview. The professionals were assigned a number and then referred to as 'Provider' or 'Advocate' plus the assigned number. Then, only fictitious names or titles were used during the interview process and in the interview notes. In addition, there were no identifiers on data files other than the fictitious names/titles. Individual consent forms, therefore, cannot be linked in any way to the data.

Strengths and Limitations

- While findings of most other studies rely on poverty experts, this research includes the voices and opinions of the poor, comparing them with two professional groups. Research such as this is of critical importance, because unless anti-poverty policies developed by professionals include the expressed needs and experiences of the poor, solutions are unlikely to be effective.

- As the focus on in-depth interviews provides detailed and powerful insights into the subjective poverty experience of a small number of participants, there is no intent of making any generalisation of the findings.

- The small number of poor participants drawn via one agency possibly presents a biased sample, so that the results are not necessarily applicable to others in poverty and might not apply to those with special needs, such as the elderly, people with disabilities or people from specific religious and cultural backgrounds.

- While the selection of the professionals was based on expertise, this small sample cannot represent a comprehensive view of all poverty experts in the field.

- Research involving disadvantaged people requires care to minimise potential risk of psychological/emotional harm to the informants. Thus, there was little probing into personal histories, in order to minimise the possibility of emotional/psychological distress. As client participants were asked to comment only on abstract or conceptual issues, this restriction may have limited some of the insights of the research.

- Some participants had trouble understanding some conceptual issues, making interviewing difficult at times and, thus, presenting another potential limitation of the study.

- While great care was taken in the client interviews to use capable and skilled interpreters, some meaning and content of peoples' stories might still have been lost in translation.

- Interviews at one moment in time provide only a snapshot in peoples' lives and their perceptions; it is, therefore, possible that if the person is interviewed again or if any characteristics of the interview are changed (e.g. different interviewer or interpreter; even slightly different wording of questions), then different results are feasible.

NOTES

PREFACE

1   Addis Ababa means 'the new flower' in Amharic (the indigenous and official language of Ethiopia), and is the capital of Ethiopia. It is often referred to as the 'political capital of Africa', and hosts the African Union and the United Nations Economic Commission for Africa. According to the last census, the city had a population of about 2.8 million in 2007 (FDREPCC 2008), which is now likely to be higher. The city has a subtropical highland climate, and, located at an altitude of around 2,400 m, 'is the third highest capital in the world' (Gordon and Carillet 2003, p. 6).

2   All informants have fictitious names.

INTRODUCTION

1   All dollar figures used are in US dollars unless otherwise stated.

2   However, estimates by Cecchetti *et al.* (2010) suggest that the debt/GDP ratios of some of the wealthiest nations will further increase for the 2010–2011 period in some of the biggest economies such as the US (92/100%), Japan (197/204%) and Germany (82/85%). While the IMF is already cautiously optimistic with its economic forecasts, it too anticipates that the debt/GDP ratios in developed countries will 'exceed 100% of GDP in 2014 based on current policies, some 35 percentage points of GDP higher than before the crisis' (IMF 2010, p. xv). However, Cecchetti *et al.* (2010) predict much more dramatic increases over the next decade, with more than 300% for Japan, 200% for the UK and 150% for Belgium, France, Ireland, Greece, Italy and the United States. These predictions do not bode well for cash-strapped states or for the populations which have been subjected to austerity measures to save money and pay back debts made by governments to bail out corporations. As these measures slash many government services and employment, hitting those who can least afford to lose them, they have been criticised as unjust, since the working population should not bear the brunt of mistakes made by the economic regimes, including economists, politicians, bankers and investors (Freeman 2010; Schultz 2010).

3   This term was first coined by Williamson (1990), describing neo-liberal economic reforms imposed in Latin America by international financial institutions in line with US government agencies such as the US Treasury.

4   The eight Millennium Development Goals (MDGs) agreed on included: 1) halving extreme poverty and hunger; 2) achieving universal primary education; 3) promoting gender equality; 4) reducing child mortality by two-thirds; 5) reducing maternal mortality by three-quarters; 6) reversing the spread of HIV/AIDS, malaria and other major diseases; 7) ensuring environmental sustainability; and 8) creating a global partnership for development.

CHAPTER 1 *POVERTY IN THE GLOBAL CONTEXT*

1   Countries such as Germany and Japan had initially different arrangements. For instance, Germany had adopted a socio-economic pact called 'Soziale Marktwirtschaft' (social market economics), and a compromise and working relationship between labour (via unions), businesses and government (via regulation). This 'Rhineland Model' achieved economic growth, high employment, high wages and good working conditions, while at the same time keeping inequality of incomes and resources in check. Equally important, in Japan there was a tradition where employers took responsibility for their workers, and companies often entered into a lifelong relationship with their employees. This was in direct contrast to the neo-liberal principles of a casual workforce that can be hired and fired on demand (UNCTAD 2010).

2   See also Walt Rostow's five stages that he thought were necessary for an economy to become mature and functional: 1) an underdeveloped nation should relinquish most of its original characteristics which impede progress. Only then was it ready for 2) the pre-takeoff society; (3) the takeoff; (4) the road to maturity; and (5) the mass consumption society (Rostow 1960). However, as critics observed, no country ever really developed using Rostow's stages (see Frank 1972; Amin *et al.* 1982; Goldthorpe 1984). Rather, the process of development opened markets and resources, made local elites rich, stimulated economic growth (as was intended), but created mass poverty precisely in those underdeveloped nations most needing assistance.

3   While people in developed countries have significant social protection via provision of welfare services, poor nations were forced by the economic adjustment policies to heavily reduce public services and benefits to the poorest (Social Watch 2010). Ironically, now, people in a number of European countries, such as Greece, are subjected to similar policies, enforced by the IMF and regional governments.

4   According to the World Development Movement Banks (no date), 'hedge funds and pension funds are betting on food prices in the financial markets, causing drastic price swings in staple foods such as wheat, maize and soy' and affecting the livelihood of millions of people.

CHAPTER 2 *POVERTY IN ETHIOPIA*

1   Surnames are not normally used in Ethiopia. Citations listed here, therefore, use the first name of the author rather than the last name. The reference list includes full names for all Ethiopian authors.

2   For many small farmers, coffee production is now only part of their income generation.

3   In 2010, the estimated volume of production was 196,119 tons, generating $841,654 million of export earnings for Ethiopia (Ministry of Trade 2010).

4   This pre-supposes that modern agricultural technology is used instead of subsistence farming to increase efficiency in production.

5   Birr is the national currency of Ethiopia, divided into 100 cents.

6   To meet the growing demand of housing in the capital, the Addis Ababa Housing Development Project, established in 2004, built 80,246 condominium houses (out of which 63,677 have been transferred to low-income households), with a further 16,569 under construction. But supply does not yet meet the demand, with 485,000 people applying for public housing in 2010 (Eden 2011, pp. 1, 31).

7   A *zebegna* is a guard who traditionally gets paid very little, sleeps in a shack inside the compound and is supposed to guard the premises 24 hours a day.

8   PASDEP has now been superseded by a new, ambitious five-year plan (2010/11–2014/15) called the Growth and Transformation Plan (GTP).

9   Ethiopia is divided into nine semi-autonomous administrative regions: Afar; Amhara; Benishangul-Gumuz; Gambela; Harari; Oromia; Somali; Southern Nations, Nationalities, and People's Region; and Tigray. There are six regional centres: 'Dire Dawa (east), Jima (south), Nekemte (west), Dese (north-central), Gonder (northwest) and Mekele (north)' (Ethiopia 2008).

CHAPTER 3 *DEFINITIONS OF POVERTY*

1   Hope Enterprises is a non-government organisation which provides *injera* six days per week for 60 cents per meal.

2   *Dihinet* is one of the words to describe poverty.

3   *Shiro wot* is a vegetarian sauce made from powdered lentils and other vegetables/spices, and is one of the cheapest sauces.

4   A *gabi* is a traditional hand-woven shawl made from thick cotton and looks like a blanket. The locals wear this to protect themselves from chilly weather.

5   While there are some social protection programmes in Ethiopia, there is no universal welfare system to assist people in need, and the unemployed, the sick and the elderly normally have to fend for themselves.

6   It is very usual for children to assist in the begging, as can be seen throughout the streets of Addis Ababa and other parts of Ethiopia.

7   This is normally white bread and not very nutritious.

8   At the time when this study was conducted, a naked boy was hiding near Hope Enterprises for two days. He had been given new clothes by a well-meaning person recently. When a band of local teenagers saw him on the streets with his new clothes, they took them from him to sell somewhere.

9   *Iddir*s are community organisations and are membership based. They assist families mainly in the burial of their family members, although some also provide various welfare programmes. All members pay a minimal fee on a monthly basis.

10 A plastic *bet* (house) is made of wooden frame covered with plastic sheets to keep the elements out. It can normally be rented for 20 birr per month (at the time of writing). While the plastic helps to protect against the rain and wind, it is very cold at night.

11 According to anecdotal evidence/local sources, public schools sometimes require contributions of around 100–150 birr per pupil per school year, depending on the level. This fee does not include the cost of books, uniforms and other school materials.

12 This kind of toilet is used by a number of households communally. It is usually locked and people have to contribute to its maintenance. Unlike the public toilets, which are run by a third party such as local administration or associations, the communal toilets are run by the people using them.

13 *Yekesel midija* is a cast iron pan where charcoal is used to cook food.

14 This is likely to be a run-down motel facility and not comparable with the Western notion of 'hotel'.

15 According to the informant, this is due to the sub-division of small plots of land, where poor young people have no access to additional land and resources.

16 *Listro* is a word used to refer to shoe shine boys in Addis Ababa and other Ethiopian cities, who earn a living by cleaning people's shoes. They normally get paid 1–2 birr per pair of shoes.

CHAPTER 4 *CAUSES OF POVERTY*

1   Refers to the military socialist government that ruled between 1974 and 1991.

2   According to some of the women, poor people often pay a certain amount e.g. 20 birr, to an employment broker in order to get a job as daily labourer, housemaid, etc. Sometimes this fee is also paid by the employer.

3   Since the study was undertaken, prices have continued to rise; it is, therefore, unlikely that figures given here still reflect the current situation.

4   According to some of the women interviewed, arranged marriages are quite common in the rural areas of Ethiopia and are still practised today. In many tribal settings, the women are the property of the men and can be sold and bought like property. Under the system of arranged marriages, they have no choice as to whom they will marry. The arrangement is made by the parents when the girl is very young (as young as 12 years old), without her knowledge or consent. The girl often marries a much older man and the arrangement is normally made to protect or enhance the wealth and property of the family.

5   While it is possible that some immigrants from poor backgrounds do 'make good' and achieve a better standard of living in Addis Ababa, the Poor in this study represent those immigrants whose lives have not been improved by their dislocation.

6   *Almaz balechira* is herpes zoster, also called shingles, an acute viral infection affecting the skin and nerves, characterised by groups of small blisters appearing along certain nerve segments (Ethiopia 2008).

7   *Chat* (Catha Edulis) is a green leafy shrub cultivated on warm, humid slopes of Ethiopia, Kenya and Yemen. People chew the leaves and suck the juice, which has a mild stimulating effect. It has been consumed for centuries in these regions and is legal in Ethiopia.

8   According to the informants, when families have children, land will be subdivided among family members. Population growth, therefore, reduces the available resources for each family, especially for small landholders, until the land can no longer support everyone.

9   Since the study was undertaken, there has been much policy development, and some of the comments made by the informants may no longer be valid/current.

10   This data on population and price of *teff* were provided during the time of the study and may now be inaccurate.

11   Located in the Horn of Africa, Ethiopia has three seasons: the dry season during September to February, a short rainy season during March and April, followed by the rainy season during June to August (Ethiopia 2008). Climate change and environmental degradation is now distorting some of the natural cycles.

12   While Advocate 4 says that this incidence occurred in Gambela, it is more likely to have taken place in Jimma.

CHAPTER 5 *BARRIERS*

1   Participating in a coffee ceremony is an important cultural tradition in Ethiopia. The ceremony is normally conducted every day and especially during religious festivities, to socialise with neighbours or as thanksgiving for good health, harvest, weddings etc. (Gozalbez and Cebrian 2004).

2   According to the informants, *tsebel* is holy water from a natural spring, usually located near an Orthodox Christian church where people gather and bath for healing. The spring water is also used for baptisms. In urban areas, tap water may be used.

3   Church (generic) here refers to all denominations.

CHAPTER 6 *SOLUTIONS OF POVERTY*

1   *Lemagn* is the term used for a beggar.
2   Four of the seven Providers in this study are employed by NGOs.

APPENDIX 1 METHODOLOGY

1   Ethiopia has a diverse culture approaching 100 different languages, of which Amharic is the official language (Ethiopia 2008).
2   Estimates compiled by the last Ethiopian census suggest that the main ethnic groupings in Ethiopia are: Oromo 34.5%, Amhara 26.9%, Somali 6.2%, Tigrie 6.1%, Sidama 4%, Guragie 2.5%, Welaita 2.3%, Hadiya 1.7%, Afar 1.7% and Gamo 1.5% (FDREPCC 2008).
3   According to the census, the main religious denominations in Ethiopia are: Christian Orthodox 43.5%, Muslim 33.9%, Protestant 18.6%, traditional 2.6%, Catholic 0.7% and other 0.7% (*ibid.*).

BIBLIOGRAPHY

Amin, S., Arrighi, G., Frank, A.G., and Wallerstein, I., 1982, *Dynamics of global crisis*, Macmillan, London.

Asmamaw Enquobahrie, 2004, 'Understanding poverty: the Ethiopian context', paper presented at the Gambia AAPAM Roundtable Conference, Banjul, Gambia, April 19-23, 2004.

Baran, P., 1973, *The political economy of growth*, Penguin, Harmondsworth.

Bello, W., 2010, 'The fundamental crisis: overaccumulation', Transnational Institute, http://www.tni.org (Accessed 22 March 2011).

Binyam Tamene, 2011, 'Fighting back. Government imposes price ceiling on major commodities to stamp out inflation', Capital, Vol. 13, No. 630, Sunday, January 9, pp. 38-39.

Booth, C., 1969, *Life and labour of the people in London*, AM Kelley, New York.

Brandt Commission, 1983, The Independent Bureau on international development issues, *Common crisis. North–south co-operation for world recovery*, The MIT Press, Cambridge, MA.

Brandt, W., 1980, (Commission Chairperson), *North–south: a programme for survival*, Pan, London.

Brown, J. C., (ed.), 1984, *Anti-poverty policy in the European community: papers prepared for a working party*, Policy Studies Institute, London.

Bundesministerium für Arbeit und Soziales (BMAS), 2008, *Lebenslagen in Deutschland*, der 3. Armuts- und Reichtumsbericht der Bundesregierung, BMAS, Bonn.

Cecchetti, S.G., Mohanty, M.S. and Zampolli, F., 2010, 'The future of public debt: prospects and implications', BIS Working Papers, No. 300, March 2010, Monetary and Economic Department, Bank for International Settlements, Basel.

Chauffour, J., 2008, 'Global food price crisis—trade policy origins and options', Trade Note 134, World Bank, Washington, DC.

CIA Factbook, 2010, *The world factbook: Ethiopia*, http://www.cia.gov/library/publications/the-world factbook/docs/notesanddefs.html?countryName=Ethiopia&countryCode =et&regionCode=af#2028 (Accessed 22 March 2011).

Corbridge, S., 1986, *Capitalist world development: a critique of radical development geography*, Macmillan Education Ltd, Houndmills.

Dag Hammarskjold Foundation, 1977, *Another development: approaches and strategies*, in P. Ekins (ed.), 1986, *The living economy: a new economics in the making*, Routledge & Keagan Paul, London.

Dennett, J., James, E., Room, G. and Watson, P., 1982, *Europe against poverty: the European poverty programme 1975–80*, Bedford Square Press, London.

Dessalegn Rahmato and Aklilu Kidanu, 1999, *A study to inform the World Development Report 2000/01, on poverty and development*, National Report: Ethiopia, World Bank, Addis Ababa.

Domhoff, G.W., 2011, 'Power in America: wealth, income and power', http://www.sociology.ucsc.edu/whorulesamerica/power/wealth.html (Accessed 1 February 2011).

Doyal, L. and Gough, I., 1991, *A theory of human need*, Macmillan Education Ltd, London.

Economic Commission for Africa (ECA), 2010, *Economic report on Africa 2010: promoting high-level sustainable growth to reduce unemployment in Africa*, ECA, Addis Ababa.

Eden Sahle, 2011, 'Lords of land: too few houses for too many in capital', Fortune, Vol. 11, No. 564, Sunday, February 20, pp. 1–2, 31.

Ellwood, W., 2006, *The no-nonsense guide to globalisation*, New Internationalist Publications in association with Verso, London.

Ethiopia 2008, Encyclopaedia Britannica 2008 Ultimate Reference Suit, Encyclopædia Britannica, Chicago.

Ethiopia Commodity Exchange Authority (ECEA), 2008, *Understanding commodities to be traded at Ethiopia Commodity Exchange. Volume I—Coffee profile analysis of coffee supply, production, utilization and marketing issues and challenges in Ethiopia*, ECEA, Addis Ababa.

European Communities, 2002, *Joint report on social inclusion*, European Commission Directorate-General for Employment and Social Affairs, Unit EMPL/E.2, Office for Official Publications of the European Communities, Luxembourg.

European Union, 2010a, *Europe in figures*, Eurostat Yearbook 2010, Publications Office of the European Union, Luxembourg, http://www.ec.europa.eu/eurostat (Accessed 22 January 2010).

European Union, 2010b, *The social situation in the European Union 2009*, Publications Office of the European Union, Luxembourg.

Eurostat, 1990, *Poverty in figures Europe in the early 1980s*, Office for the Official Publication of the European Communities, Luxembourg.

Fackler, M., 2010, 'Japan tries to face up to growing poverty problem', New York Times, April 21, 2010, http://www.nytimes.com/2010/04/22/world/asia/22poverty.html (Accessed 2 May 2010).

Federal Democratic Republic of Ethiopia Population Census Commission (FDREPCC), 2008, *Summary and statistical report of the 2007 population and housing census*, Central Statistical Agency, http://www.csa.gov.et/pdf/Cen2007_prelimineray.pdf (Accessed 17 May 2011).

Forbes, 2011, 'World's billionaires 2011: a record year in numbers, money and impact', Forbes.com/2011/03/08/world_billionnaires_2011_intro.html (Accessed 2 March 2011).

Frank, A.G., 1972, *Lumpenbourgeoisie: Lumpendevelopment*, Monthly Review Press, New York.

Frankfurter Rundschau, 2009, 'Jeder Bürger hat 20.000 Euro Schulden', 19 Oktober 2009, FR-Online, http://www.fronline.de/in_und_ausland/politik/aktuell/?em_cnt=1844967& (Accessed 19 October 2009).

Freeman, R.B., 2010, 'It's financialization!', *International Labour Review*, Vol. 149 (2010), No. 2, Journal compilation: International Labour Organisation.

Freire, P., 1970, *The pedagogy of the oppressed*, Continuum, New York.

Friedman, M., 1962, *Capitalism and freedom*, University of Chicago Press, Chicago.

Friedman, M., 1968, 'The role of monetary policy', *American Economic Review*, 58(1): 117.

Galbraith, J.K., 1995, *The world economy since the wars: a personal view*, Mandarin Paperbacks, London.

George, S., 1986, *How the other half dies*, Penguin Books Ltd, London.

George, S., 1988, *A fate worse than debt*, Penguin Books, London.

George, S., 1992, *The debt boomerang: how Third World debt harms us all*, Pluto Press, London.

George, S., 2010, 'Converging crises: reality, fear and hope', Globalizations, 7: 1, 17–22, http://www.doi.org/10.1080/14747731003593018 (Accessed 26 September 2010).

253

Goldthorpe, J.E., 1984, *The sociology of the Third World: disparity and development*, (second edition), Cambridge University Press. Cambridge.

Gordon, D., Adelman, L., Ashworth, K., Bradshaw, J., Levitas, R., Middleton, S., Pantazis, C., Patsios, D., Payne, S., Townsend, P. and Williams, L., 2000, *Poverty and social exclusion in Britain*, Joseph Rowntree Foundation, York.

Gordon, F.L. and Carillet, J.B., 2003, (second edition), *Ethiopia & Eritrea*, Lonely Planet Publications, Melbourne.

Gozalbez, J. and Cebrian, D., 2004, *Touching Ethiopia*, Shama Books, Addis Ababa.

Green, D., 2008, *From poverty to power*, Oxfam International, Oxford.

Groum Abate, 2011, 'Electric prices to increase shortly. Water tariff increased 300 percent', Capital, Vol. 13, No. 630, Sunday, January 9, p. 14.

Hancock, G., 1989, *Lords of poverty*, The Atlantic Monthly Press, New York.

Harrington, M., 1962, *The other America: poverty in the United States*, Macmillan, New York.

Harrington, M., 1984, *The new American poverty*, Penguin, New York.

Hauser, R., 1997, 'Armutsberichterstattung', in Heinz-Herbert Noll (Hrsg.), *Sozialberichterstattung in Deutschland: Konzepte, Methoden und Ergebnisse für Lebensbereiche und Bevölkerungsgruppen*, Weinheim/München.

Hayek, F., 1960, *The constitution of liberty*, Routledge, London.

Henderson, R.F., Harcourt, A. and Harper, R.J.A., 1970, *People in poverty: a Melbourne survey*, The Institute of Applied Economics and Social Research, The University of Melbourne, Melbourne.

Hesse-Biber, S.N. and Leavy, L.P., 2005, *The practice of qualitative research*, Sage Publications, Thousand Oaks, CA.

Hettne, B., 1990, *Development theory and the three worlds*, Longman Group UK, London.

Hill, J. and Scannell, H., 1983, *Due south: socialists and world development*, Pluto Press, London.

International Development Research Centre, 2003, 'Viewpoint: Tariffs and trade liberalization in Developing Countries', http://www.idrc.ca/en/ev-26739-201-1-DO_TOPIC.html (Accessed 1 March 2011).

International Labour Office (ILO), 2010, *Global employment trends 2010*, ILO, Geneva.

International Monetary Fund (IMF), 2010, *World economic outlook 2010*, IMF, Washington.

International Monetary Fund and International Development Assistance Staff, 2001, *Ethiopia: decision point document for the enhanced heavily indebted poor countries (HIPC) initiative*, IMF and IDA, http://www.imf.org/External/NP/hipc/2001/eth/ethdp.pdf (Accessed 22 December 2009).

Jones, B., 1991, *Sleepers wake*, Oxford University Press, Melbourne.

Korten, D.C., 1995, *When corporations rule the world*, Earthscan Publications Ltd, London.

Krugman, P., 2004, *The great unravelling*, Penguin Books Ltd, London.

Liamputtong, P., 2009, *Qualitative research methods*, (third edition), Oxford University Press, South Melbourne.

Mack, J. and Lansley, S., 1985, *Poor Britain*, George Allen & Unwin Publishers Ltd, London.

Mahlet Mesfin, 2011, 'Agency excludes urban planning civil servants from pay raise', Fortune, Vol. 11, No. 564, Sunday, February 20, p. 22.

Max-Neef, M., 1991, *Human scale development: conception, application and further reflections*, The Apex Press, New York.

Minichiello, V., Aroni, R., Timewell, E. and Alexander, L., 1990, *In-depth interviewing*, Longman Cheshire Pty Limited, Melbourne.

Ministry of Economic Development and Cooperation (MEDaC), 1999, *Survey of the Ethiopian economy: review of the post reform developments (1992/93–1997/98)*, MEDaC, Addis Ababa.

Ministry of Finance and Economic Development (MoFED), 2006, *Ethiopia: building on progress a Plan for Accelerated and Sustained Development to End Poverty (PASDEP)*, (2005/06–2009/10), Volume I: Main Text, MoFED, Addis Ababa.

Ministry of Finance and Economic Development (MoFED), 2010, *Ethiopia: 2010 MDGs Report. Trends and prospects for meeting MDGs by 2015*, MoFED, Addis Ababa.

Mishel, L., Bernstein, J. and Boushey, H., 2003, *The state of working America 2002–03*, Cornell University Press, Ithaca, NY.

Muchie, M., 2008, 'The impact of the Washington Consensus on democratic stability: the case of Ethiopia', in G. Lechini (ed.), *Globalization and the Washington Consensus: its influence on democracy and development in the south*, CLACSO, Consejo Latinoamericano de Ciencias Sociales, Buenos Aires.

Muluken Yewondwossen, 2011, 'Removing the price cap, Capital, Vol. 13, No. 651, Sunday, June 5, pp. 1, 14.

Narayan, D., Chambers, R., Shah, M.K. and Petesch, P., 1999, *Global synthesis. Prepared for the Global Synthesis Workshop: Consultations with the poor*, World Bank, Washington, DC.

Narayan, D., with Patel, P., Schafft, K., Rademacher, A. and Koch-Schulte, S., 2000, *Voices of the poor: can anyone hear us?*, published for the World Bank by Oxford University Press, New York.

Neumann, U. and Hertz, M., 1998, *Verdeckte Armut in Deutschland*, Friedrich-Ebert-Stiftung, Frankfurt.

Organisation for Economic Cooperation and Development (OECD), 2010, StatExtract: Income distribution—poverty, http://www.stats.oecd.org/Index.aspx?QueryId=9909 &QueryType=View (Accessed 7 January 2011).

Patel, R., 2010, *The value of nothing*, Black Inc., Melbourne.

Peel, M., 2003, *The lowest rung: voices of Australian poverty*, Cambridge University Press, Melbourne.

Pusey, M., 2003, *Experience of middle Australia: the dark side of economic reform*, Cambridge University Press, Melbourne.

Rampell, C., 2010, 'Corporate profits were highest on record last quarter', New York Times, 23 November 2010, http://www.nytimes.com/2010/11/24/business/economy/24econ.html (Accessed 15 November 2010).

Rostow, W., 1960, *The stages of economic growth*, Cambridge University, Cambridge.

Rowntree, S., 1901, *Poverty: a study of town life*, Howard, Fertig.

Saunders, P., 2005, *The poverty wars: reconnecting research with reality*, UNSW Press, Sydney.

Save the Children, 2010, *State of the world's mothers 2010*, Save the Children, Melbourne.

Schultz, S., 2010, 'Five Threats to the Common Currency', *Der Spiegel*, 11 February 2010, http://www.spiegel.de/international/europe/0,1518,677214,00.html (Accessed 28 April 2010).

Schumacher, E.F., 1973, *Small is beautiful: a study of economics as if people mattered*, Blond & Briggs Ltd, London.

Seabrook, J., 2007, *The no-nonsense guide to world poverty*, New Internationalist Publications Ltd, Oxford.

Seligson, M.A., 1984, *The gap between the rich and the poor: contending perspectives on the political economy and development*, Westview Press, London.

Sen, A.K., 1992, *Inequality re-examined*, Oxford University Press, Oxford.

Sen, A.K., 1999, *Development of freedom*, Anchor Books, New York.

Serr, K., 2001, 'Towards a theory and practice of alternative economics', *A Just Policy*, Vol. 21, March 2001, pp. 28–36.

Serr, K., 2004, 'Voices from the bottom', Australian Social Work, Vol. 57, No. 2, June 2004, pp. 137–149.

Serr, K., 2006a, *Shattered dreams,* Catholic Social Services (Vic.), Melbourne.

Serr, K., 2006b, 'Alternative anti-poverty strategies', in K. Serr (ed.), (third edition), *Thinking about poverty,* Federation Press, Sydney, pp. 183–196.

Shah, A., 2010, 'Global financial crisis', *Global Issues,* http://www.globalissues.org/article/768/global-financial-crisis (Accessed 23 September 2010).

Shaohua, C. and Ravallion, M., 2008. 'The Developing world is poorer than we thought, but no less successful in the fight against poverty', Policy Research Paper 4703, World Bank, Washington, DC.

Sharp, K., Devereux, S. and Yared Amare, 2003, *Destitution in Ethiopia's Northeastern Highlands*, Amhara National Regional State, Institute of Development Studies at the University of Sussex, Brighton.

Smeeding, T., 2005, 'Poor people in rich nations: the United States in comparative perspective', Luxembourg Income Study Working Paper Series, Working Paper No. 419, http://www.lisproject.org (Accessed 21 March 2006).

Social Watch, 2010, *Social Watch Report 2010: Time for a new deal after the fall*, Instituto Del Tercer Mundo, Montevideo, http://www.socialwatch.org/en/informeImpreso/pdfs/SocialWatch-Report-2010-eng.pdf (Accessed 20 March 2010).

Stiglitz, J., 2006, *Making globalisation work,* Penguin Books Ltd, London.

Stockholm International Peace Research Institute (**SIPRI**), 2010, *SIPRI Yearbook 2010,* **SIPRI,** Solna.

Tassew Woldehanna, 2004, 'The experiences of measuring and monitoring poverty in Ethiopia', for the inaugural meeting of the Poverty Analysis and Data Initiative (PADI), May 6–8 2004, Mombassa, Kenya.

Tassew Woldehanna, Alemu Mekonnen and Tekie Alemu, 2008, *Young lives: Ethiopia Round 2 Survey Report*, Department of International Development, University of Oxford, Oxford.

Taylor, B.K., 1992, *Imagine no possessions: towards a sociology of poverty*, Harvester Wheatsheaf, Hemel Hempstead.

Tekie Alemu, Getachew Asgedom, Liebenberg, J., Alemu Mekonnen, Seager, J., Bekele Tefera and Tassew Woldehanna, 2003, *Young lives, preliminary country report: Ethiopia*, Save the Children UK, London.

Thurow, L., 1996, *The future of capitalism*, Allen & Unwin Pty Ltd, St Leonards.

Townsend, P., 1984, 'The development of an anti-poverty strategy', in J.C. Brown (ed.), *Anti-poverty policy in the European community: papers prepared for a working party*, Policy Studies Institute, London.

Townsend, P., 1993, *The international analysis of poverty*, Harvester Wheatsheaf, New York.

Trainer, T., 1996, *Towards a sustainable economy*, Envirobook, Sydney.

United Nations Conference on Trade and Development (UNCTAD), 2010, Trade and Development Report 2010, United Nations Publications, Geneva.

United Nations Development Programme (UNDP), 1990, *Human Development Report 1990*, Oxford University Press, Oxford.

United Nations Development Programme (UNDP), 1999, *Human Development Report 1999*, Oxford University Press, Oxford.

United Nations Development Programme (UNDP), 2000, *Human Development Report 2000*, Oxford University Press, Oxford.

United Nations Development Programme (UNDP), 2001, *Human Development Report 2001*, Oxford University Press, Oxford.

United Nations Development Programme (UNDP), 2002, *Human Development Report 2002*, Oxford University Press, Oxford.

United Nations Development Programme (UNDP), 2003, *Human Development Report 2003*, Oxford University Press, Oxford.

United Nations Development Programme (UNDP), 2005, *Human Development Report 2005*, Oxford University Press, Oxford.

United Nations Development Programme (UNDP), 2009, *Human Development Report 2009*, Palgrave Macmillan, New York.

United Nations Development Programme (UNDP), 2010, *Human Development Report 2010*, Palgrave Macmillan, New York.

United Nations International Children's Education Fund (UNICEF), 1999, *The progress of nations 1999. League table: external debt as a percentage of GNP*, UNICEF, http://www.unicef.org/pon99/debtleag.htm (Accessed 12 July 2005).

Wallerstein, I., 1980, *The modern world system II*, Academic Press, New York.

Weber, M., 1985, *The protestant ethic and the spirit of capitalism*, Counterpoint, London.

Williamson, J., (ed.), 1990, *Latin American adjustment: how much has happened?*, Institute for International Economics, Washington.

World Bank, 2009, *Global monitoring report: a development emergency*, The World Bank, Washington.

World Commission on Environment and Development (WCED), 1987, *Our common future*, Oxford University Press, Oxford.

World Commission on the Social Dimension of Globalisation (WCSDG), 2004, *A fair globalisation: creating opportunities for all,* International Labour Office, Geneva.

World Development Movement Banks, (no date) 'Food speculation: what is the problem?', http://www.wdm.org.uk/stop-bankers-betting-food/what-problem (Accessed 1 February 2011).

World Health Organisation (WHO), 2010, *World Health Statistics 2010,* WHO, Geneva.

World Health Organisation (WHO), 2011, 'Factsheet No. 311', WHO, http://www.who.int/mediacentre/factsheets/f311/en/index.html (Accessed 22 February 2011).

Ziegler, J., 2005, *Das Imperium der Schande: der Kampf gegen Armut und Unterdrückung*, Bertelsmann, München.

INDEX

Against the Odds

www.ingramcontent.com/pod-product-compliance
Lightning Source LLC
Chambersburg PA
CBHW031406270326
41929CB00010BA/1345